INDIA-MYANMAR RELATIONS

INDIA-MYANMAR RELATIONS

A Strategic Perspective

Ashok Kumar

KW Publishers Pvt Ltd
New Delhi

First reprint June 2024

ISBN 978-81-952858-2-2 Hardback
ISBN 978-81-952858-7-7 ebook

Published in India by Kalpana Shukla

KW Publishers Pvt Ltd
4676/21, First Floor, Ansari Road
Daryaganj, New Delhi 110002
Phone: +91 11 43528107
Marketing: kw@kwpub.in
Editorial: production@kwpub.in
Website: www.kwpub.in

Printed and Bound in India

Dedicated
To
My Loving Wife
& Son

Contents

List of Tables, Figures and Maps

Preface

Geopolitical changes in the South and Southeast Asia have been observed with the growing flow of globalisation after the disintegration of the USSR and the end of the Cold War. This phenomenon invited the need for a new orientation in the foreign policy of India which resulted in launching India's Look (Act) East Policy. The interconnected and interdependent concepts in the new sphere of geopolitics compelled India to have closer links with regional and sub-regional powers for safeguarding the security and economic interests in the region. India's engagement with Myanmar is of utmost significance in the context of Look (Act) East Policy.

Myanmar is a geo-strategic factor for India in the Asian political dynamics. It is located at the tri-junction of South Asia, Southeast Asia and East Asia and it acts as a land bridge for both India and China—for India's Northeastern states and Southern provinces of China. Myanmar has been rightly depicted as the gateway and the bridge between the two regions or the crossroad, where India, China and Southeast Asia meet, creating an array of linkages as well as challenges and opportunities for India and other stakeholders in the region. India also realised that the non-engagement policy with the military regime had only developed congenial space for China to establish a dominant position in a crucial neighbouring country with grave implications for India's security. Since then, India has been involved in the engagement with focusing on political, economic, defence, development, connectivity, cultural, human resources and capacity building with Myanmar, providing a countervailing presence to China.

This geo-strategic location has made Myanmar a strategic convergence point between India and China, through which they can expand their connectivity and cooperative links. India's concerns over Myanmar emerges from rising Chinese footprints in India's 'Look East' While for China, Myanmar acts as a gateway to India's sphere of influence—the Bay of Bengal and the Andaman and Nicobar Islands. These factors contribute to India's rising security concerns as China's strategic interests in Myanmar pose severe threats to India's strategic and economic interests in the Indian Ocean.

India-Myanmar relations have seen upswing after the historic visit of the Indian Prime Minister to Myanmar in 2012. In the economic sphere, the trade has been doubled up between both the countries. India has enormous stakes in maintaining good relations with Myanmar for the growth and development of its Northeastern region. India-Myanmar geographical proximity offers a productive transit route for India's increasing trade with ASEAN, and also to develop its linkages with regional and sub-regional groups such as MGC and BIMSTEC. India's cooperation with Myanmar is also significant from the perspective of India's internal security as well as non-traditional security aspects, like energy security. Therefore, Myanmar is of utmost significance for India in the region.

Acknowledgements

I am highly indebted to God Almighty for giving me the inspiration, strength and blessings for this accomplishment.

First and foremost, it is a pleasure and privilege to acknowledge my profound gratitude and sincere thanks to my inspiration, Dr Kamal Kinger, Professor, Defence and Strategic Studies, Punjabi University Patiala, for his advice and guidance from a very early stage to the end. Despite his busy academic schedule, his thought-provoking suggestions and expertise in the subtle art of the subject-area enlightened me to accomplish this book in a standardised and professional manner.

I owe my special thanks to Dr Rahul Mishra, Dr Udai Bhanu Singh and Dr Pushpita Dass, who were generous and compassionate enough to share information and their views. I feel deeply indebted and extend my thanks to the staff of all the Universities and Think-Tank libraries for their kind and quick assistance.

I express my highest gratitude and feel blessed to have been surrounded by a beautiful family. I fall short of words for thanking them.

My wife, Ruhi Sarangal, deserves a heartfelt thanks for her unconditional support and affection the whole time. Without her continuous encouragement, this work would not have been possible.

Last but not the least, my little soldier, my son; Viraaj, deserves the most special mention as his bright smile gave me the courage to face each day with optimism.

List of Abbreviations

ABFSU	All Burma Federation of Students' Union
ACMECS	Ayeyawady-Chaophraya-Mekong Economic Cooperation Strategy
AIIB	Asian Infrastructure Investment Bank
ARF	ASEAN Regional Forum
ARSA	Arakan Rohingya Salvation Army
ASEAN	Association of South East Asian Nations
BARC	Bhabha Atomic Research Centre
BBIN	Bangladesh-Bhutan-India-Nepal
BCIM-EC	Bangladesh-China-India-Myanmar Economic Corridor
BIA	Burma Independence Army
BIMSTEC	Bay of Bengal Initiative for Multi Sectoral Technical and Economic Cooperation
BRI	Belt Road Initiative
BTILS	BIMSTEC Transport Infrastructure and Logistic Study
CICTT	Centre for Information and Communication Technology Trainings
CITIC	China International Trust and Investment Corporation
CNOOC	China's National Offshore Oil Corporation
CNPC	China National Petroleum Corporation
CPEC	China Petroleum and Chemical Corporation
CPEC	China-Pakistan Economic Corridor
DAC	Centre for Development of Advance Computing
EAEC	East Asia Economic Cooperation

EDII	Entrepreneurship Development Institute of India
FMR	Free Movement Regime
FTA	Free Trade Area
GAIL	Gas Authority of India Ltd.
HADR	Humanitarian Assistance and Disaster Relief
HMTI	Hindustan Machine Tools International
ICCR	Indian Council for Cultural Relations
IMBEX	India-Myanmar Bilateral Military Exercise
IMCEITS	India-Myanmar Centre for Enhancement of Information Technology Skills
IMNEX	India-Myanmar Naval Exercise
IOR	Indian Ocean Region
IRCON	Indian Railway Construction Company Ltd.
ISRO	Indian Space Research Organisation
ITEC	Indian Technical and Economic Cooperation
JeM	Jaish-e-Mohammad
JICA	Japan International Cooperation Agency
JTIF	Joint Trade and Investment Forum
KIA	Kachin Independent Army
KMMTTP	Kaladan Multi-Modal Transit Transport Project
KOICA	Korean International Cooperation Agency
LEP	Look East Policy
MADI	Myanmar Auto Mobile and Diesel Industries Ltd.
MDONER	Ministry for Development of North Eastern Region
MGC	Mekong-Ganga Cooperation
MICT	Myanmar's Information and Communication Technology
MIEDC	Myanmar-India Entrepreneurship Development Centre
MORTH	Ministry of Road Transport and Highways
NEFP	North East Frontier Province
NHPC	National Hydroelectric Power Corporation
NLD	National League for Democracy
NSAZ	Naga Self Administered Zone

NSCN-IM	National Socialist Council of Nagaland-Isak-Muviah
NSCN-K	National Socialist Council of Nagaland-Khaplang
OBOR	One Belt One Road
OIL	Oil India Ltd.
ONGC	Oil and Natural Gas Corporation
OVL	ONGC Videsh Ltd.
RCEP	Regional Comprehensive Economic Partnership
RITES	Rail India Technical and Economic Service
RLNG	Re-gasified Liquefied Natural Gas
RSIS	Research and Information System for Developing Countries
SAARC	South Asian Association for Regional Cooperation
SAFTA	South Asia Free Trade Agreement
SAPTA	South Asia Preferential Trade Agreement
SCI	Shipping Corporation of India
SCO	Shanghai Cooperation Organisation
SEAGP	South East Asia Gas Pipeline
SIGINT	Signals Intelligence
SIPRI	Stockholm International Peace Research Institute
SLORC	State Law and Order Restoration Council
SPDC	State Peace and Development Council
SREB	Silk Road Economic Belt
ULFA	United Liberation Front of Assam
UNLF	United National Liberation Front
UNODC	United Nations Office on Drugs and Crimes
UNRDS	United Nations Resources Development Services
USDP	Union Solidarity and Development Party

1
Introduction

Security is an essential constituent for a harmonious life. No one can survive without security, whether it is a living or non-living thing on earth, especially individual, society and a nation. Universally, at all fronts, security is taken for granted until an internal or external factor does not challenge it. In layman's term, security is the state of being safe from all kind of harm and threat. Three standard models of security are accepted globally: human security, national security and international security. Human security is the principal concern of all securities, whereas national security is the primary source of security and security threats.

National security and strategic studies is a prodigious and ever-evolving academic subject, which covers multi-dimensional issues. However, one of its prime section is the study and analysis of strategic and security aspects between two or more states. These aspects understand and interpret the relations between neighbour countries in the light of international and regional developments; political, economic, social, strategic, cultural and security factors; and evolution of these relations constitutes its essential part. Relations among neighbouring countries are much at stake, including development, peace, well-being and security of the peoples concerned. Unlike friends, who you can choose, neighbours and relatives cannot be chosen. This applies to states too. Hence, integrating and strengthening the bond with the neighbour is wise. Management of these bonds between neighbours excels the domain of external policy, a broader realm of mutuality of interests, identity, perception, belief and national psyche that binds two different people and societies. India's security environment develops a multiplex matrix of international and regional challenges. India's strategic position and increasing global reciprocity demand pro-active measures on a series of issues that affect national security with a vision to safeguarding vital national interests. In the twenty-first century, the world has been transformed into a multi-polar system where each nation is connected with other nations in one way or another. The national interests are the most crucial factors of foreign policy to safeguard national security, sovereignty and territorial integrity of a nation. Therefore, bilateral relations are not just a foreign policy concern instead it connects underlying layers of bonds.

India-Myanmar Relationship

The roots of the India-Myanmar relationship lie in enduring affinities developed by geographical contiguity, shared political experiences, cultural interactions and civilisational linkages. These affinities enhance mutual development perspectives, political and strategic impacts as well as prolong their relations. India and Myanmar bilateral relations are pursued by national interests, geo-strategic importance and national security aspects. India's relations with Myanmar are directed by its Look (Act) East Policy which has served as an essential instrument in foreign policy to connect with Southeast Asian nations. Myanmar is going through a democratic transition phase where it has taken several progressive steps to engage itself with global and regional powers for the development and growth of the country. In 2011, the military junta was dissolved following the general elections in 2010, and Thein Sein was sworn in as president of the new civilian government in Myanmar. Since the general elections in 2010, a series of reforms have been taking place in the country by the Myanmar government especially towards a mixed economy, reconciliation, a relaxation of the press and liberal democracy. These reforms also include the release of pro-democracy leaders from house arrest. The impact of these reforms turned into a welcoming gesture with the ASEAN chair for 2014 held by Myanmar. On November 8, 2015, the general elections were held in the country. Since 1990, these were the first open elections that took place in

Myanmar. The National League for Democracy obtained absolute majority seats in the parliamentary elections. However, Aung San Suu Kyi, could not hold president office constitutionally even after a clean sweep in the elections. Therefore, Aung Suu Kyi made Htin Kyaw the first non-military president of Myanmar in 1962, and she took charge as a state counsellor.

Strategic Significance of Myanmar

Myanmar being a factor in India's security had gone up considerably in the past two decades, especially when India turned its gaze eastwards, launching its Look (Act) East Policy and recently launched neighbourhood first policy. It was not by chance that both the strategic shift and India's Look (Act) East Policy engagement with the pro-democracy movement to stepping up the level and scale of relationship with the military regime in Myanmar occurred around the same time in the early 1990s. Myanmar's stance within ASEAN has strengthened progressively. Moreover, India and Myanmar have continued to strive for stronger cooperation and connectivity within several sub-regional structures.

In the Association of South East Asian Nations (ASEAN), Myanmar is the second largest land. Myanmar holds an area of 676,578 sq km with a population of 55 million.[1] It is a land of geographic diversity inhabiting 135 distinct recognised ethnic groups. Some sub-groups are identified along with ethnic appearances as the Bamar, Shan, Karen, Rakhine, Chinese, Indian, Mon and others. Further, it also shares the border with India and Bangladesh in the west, China in the north and Thailand and Laos in the east. It has a substantial coastline along the Bay of Bengal and the Andaman Sea, which provides Myanmar access to the Indian Ocean. The junction at which Myanmar lies is an apt bond for India to resonate its interests with prospering economies in South East Asia, East Asia and South Asia. Myanmar also occupies a critical geo-strategic position which is often perceived to be a buffer state between India and China who share a complicated relationship with elements of cooperation and competition in their engagements, especially in the Asian region.[2]

Another factor explaining Myanmar's importance for India has been the economic attractiveness. Myanmar is situated in a region which has been experiencing dynamic economic growth over the past two decades. Myanmar has abundant natural resources like forest, coal, mineral and marine resources, natural gas and petroleum.[3] Myanmar's vast oil and gas reserves are an attractive resource for India's energy quest. Despite its abundant resources, its exports are still lagging as compared to its neighbours. In Myanmar, approximately 32 per cent of the population lives in poverty, and it is one of the poorest nations in Southeast Asia with a Gross Domestic Product (GDP) of US$ 69.32 billion (2017) having 6.4 per cent economic growth rate.[4] However, the country's enormous potential can make itself one of the wealthiest country of ASEAN. Myanmar is primarily an agricultural economy which is highly dependent on rice cultivation, which alone contributes to nearly 60 per cent of the nation's export earnings. Myanmar is an economically underdeveloped nation, and its economic resources are untapped and some even unexplored. India is also looking forward to procuring cooperation in cross-border development projects—like oil, gas, power, railway, road, waterways, telecommunication, information technology, education and training. India and Myanmar have shown rapid growth in trade and commerce in recent years. Today, India is Myanmar's 4th largest trading partner after China, Thailand and Singapore.[5] A border trade agreement was signed in 1994 between India and Myanmar to enhance economic cooperation, Moreh-Tamu and Zowkhatar-Rhi, are two operational border points. A third and fourth border trade points are planned to be opened at Avakhung-Pansat/Somra and Nampong-Pangs.[6] The bilateral trade between both countries increased significantly from US$ 12.4 million in 1980-81 to US$ 1.3 billion in 2011–12. The Indian Prime Minister, during his visit to Myanmar in 2012,[7] alluded to the mutually agreed target of doubling the bilateral trade to US$ 3 billion by 2015.[8] India-Myanmar bilateral trade reached up to US$ 2.17 billion in 2016-17, out of which Indian exports were US$ 1.11 billion and Indian's imports were US$ 1.06 billion with much scope to reach.[9]

Ethnicity and religion may be regarded as the most influential factors in their relationship. A large group of Indian origin people live in Myanmar (nearly 2 per cent of the total population). To those living in Myanmar and thus exposed to the heartland of Bamar culture, proved that the Buddhist linkage has been the most appealing and lasting bond between the two societies. The International long land boundary between India and Myanmar was formally demarcated on March 10, 1967. The agreement between the two countries remains an artificial line dividing tribes such as the Singphos, Nagas, Kukis, Mizos. These tribes, however, continue to maintain strong linkages with their kin across the international divide. To maintain their age-old ties, a unique arrangement called the Free Movement Regime (FMR) has been established. Under this arrangement, the tribes can travel up to 16 km along the border without any visa obligations and can reside three days at each side. It has also become a serious problem for both the countries as Kachin Independent Army (KIA), Chin National Front (CNF) National Socialist Council of Nagaland-Khaplang (NSCN-K), National Socialist Council of Nagaland-Isak-Muviah (NSCN-IM) and United Liberation Front of Assam (ULFA) like groups have been known to have cross-border linkages and safe sanctuaries.[10] India and Myanmar share a 1,643 km long land border which is largely unfenced. Four of India's politically sensitive North-eastern states, Mizoram, Manipur, Nagaland and Arunachal Pradesh share an international border with Myanmar. On the other side Kachin, Chin, Rakhine states and Sagaing region of western Myanmar share this border with India[11] which have been facing insurgency-related problems since long. Due to their ethnic connections, insurgent groups from the Northeast of India not only receive shelter in Myanmar but also have operational bases.[12] Myanmar is a part of the Golden Triangle including Thailand and Laos, though the border region has been the theatre of criminal activities, such as smuggling, illegal trade in narcotics, fake currency and sources of arms supplies which are severe threats to India's security. India shares the strategic waters of Bay of Bengal where the critical area of Andaman and Nicobar Islands and Myanmar's Coco Islands are barely 30 km apart. This geographical proximity between the two countries translated into long-standing trade relations across land borders and the sea route.

Myanmar is of great strategic significance not only to India but as well as to China. China's growing presence and its role in Myanmar concern India. For India, it is not merely a concern of earning economic and strategic advantage, it impacts directly on India's national security. In the early years of the military regime, India pushed hard that a democratic system should establish in Myanmar. Meanwhile, China became an increasingly attractive source of low-interest loans, grants, development projects, technical assistance to Myanmar. This further enhanced the concept that the principal beneficiary of weary India-Myanmar relations was China whether it was access to all vital hydrocarbon energy sources or economic and transport corridors. China is investing heavily in infrastructure, mining projects, hydropower dams and oil-gas pipelines to help southern China's growing energy needs and gaining greater access to the Indian Ocean through Myanmar. Its presence in the Coco Islands of Myanmar in the name of ensuring the security of piracy affected Strait of Malacca through which its oil-carrying tankers pass, which is also a cause of worry for India.[13]

India is making sincere efforts to strengthen its relations with Southeast Asian nations through its Look (Act) East Policy. It is not merely an external economic policy, but a strategic move in India's view of the world and India's position in the evolving global economy.[14] In this perspective, the India-Myanmar ties have gained more importance as both nations have started interacting at regional and sub-regional levels in ASEAN, Mekong-Ganga Cooperation (MGC) and Bay of Bengal Initiative for Multi-Sectoral Technical and Economic Cooperation (BIMSTEC). BIMSTEC can become an essential contribution to security, prosperity, peace and harmony in Asia and the World as this group has a combined GDP of over US$ 2.5 trillion. Economic ties through trade, commerce and development initiatives are expected to bring prosperity to the relatively poorer bordering regions of India as well as Myanmar. Thus, among all the South East Asian nations Myanmar is vital from India's strategic and economic perspective.

Notes

1. Central Intelligence Agency "Burma", The World Fact Book. Available at https://www.cia.gov/library/ publications/the-world-factbook/geos /bm.html (Accessed on October 14, 2014).
2. A. Bhattacharya and D. Chakraborty (2011), "India's Cross-Border Infrastructure Initiatives in South and Southeast Asia," *The International Spectator: Italian Journal of International Affairs*, Vol. 46 (2), p. 110. Available at http://www.tandfonline.com/doi/pdf/10.1080/03932729.2011.576176 (Accessed on September 25, 2014).
3. Ministry of Health – Government of Myanmar, Country Profile-Natural Resources (2013). Available at http://www.moh.gov.mm/file/COUNTRY%20PROFILE.pdf (Accessed on June 5, 2014).
4. Central Intelligence Agency "Burma," The World Fact Book. Available at https://www.cia.gov/library/ publications/the-world-factbook/geos/bm.html (Accessed on Oct 14, 2018)
5. K. Yhome (2009), "India-Myanmar Relations (1998-2008)-A Decade of Redefining Bilateral Ties," ORF Occasional Paper, #10, p. 5. Available at http://www.orfonline.org/cms/export/orfonline/modules/occasionalpaper/attachments/ind-myn-OP_1236338801296.pdf (Accessed on August 21, 2014).
6. Ministry of External Affairs – GOI, "Myanmar" (2013). Available at http://www.mea.gov.in/Portal/Foreign Relation/India-Myanmar_Relations.pdf (Accessed on June 5, 2014).
7. Ministry of National Planning and Economic Development, "Myanmar-India Trade Statistics" (2012-13). Available at https://www.mnped.gov.mm/html_file/foreign_trade/s09MA0201.htm (Accessed on June 5, 2014).
8. Rajiv Bhatia (2016), *India-Myanmar Relations: Changing Contours*, Routledge, New York, p. 173.
9. Ministry of External Affairs – GOI, "India-Myanmar Relations-2017". Available at https://www.mea.gov.in/Portal/ForeignRelation/MYANMAR_August_2017_new.pdf (Accessed on May 15, 2018).
10. Pushpita Das (2013), "India-Myanmar Border Problem: Fencing not only the Solution," IDSA Comment. Available at http://idsa.in/idsacomments/IndiaMyanmarBorderProblems_pdas_151113 (Accessed on October 12, 2014).
11. R. Bhattacharya (2010), "Does Economic Cooperation Improve Security Situation: The Case of India-Myanmar Relations," *Asia-Pacific Journal of Social Sciences,* Special Issue No.1, p. 74. Available at http://www.isaps-india.org/APJSS/SP%207.%20Rakhee%20Bhattacharya.pdf (Accessed on November 22, 2014).
12. Y. Singh (2007), "India's Myanmar Policy: A Dilemma between Realism and Idealism," IPCS Special Report, No. 37. Available at http://www.ipcs.org/pdf_file/issue/928587478IPCS-Special-Report-37.pdf (Accessed on July 5, 2013).
13. Zhiquen Zhu (2010), *China's New Diplomacy: Rational, Strategies and Significance*, Ashgate Publishing Ltd., United Kingdom, p. 63.
14. Thongkholal Haokip (2012), *India Look (Act) East Policy and North East India: Achievements and Constraints*, Concept Publishing, New Delhi, p. 87.

2
Geo-strategic Significance of Myanmar and India-Myanmar Relations: A Historical View

Introduction

Myanmar[1] presents an immensely important geographic situation in Southeast Asia as the 2nd largest nation with an area of 676,578 sq km and has a population of 55 million (2019).[2] Myanmar is geographically contoured into a diamond. It is often compared to a 'kite' with a tail trailing along one side.[3] Myanmar is a nation with a variety of religions. Although the government of Myanmar declares no official religion, preference is given to Theravada Buddhism which accounts for 87.9 per cent of the total population, whereas other religions practised are: Christianity (6.2 per cent), Islam (4.3 per cent), Hinduism (0.5 per cent) and others (1.1 per cent) of the entire population. Myanmar is also a home of officially recognised 135 distinct ethnic groups and Bamar as their dominant ethnic group. The eminently identified ethnic groups are: Burmese/Bamar (68 per cent), Shan (9 per cent), Karen (7 per cent), Rakhine (4 per cent), Chinese (3 per cent), Indian (2 per cent), Mon (2 per cent) and others (5 per cent). Myanmar uses Burmese as its official language although few ethnic groups use their ethnic languages in their regions.

Geo-strategic Situation of Myanmar

Myanmar is geo-strategically located at the intersection of Southeast Asia, East Asia and South Asia, which allows it to function as a golden land bridge between India and prospering economies in Southeast Asia and East Asia. Myanmar shares its international border with India (1,643 km) and Bangladesh (193 km) in the west, with China (2,185 km) in the north, and with Thailand (1,800 km) and Laos (235 km) in the east. The maritime border (1,930 km) along the Bay of Bengal and the Andaman Sea provides Myanmar access to the Indian Ocean. It also occupies a critical geo-strategic position which is often perceived to be a buffer state between the two Asian jumbos—India and China, who share a complicated relationship, with elements of cooperation and competition in their engagements, especially in the Asian region.[4] India needs Myanmar's support to strengthen its geopolitical position in Southeast Asia. Myanmar is a crucial stepping stone in the equation at India's Look (Act) East Policy which looks forward in developing and expanding political, economic and security ties with ASEAN. Another reason that adds to the importance of Myanmar is it being a member of Mekong-Ganga Cooperation (MGC) and the Bay of Bengal Initiative for Multi-Sectoral Technical and Economic Cooperation (BIMSTEC), along with Bangladesh, Bhutan, India, Sri Lanka, Thailand and Nepal. In addition to the initiatives as mentioned above both Myanmar and India are a part of the Bangladesh, China, India and Myanmar (BCIM) Economic Corridor as well.

Geo-strategic Significance of Myanmar 'vis-à-vis' India

Myanmar is significant to India from a geo-strategic, geopolitical and geo-economic angle. Given its geographical location, Myanmar's domestic and foreign policies have a high potential to impact several significant aspects of India's strategic interests directly.

First is the protection of the territorial integrity of India in the Northeastern parts of the country. Four delicate Northeastern states of India—Arunachal Pradesh (520 km), Nagaland (215 km) Manipur (398 km) and Mizoram (510 km)—share their respective borders with Myanmar. On the other side Further, the Kachin, Chin states and Sagaing region of Myanmar share their land border with India. The problem of insurgency prevails in these parts on both sides. They share an immense porous and sensitive 1,643-km long land border with Myanmar. Due to their ethnic connections, the insurgent groups from the Northeast of India not only receive shelter in Myanmar but also have operational bases.[5] The elimination of long existing insurgencies in the Northeastern states is not possible without the proactive cooperation of Myanmar and Bangladesh. Myanmar despite being a part of the Golden Triangle,[6] including Thailand and Laos, the border region has been the spectator of criminal activities such as smuggling and illegal trade in narcotics, fake currency and sources of arms supplies which have caused severe problems to India's security. India shares the strategic sphere of Bay of Bengal including the strategically important area of the Andaman and Nicobar Islands where the two closest Andaman and Myanmar's Coco islands are barely 30 km apart. India's strategic interests in the Bay of Bengal and the Indian Ocean, as well as the security of the Andaman and Nicobar Islands, are directly linked to our sustainable relations with Myanmar.

Second, the economic development of India's Northeastern states is often linked to the relationship between India with Myanmar. It makes much good economic understanding and savings for the Northeastern states to outsource their consumable products and other daily supplies from neighbouring Myanmar rather than being dependent on other parts of India which accounts for a long distance and expensive transportation, in turn, raising the scale of economy. These states and Northwestern Myanmar can represent a natural economic zone. Therefore, a win-win situation needs to be re-established as it was present in Ancient times. The economic importance of Myanmar also consists of the fact that Myanmar strategic location provides it with an opportunity to play a fundamental role in both the geopolitics and geo-economics of South Asia and Southeast Asia. The availability of natural gas, oil, coal, zinc, precious stones, timber and some deposits of uranium in Myanmar give geo-economic dimension to its strategic significance which also makes Myanmar a favoured destination and a crossroad for India and other Southeast Asian countries.[7]

Map 2.1: Geo-strategic Position of India's Four Northeastern States with Myanmar

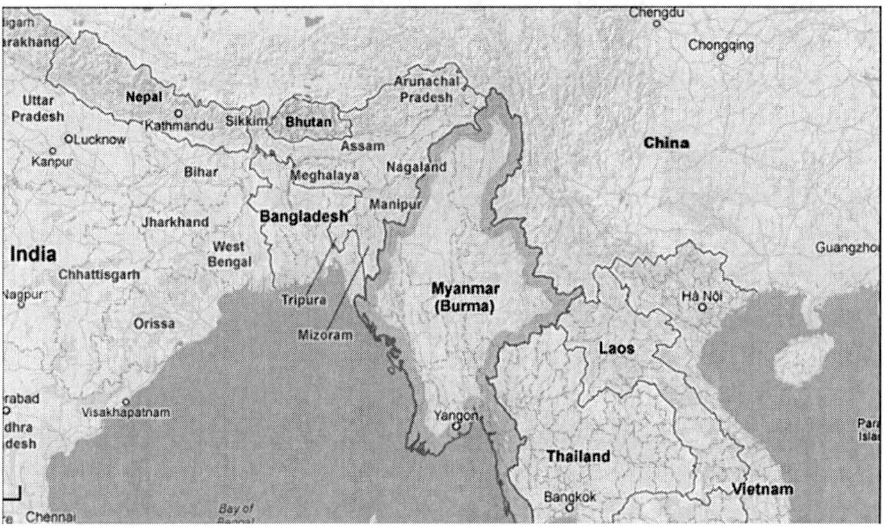

Source: Google Map.

Third, China's footmarks in Myanmar are the largest and most influential among all of India's Asian neighbours. China has been Myanmar's pre-eminent international patron especially since 1988. As per the conventional belief, there are over 2 million Chinese people live in Myanmar today. These two economies have been closely linked to each other. The Myanmar markets are flooded with Chinese goods. It also dominates the oil and gas exploration and mining sectors and has a significant contribution to the development of infrastructure and hydropower projects.[8] Four large multipurpose Special Economic Zones (SEZs) are also being developed by China there. The Chinese investments factor in Myanmar hold enormous strategic significance for India. Therefore, it is essential for India to regenerate its economic and political equations with Myanmar that safeguard its national interests vis-à-vis China.

The western countries deep-seated reservations about Myanmar's democracy initiatives now have been diluted. They have lifted long-standing sanctions and are poised to step up their economic engagements with Myanmar dramatically. Asia-Pacific region countries are also showing new interests in reviving ties with Myanmar. With time these nations will step up the game in the region. Japan also has a special relationship with Myanmar.[9] Therefore, being in the limelight with Myanmar, India has a limited opportunity in which it has to make a stronger impact and a footprint which should be much larger than its current projects and vision. It would be best achieved by providing Myanmar attractive stakes in a carefully monitored symbiotic economic relationship with India. In recent times, the bilateral visits have further strengthened the political and economic relations between the two countries and increasingly shaped the contours of diplomatic relations, laying the foundations for strategic congruence.

India is one of the oldest civilisation in the world. It is home to a diverse and a kaleidoscopic variety of population with a rich cultural heritage. Indus valley civilisation burgeoned in the third and second centuries BC. It outstretched into Northwestern India. The infiltration of Aryans in the Indian subcontinent around 1500 BC and their integration with the Dravidians generated the classic culture of India. The great Ashoka empire played an essential part for Mauryas to unite much of South Asia. Indian culture, art and science saw the blossoming during the Gupta Dynasty. Babur established the Mughal Dynasty during the 16th century after Delhi Sultanate got established by the invasion of the Turks and Afghans. After three centuries of Mughals, Europeans landed in the Indian subcontinent. Britishers became a superior political power in the landmass. With uncountable martyrdoms and sacrifices, India got independence on August 15, 1947. However, a massive and violent communal breakdown took place before the country which segregated the subcontinent into two separate states—India and Pakistan.

Since the last 73 years of independence, India has been working for a multi-dimensional and sustainable socio-economic development. India has not only achieved the status of the independent country in agriculture production but also has become one of the most successful industrialised countries in the world showing remarkable growth in science and technology, pharmacy, energy, defence, political, art and culture, tourism and many more. India is in the list of very few nations who have marked their presence in outer space to explore nature for the welfare of people. India has also achieved the nuclear power status in the world. India is the 7th largest landmass, 5th largest GDP with US$ 2.94 trillion (2019) in the world. The total area of land is 3,287,590 sq km, extending from the great snow-covered Himalayas in the north to the tropical rainforests of the south and covering the massive area from the Arabian Sea in the west to Bay of Bengal in the East. Marked off as it is by the sea and mountains, India has a distinct geographical entity, and it stands apart from the rest of the Asian Continent. It shares land borders with Pakistan (3,323 km) to the west, China (3,488 km), Nepal (1,751 km) and Bhutan (699 km) to the Northeast and Myanmar (1,643 km) and Bangladesh (4,096 km) to the east. Sri Lanka (30 km, bridge connectivity) and the Maldives are India's southern neighbours sharing maritime boundaries in the Indian Ocean.

India has a 15,106.7 km land frontier and 7,516.6 km maritime border including Lakshadweep and Andaman and Nicobar Islands. These geographical proximities provide India with abundant opportunities and challenges to play a substantial geo-strategic role as the subcontinent's landmass.[10] Due to India's position at the base of the Asian continent and the top of the Indian Ocean, it has an edge over West, Central and Southeast Asia and the littoral states of the Indian Ocean from East Africa to Indonesia. An energy-desired country, India is located close to some of the most important sources of oil and natural gas in the Gulf and Central Asia and adjacent to the Malacca Strait which is a vital sea lane through which 60,000 (approx.) ships transit every year.[11]

Map 2.2: Geographic location of India with its Neighbours in the Indian Ocean

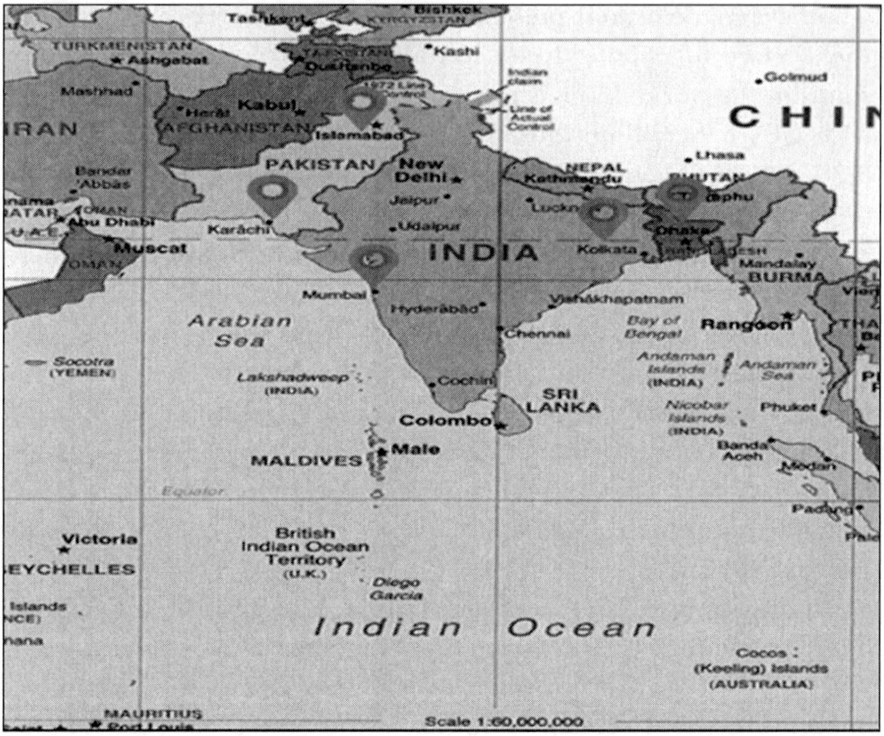

Source: COLTRACO, Strategic Partners in South Asia

India-Myanmar Relations—Historical Perspective

India and Myanmar enjoy a deep-rooted, harmonious and multi-faceted relationship. Being neighbours, the historical, cultural and societal connections are apparent. The Buddhist heritage, shared by both, is one of many lasting bonds. Being the land of Lord Buddha, Myanmar is a country of pilgrimage where around 87.9 per cent population follow Buddhism. Myanmar is home to a sizeable Indian origin people (estimated about 1.6 million). The people living across the borders share rich cultural and historical ties. There are many symbolic places that share the heritage and culture of both the nations, such as Bahadur Shah Zafar's tomb in Yangoon where the Mughal Empire was finally laid to rest, Tilak's place of confinement in Mandalay and the place of the last king of Myanmar Thibaw in Ratnagiri, Maharastra. The support received by Subhash Chandra Bose's Indian National Army (INA) in Myanmar was overwhelming. After independence, Former Prime Minister of India Jawahar Lal Nehru and Myanmar's Aung San and later U Nu embraced Non-Alignment.

India-Myanmar Connection in the Ancient Times

Since time immemorial, India had robust historical and cultural ties with Myanmar. The missionaries Sona and Uttara were sent to Suvarnabhumi to spread Buddhism during the 3rd century BC during the reign of King Ashoka.[12] With time, the religion spread and made its mark expressing itself through the construction of many beautiful temples and statues in honour of Lord Buddha. Even the name 'Suvarnabhumi' or 'Land of Gold' was coined because of the productive trading activities of Indian traders from Champa, i.e. Bhagalpur, Bharuch, and Tamralipti with Pegu, Mawlamyine and other cities of Myanmar.[13]

The reference of Suvarnabhumi or Buddhist Legends is found in the 'Jatakas'. It mentions that after attaining enlightenment Gautama Buddha was in contemplation in the Kripalu forest or grove, two brothers, named Tapusa and Palikat arrived with 500 carts of merchandise to pay their respect to Lord Buddha from the city of 'Ukkalaba' (Myanmar) which was then a port city of Suvarnabhumi.[14]

During the third Buddhist Council at Pataliputra in 241 BC when missions were sent to foreign countries to propagate religion, two revered monks Sona and Uttara were deputed to Myanmar by the Great Indian Emperor Ashoka. When they arrived to do the same, they were first violently opposed, but gradually they pacified the Myanmar community and converted the people to Buddhism.[15]

Myanmarese Dynasty: Pagan Dynasty to Konbaung Dynasty (1044-1885)

The kingdom of pagan was the first one to unify the regions that later constituted modern-day Myanmar. It was under the 250 years rule of Pagans over the Irrawaddy valley that the foundation for the ascent of

Myanmar language and culture was laid; this also contributed to the spread of Myanmar ethnicity and growth of Theravada Buddhism in Myanmar and the mainland of Southeast Asia.

Even in the early eleventh century, many familiar concepts of Indian civilisation are found in Myanmar. The great king Anawratha (1044-77 AD) was married to an Indian princess of Vaisali (which presently falls in Tirhut, Bihar). The symbols on a brick of King Anawratha in Sanskrit text have been found in various parts of Myanmar. Anawratha's interest in the fusion of Indian culture was continued by his son King Kyanzisha (1084-1112 AD) or Kyansittha in later years as a great temple builder. He desired to marry his daughter to an Indian Prince of Pattikera, although this ended in tragedy when the prince committed suicide. This love episode is still reflected in poems and songs of Myanmar.[16]

In addition to Sona and Uttara's missionary activities in Myanmar, close contacts of South Indian Pallava dynasty (560-903 AD) and Chola dynasty (850-1200 AD) could be found with Myanmar. The inscriptions found at the ancient site of 'Sri Kshetra' in Myanmar reveal inscriptions written in Sanskrit, Pali and South Indian Pallava-Grantha script with short extracts from the Abhidhamma Pitaka. Numerous figures of the Buddha in stone, bronze and terracotta have also come to light, and these are all in Indian style.[17]

There are many other connecting points between India and Myanmar in the antiquities of Myanmar. Many references of Indian people as peasants, traders, astrologers, Buddhist missionaries from India, Bodh Gaya or to the great centres of pilgrimages, Indian epics and the Ganges water, are found in ancient texts. Even the last dynasty of Myanmar founded by Alaungpaya, usually called the Konbaung Dynasty (1752-1885), revived the glories of the Myanmar kingdom by conquering Ayuthia (Thailand) and extending its boundaries beyond Arakan to cover Assam and Manipur. This eventually led to the First Anglo-Myanmar war in 1824-26 and the loss of Myanmar sovereignty in later years, followed the Indian pattern of royalty and authorised the compilation of a new Myanmar Law Code– 'Manu Ke Dhammathat' (based on the Hindu Code of Manu) including the basic principles of the modern Myanmar Buddhist law.[18]

The expansion of the Konbaung Dynasty into Arakan in the state of Assam, led to the arrival of British in Myanmar as those territories were lying in the vicinity of the India areas possessed by the British. This close contact led to the first Anglo-Myanmar War (1824-26) that ended in a British victory by the Treaty of Yandaboo. Myanmar lost previously conquered territory in Assam, Manipur and Arakan, which the British won with the help of the Siamese.[19] Teak forests in lower Myanmar and a port between Kolkata and Singapore were other sources of attraction that led to the second Anglo-Myanmar war in 1852. The Britishers won this war as well and got hold of the desired teak forests, oil and rubies of northern Myanmar. This prompted the Third Anglo-Myanmar War in 1885. This action of the British government was justified by claiming that the last independent emperor of Myanmar, Thibaw, was an autocrat and that he conspired to give France more influence in the country. Eventually, the British occupied the whole of Myanmar, hence Myanmar became a part of British India province.

Before British conquered Myanmar, India never invaded Myanmar which is better referred to as "land of disciples of Buddha." Indians have always been non-violent cultural messengers of the Indian civilisation to Myanmar. It implies even to the times of the glorious reigns of the great Mauryas or Moghuls when India was at its peak of glory, and a significant power only second in line to the Chinese empire in Asia.

Ever since India has culturally influenced the earliest of Myanmar's history, Buddhism has become such an essence of Myanmar that, "To be Myanmar is to be Buddhist." The cultural and religious adoptions have been in such a pattern that they bring out the different yet converging values of the two societies and civilisations.

British arrival in the Indian Subcontinent

After the British colonisation of both the countries, in the 18th century for India and Myanmar in the late 19th century, the remaining barriers between the two countries were broken. Both of them felt the same pain, atrocities and exploitation under the British imperialism. This gave birth to similar sentiments and a wave of anti-British instigating struggle to be liberated from the yoke of foreign rule. Conclusively the Indian nationalist movement was of dire importance to instigate Myanmar against the Britishers by providing them objectives of constitutional reforms. It also gave them a message of non-violent struggle and boycott of British systems which eventually became a part of Myanmar's mainstream struggle for freedom.

By the time, the British invaded Myanmar, the cultural influences from India became deep-rooted and matured into the attributes of Myanmar's lifestyle. As India is in closest vicinity to Myanmar among the Southeast Asian countries, it is entirely predictable that Myanmar must have been the first in Southeast Asia to receive the Indian culture traits. In the adoption of Indian practices and cultural norms, the Myanmar people exercised discretion in rejection of the Indian hierarchical caste system, giving women a high place in society, which was even noticed by Mahatma Gandhi during his visit to Myanmar in March 1929.[20]

Myanmar had a self-sufficient economy due to its agriculture. It had always been wealthy and prosperous through constant trade given its strategic location with trade routes between China and India passing straight through it. The Indian merchants and traders travelled along the coast and rivers, especially the Irrawaddy River which passes through the country along which the majority of the population lived. The impression of Indian cultural influences can be seen even today. Myanmar was the first amongst in the Southeast Asian countries to receive Buddhism, which eventually became the official patronised religion of the nation.

The Myanmar annexation aimed at the extension of complete colonial command over India and its resources. This annexation occurred in three phases of Anglo-Myanmar war, i.e. 1824, 1852 and 1885. Myanmar had a strategic significance for their imperialistic motives as it was situated between lucrative inland China's trade route that made it a vital buffer zone between French colonial possessions of mainland India-China. India's possession by the British took almost 200 years from the arrival of East India Company until the transfer of power to Queen Victoria as a Queen Empress of India in 1858. It is notable to mention that Britishers entered India as a humble trader, whereas in Myanmar as a colonial expert.

What Britishers assumed of Myanmar in the 19th century was an extension of India culturally, economically and politically. As they had a permanent and settled base in the eastern part of India until the 18th century, so they saw Myanmar as a natural grazing ground for their colonial objectives. When the civil war broke out between the forces of Alaungpaya, it was between the founder of the last Myanmar dynasty of Konbaung and the Mons in 1753. The Britishers (East India Company) took advantage and occupied the strategic island of Cape Negrais. By this, they aimed at checking French activities in the Bay of Bengal and also kept a watch on Myanmar's trade coming down the Irrawaddy. Myanmar King Alaungapaya initially protested modestly against the British interference and even wrote a letter addressed to King George II directly. The British Government did not pay any heed to it. The information from Mons prisoners about British rendering help to Mons inside the civil war provoked the Myanmar king, and he ordered the general massacre of the East India Company's officials on the Cape Negrais Island. However, then the British, who were preoccupied with the French as their traditional rival and the Indian subcontinent for their colonial possession, swallowed this humiliation resulting from the Cape Negrais episode of the Black hole and left Myanmar undisturbed for the coming decades.[21]

India-Myanmar Linkages during the British Empire

Myanmar was declared a British province in 1886 with its capital at Rangoon (present Yangoon). Myanmar's traditional society was drastically altered by the end of the monarchy and the separation of church and state. This altered the economic nature of society as well. After the opening of many trade routes, the demand for rice from Myanmar grew so huge that lands were brought under rice cultivation. However, in order to prepare the new land for cultivation, farmers were forced to borrow money from Indian money lenders at high interest rates and were often evicted for failure to pay back the loan.[22] When imported Indian labour ended up with most of the jobs, the local villages became lawless dens full of unemployment. The irony was that while the Myanmar economy grew, all the power was concentrated in the few hands that belonged to several British firms. In all this the Myanmar people ended up gaining nothing even though the economy was prospering.

Map 2.3: India and Myanmar during the period of British Rule

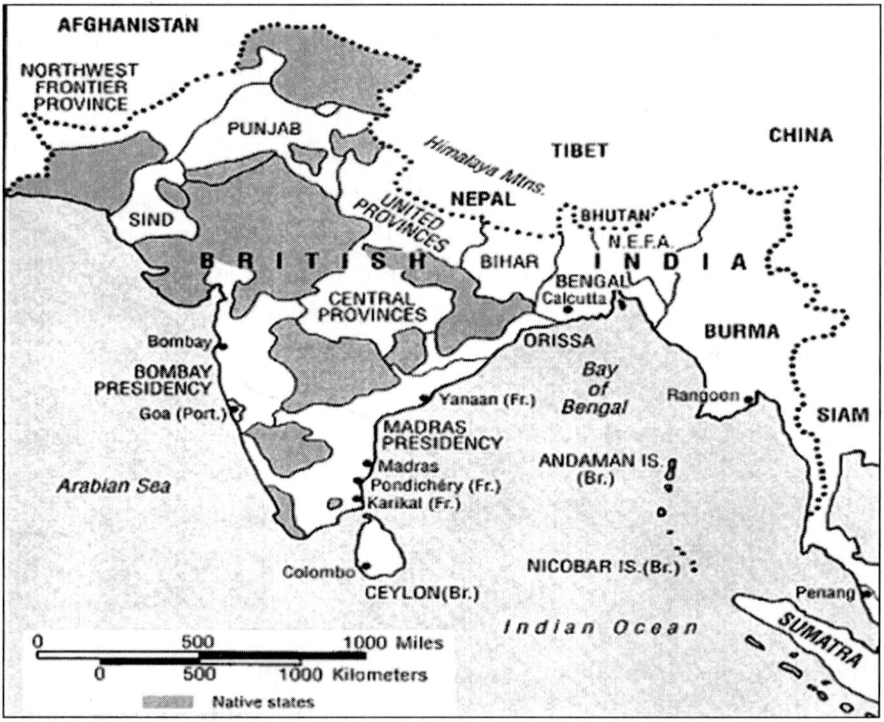

Source: www.historydiscussion.net

In the early twentieth century, few people from educated and well-to-do backgrounds went to London to study law. They returned with the belief that the situation in Myanmar at that time could only be improved through peaceful protests and table negotiations. Their advancements and peaceful strikes in the early 1920s bore fruits and led to constitutional reforms in 1923 therein creating a partially elected legislature with limited powers. However, this also made some people believe that the change in the scenario was not fast enough and the reforms not expansive. Eventually, such people replaced the older generation of London-educated elites at the head of the Myanmar nationalist movement and won the trust of the peasants as well. In 1936, they staged a thoroughly decisive strike which lead to Thakin Nu and Aung San entering the national movement. After 1937, Myanmar was acknowledged as an independent unit within the empire.[23] Myanmar was separated from India in 1937. It was granted a new constitution calling for a fully elected assembly. A few exciting events were happening at the front when Japanese invaded Myanmar and raised Burma Independence Army (BIA) with just 30 volunteers. Japanese were welcomed as liberators by Myanmarese, but very soon they were conquered by Japan. Ba Maw served as the first premier of Myanmar, but he was then forced out by U Saw in 1939, who later served as premier from 1940 to 1942 because Ba Maw was no more than a Japanese puppet in their hand. When the war turned against the Japanese, Myanmar declared a fully sovereign state in 1943, but this again came out as another facade. The sequence of these hostile events Disenchanted Aung San which led him to initiate negotiations with Lord Mountbatten in October 1943, and he officially joined the Allies with his renamed Burma National Army (BNA) in March 1945. During this period, Aung San successfully created a broad-based coalition of political parties called the Anti-Fascist Organisation renamed the Anti-Fascist People's Freedom League (AFPFL) to govern the country.[24]

The Japanese were routed out from Myanmar in May 1945. The defeat of the Japanese brought in a military administration in the country, and they demanded that Aung San must be treated in a trial as a traitor for his early collaboration with the Japanese. After the end of the war, the former civilian governor returned, and Aung San was duly arrested. This led to almost a rebellion, but the British backed off and sent Rance back to restore order and faith. Hereafter, the negotiations for Myanmar independence began which were completed successfully in January 1947. Although the agreement left both the communist and conservative branches of the AFPFL dissatisfied, however, later this sent the communists underground and the conservatives into opposition. Another party that was annoyed by this agreement was U Saw, who felt that Aung San had conceded a lot in the dialogues. Consequently, he planned the assassination of Aung San and almost the whole of his cabinet in July 1947. As a result, Thakin Nu was asked to form his new cabinet and to preside over Myanmar independence on January 4, 1948.

Figure 2.4: Nu-Attlee Burma Independence Agreement, London

Source: Google Image.

India-Myanmar Relations: 1948-1962

Having undergone the same exploitation in the hands of British, a similar struggle for independence for both Myanmar and India resulted in mutual understanding and close contacts between the leadership of the two nations after India got independence from the British on August 15, 1947 and Myanmar on January 4, 1948.

On the day of Myanmar's independence, Indian Prime Minister Jawaharlal Nehru said:

> As in the past, so in the future, the people of India will stand shoulder to shoulder with the people of Myanmar, and whether we have to

> share good fortune or ill fortune, we shall share it. This is a great and solemn day not only for Myanmar, but for India, and the whole of Asia.[25]

Ever since independence, the two countries have coexisted in mutual harmony and shared a fiduciary relationship with each other as nations, even though the relationship faced critical issues: boundary demarcation, the impact of insurgencies in border regions, nationalisation of India's legal bar and businesses on their ownership of land, managing and establishing relations with the powerful neighbour as well as with superpowers. Under the stewardship of Prime Ministers U Nu and Jawaharlal Nehru, who shared a close friendship, the bond between the two nations became even more friendly and cooperative.

Owing to the friendly ambience between the two leaders, whenever a troublesome issue surfaced the two personalities worked closely with mutual trust and friendship to resolve the issues, whereas the-post colonial relations between India and Myanmar influenced the fate of people of Indian origin in Myanmar. However, post-independence of the Myanmar government had worked upon protecting the fate of Myanmar people against the foreigners and to strengthen its economic interests as well. These measures hit the Indians living in Myanmar most adversely as the Indians constituted the most extensive section in the foreign population of independent Myanmar. In 1948, amongst a few acts passed by the Myanmar Government was the Land Alienation Act that forbade the sale of land to non-Myanmar nationals. The Myanmar Land Nationalisation Bill which was passed on October 11, 1949 aroused deep resentment and strong protest among Indians in both Myanmar and India.[26] However, the cordial friendship between Nehru and U Nu averted any unpleasant confrontation between the two allies. Nehru observed that the Land Nationalisation Acts of Myanmar were non-discriminatory, although they mostly affected Indians. However, Nehru also stood firm on the fact that instead of this act adequate compensation should be paid by Myanmar to the affected people, although the agreement that was reached was half-heartedly carried out by Myanmar Government.

The rice export from Myanmar to India intensively contributed to the cordial relationship between the two countries. In the 1950s, India was the largest rice customer for Myanmar; even India agreed to take more rice from Myanmar at a higher rate.

After gaining Myanmar's independence in 1948, Myanmar confronted an internal crisis and to counter this India extended assistance whatever it could offer to restore peace and normalcy in its neighbourhood. In 1949, the Myanmar Government was in crucial need of cash to meet its military expenses for suppressing the insurgency in the country. In such a critical need India provided arms and ammunition to the Myanmar Government which prevented the fall of Rangoon into the hands of the rebels. Later, in April 1950, the Indian minister of industry and supply Mr Gadgil confirmed the sale of six Dakota aeroplanes to Myanmar, which helped the government of Myanmar to maintain liaison with the towns that remained in their control during the hours of need.

With Myanmar's constructive efforts the Indian concern over the treatment of Indians receded. The two Prime Ministers started a practice of regular consultation and cooperation on the issues that concerned both countries and also on the broader issues like world peace and international issues. Another cordial move between the two nations was a Treaty of Friendship signed by both countries on July 7, 1951. This treaty was for five years and was supposed to hold in force "forever after that" if neither of the sides would give a notice desiring its termination six months before its expiry. The Treaty of Friendship came into force on January 31, 1952, with the exchange of instruments of ratification in Rangoon by Article VII of the treaty.[27]

A bicameral parliament was formed, consisting of House of Representatives and the House of Nationalities, elections were held in 1951-1952, 1956 and 1960. In 1960, General Ne Win led the government as a care taker in Myanmar. During his term, A Sino-Myanmar border agreement and a treaty of friendship and mutual non-aggression were signed on January 28, 1960. However, a Sino-Indian border conflict broke out in October 1962. Myanmar showed a neutral stand on the issue, not wanting to incur the hostility of either of the two. This neutral stand of Myanmar was interpreted as 'pro-Chinese' by India, and it naturally disturbed the harmonious relations between the two countries.

India-Myanmar Relations: 1963-1987

The India-Myanmar friendship post-independence served the interests of both the countries. Eventually, this relationship was disturbed when General Ne Win came to power by staging a military coup on March 2, 1962. This marked a stark change in Myanmar's foreign policy towards China which in turn had repercussions on India-Myanmar relations. This trend continued until the end of 1964. According to the economic policy of the nation, General Ne Win government showed nationalistic fervour. In the early phase of 1964, the Ne Win government nationalised shops and stores thus hitting small traders. The previous nationalisation measures of U Nu government had adversely hit the majority of Indian landlords, and the big financiers. It was the Indians who were the worst hit by Ne Win's nationalisation measures. According to the spokesman of the Myanmar Displaced Persons Association, over 12,000 Indian concerns with assets worth Rs 15 crore were affected.[28] These nationalisation measures were so vigorous that many Indians were deprived of even their means of livelihood. They were not given any compensation at the time of nationalisation, and many of them wanted to return to India. However, even this could not be possible as they could hardly pay for their passage as the Government of Myanmar did not even pay their passage facilities to them. When permitted to leave Myanmar, they were restrained to take anything along with them to India. Such grave situations of the Indians in Myanmar brought a near breakdown in the relationship of the two countries. However, the relationship began to regain its former stance towards the end of 1964.

In February 1965, General Ne Win visited India and the two countries issued a joint communiqué which stated: "A common outlook on international issues resulting from the pursuit of a policy of non-alignment has helped in the development of close and good neighbourly relations between the two countries."[29] The shift in Myanmar's attitude was due to the strained relationship between China and Myanmar then because of China's support to Myanmar insurgents. Later in June 1967, anti-Chinese riots broke out in Myanmar, although no evidence pointed to the involvement of Myanmar's Government in inspiring the riots. During this period, the close ties that India's Prime Minister Indira Gandhi and Myanmar's new leader General Ne Win shared played an essential role in the relationship of the two nations. On March 10, 1967, India and Myanmar signed the boundary agreement to demarcate the entire boundary between the two countries formally.[30] The agreement was ratified, and the instruments of ratification were exchanged by both the governments on May 30, 1967. It was believed that General Ne Win on his six days visit to India discussed the threat that China was posing to both the nations and the possibility to promote close political cooperation between them to meet the common danger.

A positive move to promote India-Myanmar trade was initiated with General Ne Win's visit to India on the invitation of Indian President during January 15-22, 1970. The bilateral trade relations and regional economic cooperation were among the major issues which were discussed. A new payment agreement on August 10, 1974, between India and Myanmar enabled Myanmar to buy goods from India like electrical goods, cotton textiles, pharmaceutical products and hardware worth Rs 7.5 crore, and in return India would import commodities like urea and mineral ores from Myanmar. It was the condition for Rs 2.17 crore project in October 1979, under which India would set up 21 pilot projects in Myanmar in areas ranging from plants for menthol, calcium carbide, glue and gelatin, to electro-chemical metallurgy, orange juice and Ferro-tungsten. The two-way trade turnover during 1987 was about Rs 36 crore.[31] During this period, another landmark in India-Myanmar relations was the problems posed by insurgents in Northeast India on the Naga and Mizo border. Both Mizos and Nagas are living on both the sides of the border of the countries. Myanmar rendered great help to India to counter the insurgency in the Northeast.

Myanmar's foreign policy from 1962, particularly after 1972, could be termed as an isolationist policy. Even during this period of isolation, Indian leaders paid visits to Myanmar. Indian External Affairs Minister Swaran Singh visited Myanmar in April 1973 and also Atal Bihari Vajpayee, the former External Affairs Minister, paid a visit to Myanmar in August 1977. However, India-Myanmar relationship suffered a setback from 1977 till 1988 as Myanmar nurtured friendship with China. Moreover, by 1987, Myanmar acted in expanding its relations with other countries by paying visits, such as General Ne Win visited the United States and the Federal Republic of Germany. Indian Prime Minister Rajiv Gandhi visited Myanmar in December 1987, but it did not contribute towards improvement in India-Myanmar relations.

India-Myanmar Relations: 1988-1998

India-Myanmar relations hit the lowest when India supported the pro-democratic upsurge in 1988 in Myanmar. In 1988, questions were raised, and there was growing unrest against the government's poor policies for rebuilding and restructuring the economic framework, including controls over Foreign Direct Investment (FDI). This led to pro-democracy demonstrations throughout the state, which was known as the 8888 Uprising, named after the date of the protest, August 8, 1988. Thousands of protester were killed on the same day. Martial law was implemented with immediate effects in the country, and State Law and Order Restoration Council (SLORC) took over Ne Win's constitutional government. In 1989, after taking over, SLORC also converted the official name of "Socialist Republic of Union of Burma" to "Union of Myanmar". Presently, its official name is "The Republic of the Union of Myanmar."

India was the first neighbouring country who stood firmly on the side of democracy when the 1988 uprising took place in Myanmar. The Indian Embassy in Rangoon actively helped the pro-democracy activists, and the officials were in touch with opposition groups like Aung San Suu Kyi, U Nu and the All Burma Federation of Students' Unions (ABFSU) during the uprising. The support was to such an extent that when the Myanmar student activists fled to the India-Myanmar border, the Indian Embassy in Rangoon provided them financial assistance to return to India. Indian government opened refugee camps in Manipur and Mizoram states for these students.

In 1989 External Affairs Minister Narasimha Rao informed a parliamentary panel that "strict instructions" had been given not to turn back any genuine Myanmar refugees seeking shelter in India.[32] The Indian government along with USA and Western countries, isolated the Myanmar military regime. India was also a sponsor of United Nations resolution condemning the Myanmar military junta for its violations of human rights in 1992. In 1990, general election in Myanmar, the National League for Democracy (NLD) had a landslide victory, and thereafter the Myanmar government escalated the repression on the democratic protesters in general and the NLD in particular. However, between 1991 and 1992, the foreign policy had a strategic shift and reviewed the foreign policy towards Myanmar and following the breakup of the Soviet Union the Indian government launched its "Look (Act) East Policy," which was defined by the then prime minister as "a strategic shift in India's vision of the world and India's place in the evolving global economy."[33] Since then, many initiatives have been pursued to improve ties, especially in trade relations among members of the Association of South East Asian Nations (ASEAN), India and other Asian states. As India's gateway to East Asia, the Myanmar military regime has been at a critical geo-strategic position, giving it a strong hold in negotiations with India.

There were times when Myanmar army personnel crossed the Indian border in pursuit of the Myanmar rebels. When the Myanmar government started paying attention to Kachin insurgents on the India-Myanmar border, an unwritten understanding developed between the authorities of the two countries: troops from either side could cross the border to a certain limit in pursuit of the insurgents.[34] India realised that it was need of the hour to have a friendly relationship with the Government of Myanmar for tackling their insurgency in the Northeast as some of these groups had their camps established in Myanmar. India had the vision to embrace globalisation after 1990 and to develop economically; it had to serve economic cooperation with its neighbour including Myanmar. Moreover, the close military and economic cooperation between

Myanmar and China were the cause of concern for Indian policies since 1988. In 1990, India extended its willingness to stabilise the relationship with Myanmar. However, the Myanmar government initially went against these attempts. In 1992, the Myanmar government showed some positive moves towards India's attempts to promote the bilateral relationship. From August 11-14, 1992, an 8-member Myanmar delegation of the Political Affairs Department of the Ministry of Foreign Affairs visited India and met the senior officials in the ministries of Home, External Affairs, Commerce and Defence of the Government of India. It was the first time any official Indo-Myanmar senior-level meeting was held since Rajiv Gandhi's visit to Myanmar in 1987.

In January 1994, Myanmar's Deputy Foreign Minister U Nyunt Swe visited India. During his 6-day visit, a series of meetings with Indian ministerial officials discussed wide-ranging issues to improve the relationship between the two countries. A Memorandum of Understanding was signed on January 21, 1994. Its primary objective is to promote cooperation between the civilian border authorities of the two countries and to prevent "illegal and insurgent activities." A bilateral agreement was also signed to regularise and promote border trade to be conducted through Moreh in Manipur State of India and Champhai in Mizoram State of India corresponding to Tamu and Hri on the Myanmar side.[35] The border trade officially opened on April 12, 1995, at Moreh in the presence of the then Indian Commerce Minister P. Chidambaram and the Myanmar trade minister Lt. General Tun Kyi. Since then, the India and Myanmar relationship has been steadily improving, and this has been marked some non-officials and officials visits of the senior officials and ministers of the two countries.

The people of India overwhelmingly welcomed the presentation of Noble Peace Prize winner Aung San Suu Kyi in October 1991 while she was under house arrest in her own country. The prominent citizens and leaders of political parties from India expressed their support to the democratic movement in Myanmar and even urged the military government to release her from house arrest. India conferred its prestigious Jawaharlal Nehru Award for International Understanding for 1993 to

Aung San Suu Kyi on November 14, 1995, in India.[36] Meanwhile, the relationships between the two countries improved incredibly as regular meetings, exchange visits and sharing of intelligence became more frequent. The bilateral trade between India and Myanmar increased substantially which in turn had a positive impression on the political relations of both countries. It can be rightly said that trade relations between India and Myanmar were a right step towards reconciliation and cooperation. The Myanmar military junta was looking for recognition, especially from India, and other Asian countries. India was cautious of reports that Myanmar permitted a military base in the Bay of Bengal and sea access to the Indian Ocean. On the other end, Myanmar's military leadership was unsure about India's position on the pro-democracy movement in Myanmar.

Although the Myanmar junta had always been cautious of India's moves and actions they were also uncomfortable with its dependence over China. India reaped the benefits by leaping on the confluence of national interests between the two countries to give an added push to its ties with Myanmar. The comfort level between the two countries saw a gradual increase after 1988, although until that time, the ties were influenced by the internal factors. India and Myanmar were all set to take their relations to the next platform in 1996. However, the incumbent Indian government was voted out of power in May 1996 till March 1998. The country saw three prime ministers coming to power, and none of their governments could stay long enough to take decisive policy decisions and so the process of enhancing bilateral relations stagnated.[37]

India-Myanmar Relations: 1999-2010

Indian policy makers took a swift turn and enhanced their policies concerning 'Eastern Strategy'. A high-level interaction was held between Home Ministers of both the countries in India to specifically strengthen the areas of cooperation in issues like cross-border terrorism and having better communication links. India conveyed her consent to arrange a training programme for anti-narcotics officials of Myanmar. In the early period of 2000, a military general high-level meeting was held between General VP Malik and General Maung Aye to give an initiate of Military to Military contacts after a gap of twelve years since 1988. In this meeting business and security were also the main section of the agenda.[38]

In October 2004, India and Myanmar signed an agreement on hydro-electric power, cultural exchanges and security, headed by Myanmar's General Than Shwe with his delegation of cabinet ministers held for six days in India. The then President of India, Abdul Kalam, visited Myanmar to sign an accord on cooperation in remote-sensing technology, two MoUs on cooperation and coordination in the petroleum sector and in the field of Buddhist studies in March 2006. As an extension to these visits, more meetings were held between both the nations focusing on the sensitive border and defence dialogues, along with discussions on arms sales. On April 23, 2007, an 18-member Myanmar Army delegation led by Brigadier General Tin Maung Ohn visited Calcutta for the 30th biannual liaison meeting of army officials from both countries.[39] Relations got boosted after getting the political support from India to the military junta's political transition plan after the revolt of September 2007. India also supported Myanmar's desire to become a full member of SAARC and welcomed its joining in the regional grouping.[40]

India-Myanmar Relations: 2011 and Beyond

Since 2011, there have been numerous effective changes, such as freedom of political prisoners, including the known figure Aung San Suu Kyi, various reforms in the economic sector with media freedom, social and administrative domain have been brought about by Thein Sein government. However, 25 per cent seats are reserved for the military, and the strong presence of Members of Parliament from the military-rooted ruling Union Solidarity and Development Party (USDP) Parliament too has evolved into an active deliberative and lawmaking forum. The changes brought Myanmar back into the international mainstream after five decades of military rule and its chairmanship of ASEAN in the year (2014) has gone off quite smoothly. Myanmar is now our most rapidly growing neighbour experiencing 6.4 per cent

GDP growth rates (2019). There can be mutual benefit if both India and Myanmar can work together to truly transform the evolving connectivity corridors into development corridors which demonstrate 'Act East' policy. Building an interlaced economic partnership across the border can form an enduring bond between the two countries that already enjoy harmonious political ties. India's Act East Policy should mainly focus in the long run and must include not only the booming Southeast Asian economies but also Myanmar and countries in the Asia Pacific, such as Vietnam, Laos, Cambodia, North and South Korea. Engaging Japan shall be particularly helpful in honing the counter-China strategies. Unless a proactive realist approach is taken, it shall be quite hard to become a permanent or substantial fixture in the East Asian political-economic landscape.

A diversity of Foreign Direct Investment in Myanmar shall undoubtedly be a more desirable option for India than reckoning with an ominous monopoly. The beginning of a new Foreign Investment Law aimed at attracting outside companies to establish businesses in Myanmar and provide much-needed employment and infrastructure were significant reforms passed in November 2012. The legislation permits foreign-owned firms to operate in the country. India was invited to invest in infrastructure by Myanmar. Accordingly, India and Myanmar signed several agreements and MoUs to improve the connectivity by road, air and multi-modal transport. A year later, post-World Economic Forum meeting, India offered Myanmar US$ 150 million to set up a Special Economic Zone in Sittwe which will connect Kolkata via sea. Crucially, Myanmar's infrastructure will also connect India to Southeast Asia. The development and infrastructure investment projects aided by India were in continuation to the 2012 deal between the two nations. India also increased the US$ 500 million credit line for developmental projects.

India is keen to continue its FDI policy with Myanmar in a number of other areas. Myanmar being a transitioning economy which also requires investments from India like country. The Indian government had announced its investments, accounted to US$ 2.6 billion in 2013 in Myanmar. Both countries have fixed a bilateral objective to increase trade volume, US$ 1.872 billion in 2012 to US$ 3 billion by 2015. To accomplish this objective, India increased its low exports of only US$ 542 million. India-Myanmar bilateral trade reached up to US$ 2.17 billion for 2016-17, out of which India's export contributed US$ 1.11 billion and India's import accounts US$ 1.06 billion. Indian investors have a supremacy in the service sectors of Information Technology and education. They will support the burgeoning investments in manufacturing, agriculture, automobiles, pharmaceuticals and healthcare.[41]

Map 2.4: India and China Oil/Gas pipelines and highways in Myanmar

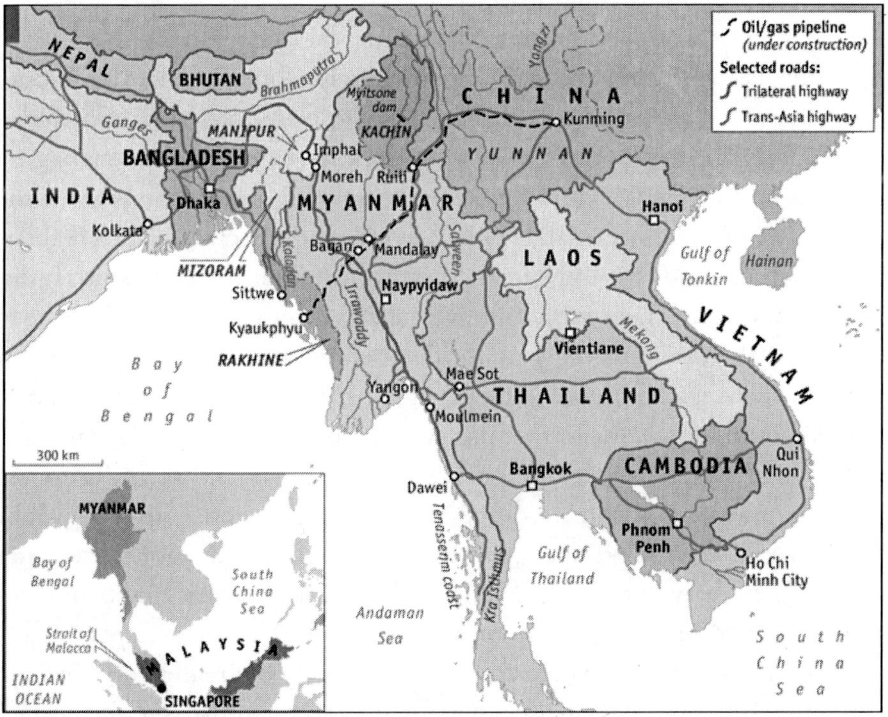

Source: *The Economist.*

There are Projects executed by Indian companies in recent years in a variety of sectors such as roads, railways, telecommunication, automotive, energy and remote sensing. Construction and upgrading of Tamu-Kalemyo-Kalewa road have been completed. RITES have been assisting Myanmar in improving its railway transport system. ISRO subsequently upgraded a data processing centre for remote sensing applications. Tata has set up a turbo-truck assembly plant with assistance from a line of credit by the Indian government. Earlier, a project for the high-speed link in 32 Myanmar cities was completed by the telecommunication company (TCIL). Three leading companies—OVL, GAIL and Essar—have been active in the energy sector. Setting up of a massive turbo-truck assembly plant by TATA Motors, setting up of India-Myanmar Industrial Training Centre, and Myanmar-India Entrepreneurship Development Centre, India-Myanmar Centre for Enhancement of IT Skills were some initiatives by both the nations.[42]

A democratic Myanmar offers scope for engagement over wide-ranging issues of governance and institution-building to the Indian government. Democratic India remains the best-practising and robust democracy in its environs, acquiring decades of practice of managing dissent and diversity. Moreover, a democratising Myanmar bridges the gap between India's normative positions of pro-democracy and its realistic approach of productive engagement with the military leadership. India, despite its engagement with military-ruled Myanmar, found it difficult to reconcile the domestic support for democratic movements in Myanmar and the strategic imperative of engaging the latter. This reconciliation can allow India to concentrate its resources on developing relations with Myanmar. Ultimately, a democratising Myanmar allows India to tap into the most significant resource base of engagement—pro-democracy leaders and support groups operating in India. The return of these exiles to their country can further help India strengthen its constituencies within the political leadership of Myanmar.

India can also get benefit from the possibility of greater coordination in combating transnational crimes in India's Northeast, such as armed insurgency, trafficking in drugs, arms and human beings, and illegal cross-border migration. Moreover, the positive changes in Myanmar may reduce the flow of illegal cross-border movement of people that proved to be an essential carrier and conduit of cross-border trafficking in arms and drugs and overall instability along the border.

In the current scenario, India can engage Myanmar more freely and widen the arena of engagement including defence and security cooperation. Nevertheless, the opening up of Myanmar also poses a critical challenge to India's engagement with Myanmar. In the presence of other players, India has to be more attentive to Myanmar's concerns and proactive in its policy initiatives for bilateral and multilateral cooperation. Otherwise, India might see the strategic space being taken over by other players from both the West as well as the East.

Notes

1. *Myanmar* also refers to a citizen of Myanmar, or more specifically, a person from the majority of Bamar ethnic group. In 1989, the military junta officially changed the English version of its name from Burma to Myanmar.
2. Central Intelligence Agency "Burma," The World Fact Book. Available at https://www.cia.gov/library/ publications/the-world-factbook/geos /bm.html (Accessed on October 14, 2014).
3. Aung San Suu Kyi (1991), *Freedom from Fear and other Writings*, Penguin Books, London, p. 5.
4. A. Bhattacharya and D. Chakraborty (2011), "India's Cross-Border Infrastructure Initiatives in South and Southeast Asia," *The International Spectator: Italian Journal of International Affairs*, Vol. 46 (2), pp. 109-25.
5. Y. Singh (2007), "India's Myanmar Policy: A Dilemma between Realism and Idealism," IPCS Special Report, No. 37, p.3. Available at http://www.ipcs.org/pdf_file/issue/928587478IPCS-Special-Report-37.pdf (Accessed on March 12, 2015).
6. The Golden Triangle is one of the world's most illicit opium producing regions, incorporating Myanmar, Thailand and Laos. Myanmar is the world's second largest producer of illicit opium, after Afghanistan.
7. Ministry of Health – Government of Myanmar, Country Profile-Natural Resources (2013). Available at http://www.moh.gov.mm/file/COUNTRY%20PROFILE.pdf (Accessed on June 5, 2014).
8. Ranjit Gupta (2013), "China, Myanmar and India: A Strategic Perspective," *Indian Foreign Affairs Journal* Vol. 8(1). Available at https://www.questia.com/library/journal/1P3-3079009831/china-myanmar-and-india-a-strategic-perspective (Accessed on April 7, 2015).
9. Toshihiro Kudo (2007), "Myanmar and Japan: How close Friends become estranged," *Institute of Developing Economies,* IDE Discussion Paper No. 118, p. 4. Available at http://www.ide.go.jp/English/Publish/Download/Dp/pdf/118.pdf (Accessed on June 15, 2015).
10. National Portal of India, http://india.gov.in/india-glance/profile (Accessed on July 15, 2016).
11. Address by Former Defence Minister (2005), Pranab Mukherjee at the Carnegie Endowment for International Peace, India's Strategic Perspective, Washington D.C. Available at http://www.indianembassy.org/press_release/2005/%20June/11.htm (Accessed on November 11, 2016).

12. Romila Thapar (1963), *Ashoka & the Decline of the Mauryas*, Oxford University Press, New Delhi, p. 54.
13. Dr. P.N. Chopra (ed.) (1990), "The Gazetteer of India: History and Culture," Vol. 2, Publication Division, *Ministry Information and Broadcasting*, GOI.
14. P Arthur Phayre (2013), *History of Burma: From the earliest time to the end of First war with British India*, Hardpress Ltd. Publication, United States, p. 106.
15. P Arthur Phayre (1883), *History of Burma including Myanmar proper Pegu, Taungu, Tenasserim and Arakan*, Trubner & Co., Ludgate Hill Publication, London, p. 93.
16. Ibid., p. 38.
17. Ibid., p. 99.
18. Andrew Huxley (1995), "Buddhism and Law: The view from Mandalay", *Journal of the International Association of Buddhist Studies*, Vol. 18(1), p. 78.
19. Jim Russell (2005), "Bangladesh and Myanmar", *Travel Diaries*, p. 18. Available at http://jimrussell.id.au/2005_ bangladesh_&_myanmar.htm (Accessed on August 20, 2016).
20. Ministry of Information & Broadcasting, Government of India (1970), "The Collected Works of Mahatma Gandhi Vol.40 February-May 1929", The Publication Division. Available at https://www.gandhiheritageportal.org/the-collected-works-of-mahatma-gandhi (Accessed on May 21, 2016).
21. D.R. Sardesai (1977), *British Trade and Expansion in Southeast Asia 1830-1914*, Allied Publication, Maharashtra, India, p. 43.
22. Lee Bih Ne (2013), *Brief History of Myanmar and Thailand*, Desktop Publisher, Philadelphia, p. 56.
23. As of 1923 Myanmar had a distinct government within the framework of British India. The separation of Myanmar from India was decided under the Government of Myanmar Act of 1935 which came into force on the 1st of April 1937.
24. Konrad Mitchell Lawson (2012), "Wartime atrocities and the politics of Treason in the Ruins of the Japnese Empire, 1937-1953", Ph.D thesis, Department of History, Harvard University, Cambridge, p. 172. Available at http://nrs.harvard.edu/urn-3:HUL.InstRepos:9795484 (Accessed on June 12, 2015).
25. Bibhu Prasad Routray (2011), "India-Myanmar Relations: triumph of Pragmatism", Vol. 1(1), p. 301.
26. Thin Thin Aung and Soe Myint (2001), "India-Burma Relations", *International Institute for Democracy and Electoral Assistance*, p. 89. Available at http://www.idea.int/asia_pacific/burma/upload/chap4.pdf (Accessed on June 12, 2016).
27. Annexure A.
28. Thin Thin Aung and Soe Myint (2001), "India-Burma Relations", *International Institute for Democracy and Electoral Assistance*, p. 91. Available at http://www.idea.int/asia_pacific/burma/upload/chap4.pdf (Accessed on June 12, 2016).
29. R Venkataraman (2001), "Research on Indo-Burma Relations". Available at http://www.zoominfo.com/p/India-Venkataraman/211168326 (Accessed on July 15, 2016).
30. See Annexure B.
31. Thin Thin Aung and Soe Myint (2001), "India-Burma Relations", *International Institute for Democracy and Electoral Assistance*, p. 92. Available at http://www.idea.int/asia_pacific/burma/upload/chap4.pdf (Accessed on June 12, 2016).

32. Soe Myint (2003), "India Should do more for Myanmar's Democracy", Mizzima News. Available at http://www.burmatoday.net/mizzima2003/mizzima/2003/06/030610_india_mizzima.htm (Accessed on May 22, 2016).
33. B Ghoshal (2013), "China's perception of India's Look (Act) East Policy and Its Implication," IDSA Monograph Series, No. 26, p. 21.
34. Nikoline Fon Holmoy (2013), "Recurring Conflicts in Northeast India," An analysis at the International, Federal and Group level, Master Thesis in Political Science, NTNU, Trondheim, p. 47.
35. Bibhu Prasad Routray (2011), "India-Myanmar Relations: triumph of Pragmatism," *Jindal Journal of International Affairs*, Vol. 1(1), p. 319.
36. Ministry of External Affairs, Government of India, Annual Report 1995-96. Available online at http://mealib.nic.in/?2524?000 (Accessed on March 25, 2017).
37. R Hariharan (2004), "Taking a Re-Look at India-Myanmar Relations," *South Asia Analysis Group*, Paper No. 1141. Available at http://www.southasiaanalysis.org/paper1141 (Accessed on May 26, 2016).
38. Renaud Egreteau (2005), *Wooing the Generals: India's New Burma policy*, Authors Press and Centre for Social Sciences and Humanities, Aséanie, India, p. 179. Available at http://www.persee.fr/web/revues/home/prescript/article/asean_08599009_2005_num_15_1_1856 (Accessed on December 16, 2016).
39. Marie Lall (2008), "India-Myanmar Relations-Geopolitics and Energy in Light of the New Balance of Power in Asia," *Institute of South Asian Studies*, Working Paper No. 29. Available at http://www.burmalibrary.org/docs09/Geopolitics&Energy-Lall-red.pdf (Accessed on June 9, 2016).
40. K Yhome (2009), "India-Myanmar Relations (1998-2008) A decade of re defining bilateral ties," Observer Research Foundation, ORF Paper #10. Available at https://www.orfonline.org/research/india-myanmar-relations-1998-2008-a-decade-of-redefining-bilateral-relations/ (Accessed on June 15, 2016).
41. Asma Masood (2013), "Myanmar: Achieving India's Economic Interests," *Institute of Peace and Conflict Studies*, Article No. 4037. Available at http://www.ipcs.org/print_article-details.php?recNo=4071 (Accessed on June 20, 2016).
42. B P Routrey (2011), "India-Myanmar Relations: Triumph of pragmatism," *Jindal School of International Affair*, Vol 1(1), pp. 301-22.

3
Areas of Cooperation and Concern between India and Myanmar

Introduction

India and Myanmar share strong friendly relations from centuries, connected by strong linkages of past and commonness in spirituality and culture. During the early 1990s, however, a new momentum had been generated in their relationship. In the same period, India ignited its well-known Look (Act) East Policy (LEP), symbolising a necessary move in India's strategic vision in its external policy and its position in the international domain. Since then, India and Myanmar's relations have received a boost from more aggressive initiatives in forging formal agreements and deepening economic, strategic, political, cultural and people-to-people ties between them.[1] Prime Minister of India, Narendra Modi came into power in 2014 and continued the commitment to the Look East Policy and renamed it 'Act East Policy' since then.

India and Myanmar are important to each other from strategic and economic angles. Myanmar is located at a critical geo-strategic place in the world. Both nations edge each other with long 1,643 km land border and also have a long maritime boundary in the Bay of Bengal and the Andaman Sea. This geographic contiguity has transformed their multi-dimensional relation. Both nations have become strategically essential for one another. Myanmar is often regarded as a land-bridge between India and Southeast Asia and beyond East Asia. It acts as a precursor for India and the neighbouring countries in the region. India and Myanmar relationship is integral to India's Look (Act) East Policy, in the view of a more firm and flourishing Asia and encircling influence in the Indian Ocean and the Pacific Ocean. Therefore, Connectivity is essential between India and Myanmar. With the end of military rule in 2011 in Myanmar, India-Myanmar relations witnessed more promises for closer ties in the ongoing journey towards democratisation and embarked on economic and political reforms. In recent years, elected candidates of Myanmar have been approaching India to explore and learn the procedures and practices of parliament. India, above all, is the largest democracy in the world and may edify fundamental knowledge to its neighbour nation whose progress was decelerated by the absence of democracy. India-Myanmar partnership has shown growth, which can be defined not only by development associations but also by its matched capacity building.

India and Myanmar representatives and leaders have been warmly exchanging their opinions on enhancing their current benign relations. In October 2020, India and Myanmar seeking to boost bilateral ties through a high level visit by Foreign Secretary Harsh Vardhan Shringla and Chief of Army Staff Gen. M.M. Naravane to the eastern neighbour; Myanmar, the Northeast remains the focus of India's geopolitical strategy towards the east. The key factors like connectivity, security and defence cooperation, boundaries, development aid, energy cooperation, trade and commerce and people-to-people ties were the focus areas of interaction. In early 2012, India extended a US$ 500-million loan to Myanmar for development in various sectors like health, infrastructure and power generation of which US$ 140 million is for infrastructure.[2]

India-Myanmar Bilateral Engagements

India and Myanmar's geographical proximity has provided the stances to each nation in developing and sustaining friendly and robust relations. This also facilitated the people-to-people contact in border areas. Both nations bilateral relation took off when India and Myanmar signed a Treaty of Friendship in 1951.[3]

Since then various agreements have been signed between both the nations to enhance bilateral Cooperation. To facilitate the regular dialogue on a stretch of issues of common interests Institutional mechanisms have been installed. In 2002, Indian Consulate General in Mandalay was re-opened, and a new Consulate General of Myanmar was set up in Kolkata. India has been responsive to the needs of friendly people of Myanmar and has been providing relief materials and assistance.[4] For instance, India provided aid of US$ 1 million for humanitarian relief and rehabilitation for the areas affected by the severe earthquake in Shan State in March 2011. India also assisted the communal riot-affected people of Rakhine State with a contribution of US$ 1.2 million.[5]

India and Myanmar are determined to upgrade their land connectivity. Myanmar is considered as India's gateway to ASEAN. India's approach in India-ASEAN engagement underlining a vital issue in their dialogues such as on enhanced road and rail connectivity between them for rapid progress. A transformation is underway in Myanmar towards an actual democratic structure, and trade and investment provide the platforms to a market economy which will enhance connectivity and may help both countries to exploit the benefits. India's four Northeastern states,, Nagaland, Manipur, Mizoram and Arunachal Pradesh, share borders with Myanmar. They have been weighing how connectivity can assist to strengthen the choices for addressing the improvement concerns to their states. This has also been highlighted in the NER Vision 2020 document spelling out strategies for peace, progress and prosperity in the North Eastern Region.[6]

The enhanced relations have been exhibiting results in terms of multilateral trade which has matured, and Indian companies have established their poles in Myanmar. Best Indian companies are looking forward to investing in energy and aviation industries, including telecommunications. Nurturing Better relations with Myanmar is crucial to the economic enrichment of India's North-eastern states. The undeveloped and troubled Northeast India has been the result of its acute failure of connectivity and market establishment. India's Look (Act) East Policy with its approach has the potential to target a paradigm turn in the overall progress of the nation in building a stronger relationship with Myanmar. However, slow implementation and execution in projects might be a sour note amidst the developments in India-Myanmar relations. Sometimes, certain agreements have been established without specific consideration of the realistic prospects of their execution and functionalisation. Moreover, this has been accepted by the Myanmar government, which tends to think that India is inactive in performance. India must prove such a conceptualisation incorrect. At the same time, India is also viewed as a 'good omen' due to its historical and spiritual connection. Relations between the two countries are at present stable, so India needs to leverage this for better links and more constructive bilateral ties.[7]

Development Cooperation between India and Myanmar

Development cooperation is a key to the relationship. India has offered technical and financial assistance for projects in Myanmar, both in infrastructural and in the areas of Human Resource Development and institutional capacity building.[8] India and Myanmar have a number of successful projects in the areas of agriculture, infrastructure, industrial development, human resource development, power, health. The development cooperation between the two countries is being financed under grants and concessional loans amounting to US$ 1.2 billion.[9] India and Myanmar have signed the MoU on the US$ 500 million Line of Credit to be utilised in the infrastructure development projects, including in the fields of Agriculture and Irrigation, Rail transportation, Electric power and many more sectors in Myanmar.[10]

Multi-Mode Connectivity

The present era belongs to connectivity. Tangible connectivity is the foundation of all other forms of connectivity such as socio-economic connections and people-to-people linkages. Due to India-Myanmar's geographical proximity, the rail, road, inland waterway, air and maritime bridging are significant for integrating the region as well as to boost and grow economic cooperation which would contribute to the socio-economic development of the region. Myanmar has a sizeable network of domestic road connectivity, but all these roads are not in good state. Therefore, upgrading the existing network in the country has become one of the primary tasks to strengthen them so that they can withstand traffic. Existing national road networks connected with international highways, must also be built at par with international standards and become more reliable to bear cross-country trade and traffic. India, Myanmar and Thailand would be connected by the Trilateral Highway after completion. It has many stretches that are in terrible driving condition, adding, for instance, the Kalewa-Yagi stretch. The trade prospects are failing in Kalewa even after having Indian goods at little costs due to the lousy road conditions making the area inaccessible. There is also a school of thought who recommends that this is the correct time to revive and develop the Stilwell road. This strategic road was constructed for allied forces during WW-II to carry logistic supplies to China. This stretch bridges Kunming in China with Assam in India through Myanmar. Myanmar portion of the road descends in Kachin state. The road in the Indian territory remains less usable as the government of India kept it classified and didn't release any statement on it. The Indian government is taking benefit of the doubt that anti-India insurgents and rebels can exploit the road. Look (Act) East Policy has envisioned many projects to explore and establish a greater network of physical connectivity.[11] There is no dearth of literature relating to the possibilities of these links with the assessment of such projects, but effective implementation on these projects remains a challenge. The maximum benefits of these projects can be achieved only through the integration of these projects through proper planning. Physical links between the two countries can also be transformed into development corridors. The concept of such corridors is beneficial for the economic growth of the two countries, so there is a need to meet the demands from enlarged connectivity to develop expected outcomes.

The Kaladan Multi-Modal Transit Transport Project

The Kaladan Multi-Modal Transit Transport Project (hereafter Kaladan Project) would bridge eastern flank seaports of Kolkata of India to its less utilised landlocked Northeastern state of Mizoram of India by crossing Arakan, Sittwe and Chin States of Myanmar via a recently constructed river and highway transportation arrangement. India conceived the project intended to develop a route between its mainland and India's Northeast region for trade purposes which is a crucial component of India's Look (Act) East Policy. The Kaladan Project is expected to strengthen the economic linkages with Myanmar and the rest of Southeast Asia. The original map conceptualised the Kaladan Project as a precursor to establishing a gas pipeline along the same route, and financing for the entire Project—currently estimated at US$ 214 million—is being provided through the Indian Ministry of External Affairs (MEA).[12] In April 2008, Myanmar and India signed a foundational agreement titled the Framework Agreement between the Government of the Republic of India and the Government of the Union of Myanmar for the construction and operation of a multi-modal transit transport facility on Kaladan River connecting the Sittwe port in Myanmar with the state of Mizoram in India.[13] Since the Framework Agreement work has progressed sporadically, and the Project is expected to be fully operational by the end of 2020 after many delays.[14]

The Kaladan Project has geo-strategic significance for India as it is one of the endeavours by India to safeguard its interests in Southeast and East Asia by connecting the Mizoram state of India to Sittwe port of Myanmar.[15] Indian scholars often raise the point that China's presence is expanding rapidly in the region, so simultaneously India must make some moves before it is left behind in the race. To counter-balance China's growing influence in the region, especially in the Bay of Bengal, the Kaladan Project and port at Sittwe can be utilised by India. China's famously known 'String of Pearls' strategy has Sittwe—along with the Coco Islands and Kyauk Phyu—which is often considered the major bases in its strategy. India has considered the Bay of Bengal its domain of influence and had always put efforts to maintain the status quo., India-Myanmar have been increasing their naval cooperation by engaging themselves in the IMNEX-March 2018 bilateral naval exercise in the Bay of Bengal to secure maritime borders.

The Kaladan Project Impact Area

About one million people live near the Kaladan River, who are mainly dependent on the river for their bread and butter by fishing, as a way of transportation, as a source of water for irrigation and family usages.

Map 3.1: The Directions of the KMMTTP

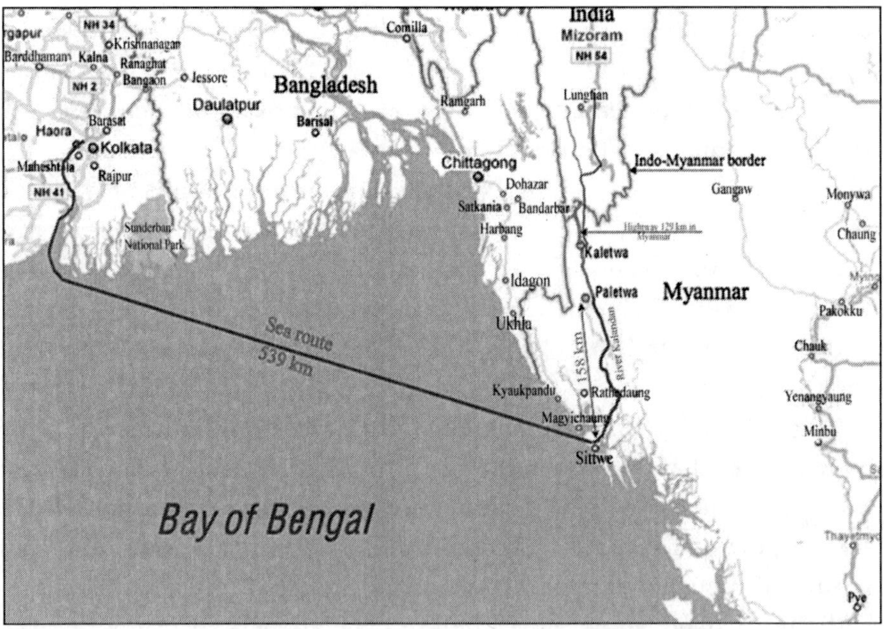

Source: www.researchgate.net

Different Phases of the Kaladan Project and its Current Status

Work developments on the four phases of the Project are as follows:

Phase 1: A Seaport and Transhipment Terminal at Sittwe

A new port is expected to be constructed on 60,000 sq m of public land at Sittwe in the Arakan State. An old jetty is currently being used by the Myanmar Port Authority to serve domestic ships travelling from Yangon, Mon State and Tanintharyi Region. Next to the existing jetty is the Myo Ma fish market where local fishers sell their catch. The Township Governmental Municipality Office manages the Myo Ma market. The new Sittwe deep sea port—locally referred to as the "Indian Port"—will feature two large jetties measuring 219 m by 15 m and 54 m by 15 m to accommodate giant cargo ships.[16] An area of 48,000 sq m has been reclaimed from the harbour nearby. Myanmar government has provided 6 hectares of public land which includes coastal/deltas land. This delta land was earlier used by local fisherman and some residents for recreational purposes out of the reclaimed area for the new port 560,000 cubic tonnes of soil which was dredged from the adjacent channel near the

Figure 3.1: Satellite Image of Sittwe Port, Myanmar

Source: Google Image.

face of Kaladan River. The dredging operation is meant to provide aggregate material used for reclaiming the land at Sittwe port and transformer nearby and 55 hectares of harbour water into a deep-sea port to accommodate larger cargo ships. The new port will have the capacity for service ships up to 20,000 deadweight tonnage. There will also be a transhipment terminal, including off/on leading equipment and a complex of 29 warehouses to be constructed at the Sittwe port. The port will also be used to shift cargo from large ships to small vessels which can navigate in the Kaladan River. Navigation will be done from Platewa town in chin state to Kaladan River. It is a very ambitious project which is being built jointly by the inland waterways authority of India and Essar Project Ltd. The project has been completed.

Phase 2: Development of Kaladan River Inland Waterway Infrastructure from Sittwe to Paletwa

The second stage is the widening and dredging of stretches of the Kaladan river that has been turned into a 160 km inland waterway conveyance structure for cargo ships. Stage two also includes the construction of a transhipment terminal and a port at Paletwa Town, along building six cargo vessels which will cater to the waterway between the Paletwa ports and Sittwe. In May 2010, the India-Myanmar Multi-Sectoral Group decided to deviate from the original Detailed Project Report by shifting the terminal-point of the inland waterway transport system from Kaletwa to Paletwa.[17] The width and depth of Kaladan River were not uniform throughout its long journey. Somewhere it was less deep and at some places, it was less broad. So, for the safer passage of cargo ships, it is necessary that width and depth should be the same throughout the journey. The stretch of Kaladan River between Paletwa and Kaletwa requires a handsome amount of dredging and widening due to the existence of many shallow shoals and exposed rocks and boulders. Initially, no one had estimated that dredging and widening of the river would also be required at a lateral stage. However, In 2017 the Indian Ambassador to Myanmar announced that dredging is going to take place at four or five points between Sittwe and Paletwa. The aggregative material created during these dredging operations will be shifted into the designated surface or underwater dumping field. Additional riverine infrastructure to be built in Phase Two includes ten navigational buoys placed in the stretch of river between Sittwe and Kyauktaw and 70 fixed shore markers—permanent six-metre concrete posts on the river banks—installed in the stretch of river between Kyauktaw and Paletwa.[18] At Paletwa town, it is also proposed to build a port complex at the terminal point of the waterway transport system. The new port at Sittwe is expected to accommodate several cargo ships which have a length of 200 m and have a capacity of 6000 DWT. The transhipment terminal will also be installed at the port complex to transfer cargo from waterway to trucks and to ply on the new highway from Myanmar to Indian borders. It is proposed to construct a river bed near Paletwa port which will be built 2 m deep to make the easy access and pass of the IWT cargo ships. Myanmar government has also allotted 3 hectares of land for the port complex on this land. Eventually, Phase two consider the construction of six each; 260-tonne cargo vessels which would bridge the stretch between the Sittwe Port and the Paletwa Port along the Kaladan River. The project was completed on June 2014 as estimated.

Phase 3: A highway between Paletwa and the Mizoram Border

The construction of a two-lane highway of 130 km is the part of the Kaladan Project. This road runs from Paletwa town to Myeikwa at the Indian border. The length of the above highway was doubled from 61 to 130 km when the decision was taken to move the terminal point of the inland waterway system from Kaletwa to Paletwa. Myanmar government is liable to provide the required land for the project. Phase three is an intensively land-oriented project in which the Ministry of Construction of Myanmar is directly looking after the project. Ministry of Construction along with the Max Myanmar Group of companies is the implementing partner in the project for road construction in Paletwa Township. In 2018, Phase three construction work has been started It includes 61 km

Kaletwa-Myeikwa highway which would be built in a valley parallel to the Kalet River covering 15 villages on the route. Construction of 387 culverts, 11 bridges on the stream and a protection wall was involved in the original highway DPR along eleven buses and three trucks rest stands. The proposal meant to provide road construction material by dredging aggregates from nearby rivers would simultaneously help India in arranging. There is a dearth of local labour and imported labour as there is an unwillingness in working in such a remote and malaria-prone field. Therefore, heavy machinery is passed to use and construct the highway. It is learned from the status of phase three that there is no clarity to anyone. It seems likely that the Kaletwa-Myeikwa stretch would be the same, but residents may have an idea to the route of the Paletwa-Kaletwa section. One possible route for the Paletwa-Kaletwa highway would be along the Kaladan River valley. Southern Paletwa township is highly crowded than the Northern part, and this route would pass through around 50 villages. With the expanding of the Phase Three highway from 61 to 130 km, the land and dredged aggregates required for construction would go high. An EIA for the new project route in Chin State is necessary, mainly if the highway needs extensive aggregate mining from nearby creeks, streams and rivers.

Phase 4: Construction of Highway from Lawngtlai to Lomasu

The construction of a two-lane highway from Lawngtlai to Lomasu is the fourth stage of the Kaladan Project at the India-Myanmar border covering 100 km distance approximately. It is an extension of Indian National Highway no. 54. Its construction is being done by Ministry of Development of North Eastern Region's special accelerated road development programme of the Northeast of India. The Lawngtlai and Lomasu highway would be broader in specific areas, and otherwise, breadth of the highway is set 12 meters. ARSS-Atlanta and RDS project are two Indian contractors who will work under the Mizoram public works department. Both will construct different lengths, parcels and stretches which start from Lawngtlai to 38th km and next from 38th to 71.50 by ARSS-Atlanta, RDS would construct the next stretch up to

99.83. In February 2020, the reports came out that this project has been waiting for environment and forest departments approval and recently it was reiterated by the Ministry of Transport and Highways of India as well. Land Customs Station at Zorinpui on a 112,200 square meters is also a portion of phase four in Kaladan project. As earlier said local contractors Ram Dayal Sharma and ARSS-Atlanta are implementing partners in this phase. The project is expected to end by 2020.

Map 3.2: Four Phases of Kaladan Multi-Modal Transit Transport Project

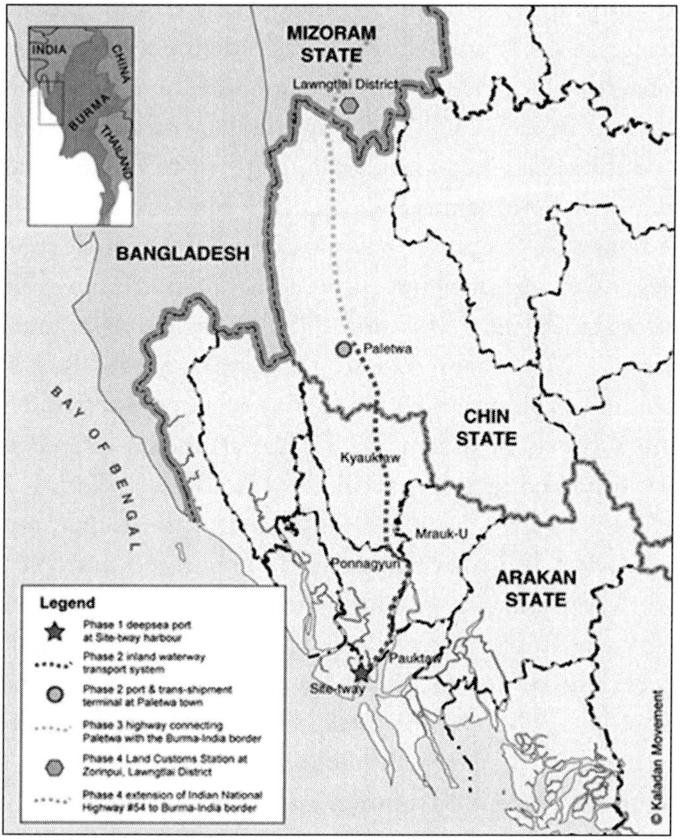

Source: North East Federation on International Trade.

The Sittwe port will be directly connected with the Kolkata port after completion of the project and provide further impetus to the connectivity between eastern India and Myanmar.[19] It would prove a necessary move in linking India's Northeast with sea routes commercially. As Swapna Bhattacharya says:

> This entire circle of land and waterways connecting the two countries with multiple purposes should be seen as one of the most important landmark events in India-Myanmar relationship in the 21st century.[20]

The precursor to a Pipeline

The Kaladan project is highly significant and has additional strategic objectives for India. It was felt that a gas pipeline would be made along the same route as shown by the former ambassador of India to Myanmar, Shyam Sharan in 2011. While the immediacy of the Myanmar-India pipeline plan has lessened since India lost-out to China's state-owned China National Petroleum Company in a bid to secure buying rights to the A-1 and A-3 natural gas blocks off the Sittwe coast, Indian companies and government bodies maintain an interest to exploit oil and gas resources in Western Myanmar.[21] Some Indian firms are interested in investing in Myanmar's oil and gas sectors. Presently, ESSAR Oil Ltd. is holding exploration rights in Bay of Bengal offshore block A2 and onshore Block L. Indian Oil Corporation has offered to explore oil in Myanmar collectively with ONGC Videsh Ltd. (OVL) and Oil India Ltd. (OIL)—both are connected to the Indian government and have made a bid for offshore and onshore oil and gas blocks in Myanmar. Myanmar is a resource-rich country whose resources are largely untapped. The Bangladesh-China-India-Myanmar regional grouping reinforced the fact that Myanmar is viewed as the bowl of resources and neighbouring countries can collaborate to make the most of these resources. It is also notable that all countries are facing an energy shortage, except Myanmar, and by joint ventures, their needs can be fulfilled within the group.

Rihkhawdar-Tedim-Falam Road Project

Champhai in Mizoram is being connected to Rihkhawdar in Myanmar through a 225 km Rihkhawdar-Tedim-Falam (RTF) road. There are two very significant border trade points on the Indo-Myanmar border at Moreh and Champhai which were operationalised in 1994 and 2004, respectively. It has also been proposed by Indian railway that a railway link should be established with Myanmar through Northeast in the Jiribam-Imphal-Moreh sector. It is proposed to extend this line up to Mandalay on the Delhi-Hanoi railway link. There is already an 80 km Rihkhawdar-Tedim road which connects Myanmar with Mizoram. It is also called an essential lifeline for increasing trade and commerce between the two countries and measure gain in Champhai district of Mizoram. After declaring open for all, the Rihkhawdar-Tedim road will take its course and boost up trade and development between both the countries. There are confined businesses at the trade centre in Champhai due to the pity road connectivity on the Myanmar side. During the July 2010 visit of the Senior General Than Shwe, Chairman, State Peace and Development Council of Myanmar to India, it was decided that the construction and revamping of the Rihkhawdar-Tedim road in Myanmar would be financed through grant assistance of US$ 60 million from India.[22] The proposed project has not taken shape because the road is in a poor condition at present. India can assist Myanmar to make it single lane road. By doing so, there will be a direct train and travel connections between Myanmar and Mizoram. There would be maximum benefits of making investments in the Zokhawthar LCS in Mizoram. Rihkhawdar is the adjoining town on the Myanmar sides and there is no proper road from Rihkhawdar to Myanmar. There is no mettled road from Kalemyo via Tedim to Myanmar. It is a kutcha road in literal terms which can be used only in dry weather. The road between the Indian border, Zokhawthar and Rihkhawdar town in Myanmar for 5 km required repairs and upgradation.

Rihkhawdar-Tedim road connects Mandalay through Monywa. This is the only stretch between Zokhawthar and Mandalay in Myanmar. Indian Railway Construction Company Ltd (IRCON) has formulated the detailed proposal of the Rihkhawdar-Tedim, 80 km road worth Rs 298 crore. The Committee of Non-Plan Expenditure (CNE) has already approved the proposal. The task has been decided to meet the completion after three years of requisite approvals. Another project that India has agreed to fulfill of Rihkhawdar-Tedim road development project in Myanmar. The Ministry of External Affairs has demanded technical support from the Ministry of Road Transport and Highways (MORTH) for the above mentioned road. Trade between India and Myanmar takes place on a regular basis but in limited volume via the Zokhawthar LCS. The Zokhawthar-Rihkhawdar trading point is more peaceful than the Moreh-Tamu border point even though there is a larger volume of trade exchange. Champhai is the closest town from the border, nearly an hour drive of 33 km at Zokhawthar in Mizoram. The road from Champhai to Zokhawthar is under construction and near completion with the assistance of ADB. This road has been proposed to be widened at several points due to its likely use by the people. Champhai is 186 km away from Aizwal, the capital of Mizoram. It takes about 6 hours to

Map 3.3: Champhai-Rihkhawdar-Tedim-Falam Road

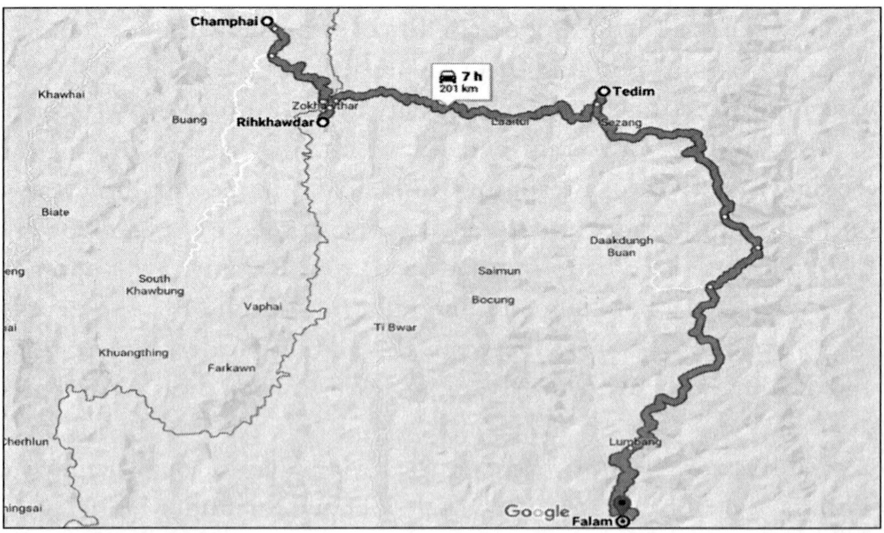

Source: Google Map.

cover the journey by bus. The road has to be upgraded on the Manipur side and made capable of handling heavy vehicles if an increase in trade is expected through border point at Mizoram. At present, the real picture differs but Zokhawthar-Rihkhawdar border point has high potential to increase the interaction between India's Northeast and Myanmar. The opening of the Rihkhawdar-Tedim road is also expected to boost bilateral trade between the two countries.[23]

India-Myanmar-Thailand Trilateral Highway

It has utmost significance for all the three countries involved. Its primary purpose is to make connectivity from Moreh (India) to Mae Sot (Thailand) through Myanmar. The authorities have been proposed two routes—one through Mandalay and another one is bypassing Mandalay. Myanmar is interested in Mandalay route and requested the

Map 3.4: Asian Highway Routes passing through Myanmar

Source: North East Federation on International Trade

same to India. Myanmar's importance in Mandalay route lies in the significance of commerce angle for Mandalay which is the commercial city of the country. The two routes are:

- Moreh (India)-Tamu-Kalewa-Chaungma-Yinmabin-Pale-Kyadet-Lingadaw-Bagan-Kyaukpadaung-Meiktilabypass-Taungoo-Oktwin-Payagyi-Theinzayat-Thaton-Hpaan-Kawareik-Myawaddy-MaeSot(Thailand) (bypassing Mandalay)
- Moreh (India)-Tamu-Kalewa-Yagyi-Chaungma-Monywa-Mandalay-Meiktila bypassTaungoo-Oktwin-Payagyi-Theinzayat-Thaton-HpaanKawkareik-Myawaddy-Mae Sot (through Mandalay).

Stretches: AH 1- 1650 km (Myawaddy-Yangon-Mandalay-Tamu)
AH 2 – 807 km (Tachileik-Meikhtila-Tamu)
AH 3 – 93 km (Mongla-Kyaing Tong)
AH 14 – 453 km (Muse-Mandalay)

The road between Kalewa-Yagyi-Chaungma-Monywa is not adequately developed. It has been estimated an amount of US$ 140 million would be spent on building the 3,200 km of trilateral highway using her good offices. India has promised to extend a loan amount of US$ 500 million for constructing area of the road connecting India and Thailand via Myanmar. The Manipur sight has been visited by the officials of ADB to do a technical survey and assess the total cost on the ground. The preliminary reports have also been submitted and examined by the Roadways Ministry, and then it would be forwarded to the Department of Economic Affairs (DEA) after passing all the technical aspects. It has also been made clear by the ADB to finance Northeast-Myanmar connectivity road project. Northeast inner connectivity with Myanmar via Moreh border town has vital importance from the economic growth angle. The distance from Moreh to Imphal is 110 km, and both places are connected by NH 39. It takes two hours to reach Imphal from Moreh. Imphal is also connected with Guwahati by NH 36, 37 and 39. The journey from Guwahati to Imphal nearly takes 12 hours to reach at present, with many stretches being in a poor state. Another option for travelling from Imphal to Guwahati via Haflong is also being considered, which is a shorter but more difficult route and suggestions for upgrading this Imphal-Silchar road are also being considered.[24] Both countries should consider this project on priority as this connectivity would improve and boost up the economic flow.

India has also given the proposal to connect Vietnam, Cambodia and Laos with ports and Special Economic Zones (SEZ) of the ASEAN under the Trilateral Highway. This will work upon innovative financial and institutional mechanism. There is enormous scope for expansion of physical connectivity due to the development of soft infrastructure along these corridors.

The Moreh-Tamu-Kalewa-Kalemyo Road Project

The India-Myanmar Friendship Road (160 km) was conceived in 1993 and was inaugurated in 2001. The road was entirely built by India, a gift to Myanmar, and now it's a part of the Asian Highway.[25] India's BRO has built the Moreh-Tamu-Kalewa-Kalemyo Friendship Road across the border from Moreh. For upgrading road network in the Northeast, a loan of US$ 125.2 million has been signed between India and ADB. The maintenance task of this road has been handed over to Myanmar. However, there are 70 weak bridges along the road, of which only one has been repaired by Myanmar so far, while the remaining 69 bridges

Map 3.5: The Moreh-Tamu-Kalewa-Kalemyo (India-Myanmar Friendship) Road

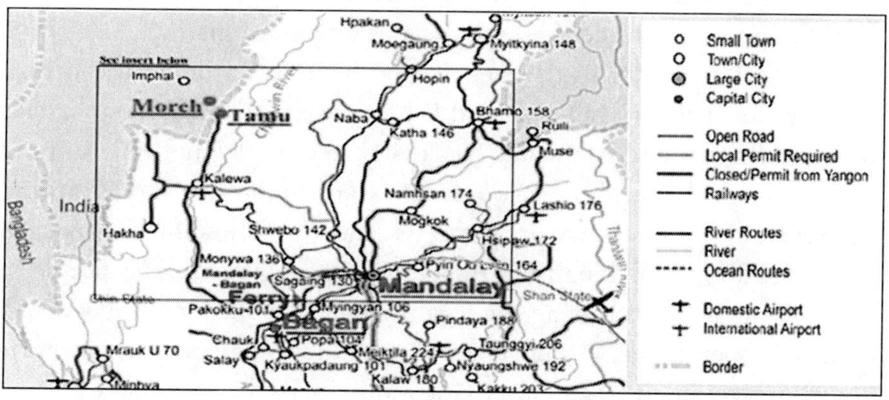

Source: Research and Information System for Developing Countries.

need repair and upgradation.[26] The Border Road Organisation would not take responsibility for repairing them, rather it is the Myanmar government's responsibility. It is also included in the Trilateral Highway.

Proposed Imphal-Mandalay Bus Service

In early 2015, a field survey for the proposed 579 km Imphal-Mandalay bus service began comprising a joint team from India and Myanmar which was initially submitted to the MORTH and the MDONER in 2009.[27] The entire range is expected to be the all-weather road. Three routes are under consideration in this proposal. The Imphal-The Moreh stretch is of about 110 km while the rest of the stretch from Moreh to Mandalay is of about 469 km. Both sides have signed the MOU for bus service from Imphal to Moreh and Moreh to Mandalay which was amended in 2012 and then in 2014, after the second meeting of the technical committee. The members of the joint special team from both the countries had looked into the problems of construction of the road. The findings of the joint team recommend that the patch from Imphal to Moreh was in a good state, but as far as the route from Moreh to Yagi and Moreh to Gangawis is concerned, it was not in a good state. The above said MOU is yet to be ratified by both the parties. The technical committee proposed three routes for the bus service. However, the second route was not usable, especially in the rainy season. The committee has also observed that 70 bridges in the Yagi-Kalewa stretch required repairs and upgradations.

There is no doubt in the fact that both countries under the British rule did not have any rail and road links between them. The bus service between Imphal and Mandalay has a vital role to play not only in their bilateral trade but for the development of tourism in India and Myanmar. However, illegal trade remained the issue as this is one of the engaged routes for drug trafficking from Asia to Europe. This route is expected to be the impetus in increasing the legal trade and reducing the illegal one once it is operational. Passengers are required to possess valid passports and may be granted single-entry visas valid for 28 days on arrival.[28]

In 2014, Route 1 was finalised and the bus-service was supposed to get operationalised from April 7, 2020 but it was disrupted due to COVID-19 pandemic. The length of this route is 579 km long which can be covered in 14 hours. India and Myanmar are keen to enhance people-to-people contact on both sides to improve linkages. It has been decided that visa on arrival facility must be made available to travellers to ensure them easy access on both sides. Many people from the Indian state of Manipur have their relatives and businesses in Mandalay, Myanmar. It has also been felt by the experts that linking India with Myanmar and then to Southeast Asia is of utmost significance for India. However, there has been no progress in this direction and it is still documented only. According to Myanmar's Ministry of Construction, there are plans in place to increase roads

Map 3.6: Proposed Routes for Imphal-Mandalay Bus Service

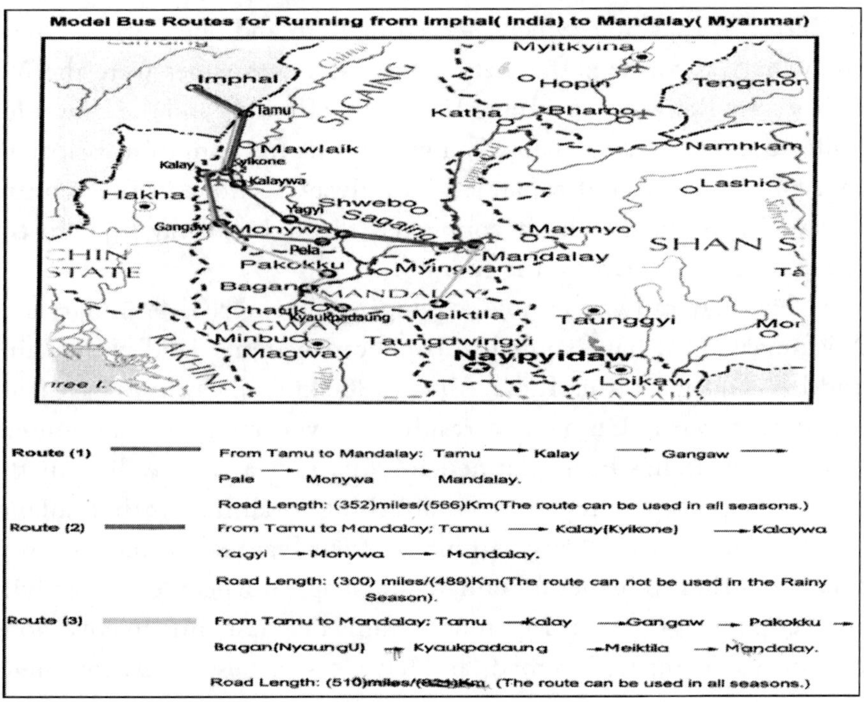

Source: Ministry of Transport, Myanmar.

within the country, which will connect bilateral and multilateral projects in the tunnel and primarily benefit India's Northeast and neighbouring states like Thailand. Myanmar has significant national transport connectivity corridors in the tunnel, Mandalay-Tamu is one of the vital corridors. Once the Ministry of Construction of Myanmar will take the approval from the Parliament, implementation of the project will be started. The expected time for completion of all projects is estimated to be around 30 years. India has signed an agreement with Myanmar to upgrade the road links in Rakhine state in Myanmar worth US$ 20 million and the Myiktina-Putao worth US$ 140 million.

Railway Connectivity

The very first railway line in the then Burma was constructed during the 19th century under British rule. There were three local rail companies in Burma at that time which merged in 1896 and one Burma railway company was formed. These three local rail companies were the Mu Valley state Railway, the Sittang Valley state Railway and the Irrawaddy Valley State Railway. When Myanmar got its freedom from Britishers in 1948, it rebuilt and expanded its railway network in the country. Today, Myanmar has been connected through railway lines in the major cities and towns of the country.

Myanmar railway is now expanding to external boundaries of Myanmar and it has planned to connect Myanmar land with China and Thailand apart from India. Already 800 km railway lines have been installed towards China as a result of government-to-government interaction. It has been planned to construct a railway line in the Dawei deep seaport region to establishing a rail link with Thailand. Today, it has become very significant for Myanmar to have railway link with other countries for enhancing people-to-people connectivity and economic growth of Myanmar. Trains take less time to cover long distances as compared to roads and have less cost especially for longer distances.

In 2005, a survey was conducted by RITES for rail connectivity between Mandalay (Myanmar) to Jiribam (Manipur). According to the feasibility report, the length of Section I of the rail link, (Jiribam-Imphal-Moreh) is 219 km and the length of Section II (Tamu-Kalay) is 127.4 km.[29] Thus, Jiribam to Mandalay covers a railway link of 885.4 km. After 2013, there has not been any development in this direction. Once it is completed, it would join the Southern corridor of the Trans Asian Railway network. Both countries also observed the absence of any rail link between Jiribam and Moreh on the Indian side while Tamu and Kalay on Myanmar side. Railway connectivity between these pillars would certainly boost up the commerce and communication activities. The Jiribam-Tupul-Imphal broad gauge line was expected to be completed by 2016.[30] The route will involve several minor and major bridges and tunnels, of which a unique feature will be Bridge No. 164 having a pier height of 141 m and thus becoming the tallest girder rail bridge in the world.[31] Northeast Frontier Railway has been conducted a broad gauge rail link survey between Imphal and Moreh which will be operational by the end of March 2022.

Map 3.7: Tamu-Kalay-Mandalay Rail Link

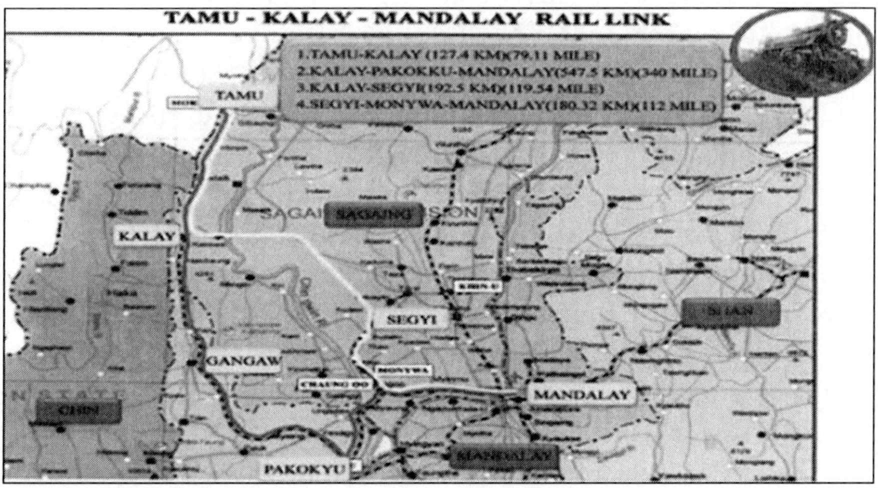

Source: Ministry of Rail Transportation, Nay Pyi Taw, Myanmar.

Investments from international bodies like the Japan International Cooperation Agency (JICA) are being welcomed for improving physical connectivity by establishing and upgrading rail and road links.[32] The Korea International Cooperation Agency (KOICA) has shown interest in upgrading the railway network in Myanmar.

As a matter of long-term planning for the coming 30 years, the Ministry of Transport, Myanmar has framed an integrated national transport master plan for spreading railway links within the country and with other countries. There is a proposal for integrating ten primary transport and development corridors, Tamu-Mandalay corridor is on the top of the list. This project is meant to be completed within the span of 15 years. There is an urgent requirement to upgrade and improve the quality of existing road transport links on Myanmar's border areas. India is actively involved in providing infrastructure and development support to Myanmar to expand physical connectivity in Myanmar with primary financial help from private sectors and as loan and aids from friendly countries and Institution such as ADB. Japan and China are profoundly helping in cooperation programmes such as maritime searching and rescue operations.

In 2013, India's Northeast Frontier Railway (NFR) composed a proposal to connect India's Northeast with Myanmar and Bangladesh. According to the proposal, 252 km of railway tracks would be laid connecting "Jawaharnagar, the headquarters of Dhalai district in Tripura, and the Darlong city of Myanmar through Kolasib, a town in Mizoram."[33]

India Coastal Shipping Service with Myanmar

India and Myanmar have started a cargo ferry service between them since October 2014. The ferry service has been launched by the Shipping Corporation of India (SCI) which functions from Chennai to Yangon, and it plies on the Colombo-Chennai-Krishnapatnam-Yangon route, calling on the Chennai port once every fortnight.[34]

The service includes container ships, and is expected to significantly reduce the journey time for goods to reach Myanmar through land routes. It will be advantageous for both countries as they agreed to increase bilateral trade to US$ 3 billion.[35] This is going to reduce the trading and transport cost sharply as it would decrease distance and time, which will further save the cost involved in it.

Map 3.8: India New Shipping Links to Myanmar

Source: *The Times of India.*

India-Myanmar Air Connectivity

India and Myanmar urgently need to improve their air connectivity. The absence of direct flights is the current issue in connectivity and it impacts flight duration as the connecting flights have halts. India's air connectivity with Myanmar will mainly benefit the monks, pilgrims and tourists to visit Bodh Gaya. At present, Air India flights are available from Kolkata to Yangon twice every week, and besides this, there is another one which flies once a week between New Delhi to Yangon via Gaya.[36]

Air connectivity between India and Myanmar is not so much frequent so both the countries would have to take necessary steps to improve the same. Flights from Thailand, by Thai Airways, reach Yangon via Bangkok only. Similarly, Myanmar has regular flights to Singapore, Malaysia, Taiwan, Japan and Bangkok which make it possible for Myanmar to have good relations with neighbour countries. During October to March every year, Myanmar Airways and another privately operated service, the

Myanmar Golden Airlines, operate flights thrice a week from Yangon to Gaya for Buddhist pilgrims in Myanmar.[37]

Today Myanmar does not have adequate direct flights. Myanmar airlines is set to promote religious tourism by initiating a new flight on Kolkata-Bodh Gaya-Yangon route. The Indian diaspora is precisely focusing on Mandalay and Yangon as it is employed in numerous areas such as trade and commerce, education and civil services. Many India-based families are engaged in import and export businesses. Therefore, there is a broader scope and opportunity for economic exchange, furthering it to another level of social interactions. A notable annual growth of 20 per cent has been shown in the aviation industry in Myanmar. Both the countries would explore the advantage of the progress. Myanmar is enlarging its sphere by multiplying international air services, especially to India.

Air connectivity has a vital character in multi-modal connectivity. A report published by the Research and Information System for Developing Countries states that with Imphal now becoming an international airport, it will be important to include it as an option in the Bilateral Air Services Agreement to enable airline companies to consider operating flights between Imphal and Mandalay.[38] Likewise, flights from Aizawl to Kalemyo and Mandalay would promote trade once the Zokhawthar border point shows positive activity with the running status of Rihkhawdar-Tedim road. This has already been announced by Myanmar government that they would strengthen the Kalemyo airport.

Hydrocarbon, Energy and Petroleum Cooperation between India and Myanmar

Energy cooperation holds an enormous calibre for India and Myanmar, and this would certainly have a growing impact on their overall bilateral relationship. The energy sector of India, one of the world's fastest-growing economies, sees an average of 6.5 per cent growth in demand yearly.[39] Energy demand is increasing day by day, and will be even higher in India in the coming years. India's energy security is primarily about ensuring continuous availability of commercial energy at competitive prices to support its economic growth and meet the lifeline energy needs of its households with safe, clean and affordable forms of energy.[40] Efforts are being made at increasing production and exploitation of all available domestic energy resources along with thrust on measures to increase energy efficiency and managing the demand through suitable fiscal and pricing policies.[41]

There are various sources of energy like hydroelectricity, nuclear energy, oil and coal. As far as India's energy supply is concerned, it is highly dependent on coal, and this situation is going to remain the same. However, natural gas is expected to increase the supply portfolio. The various segments supply natural gas with a competitive advantage, such as lack of finance in coal mining, growing concerns over environmental impurity, non-accessibility of cheap good quality coal, disarray over-allotment of coal beds for mining and coal prices. Moreover, climate change obligations are also pushing the country in intense pressure to lessen dependency on coal. It is estimated that by 2032 India will be dependent on imports for most of its oil needs (90 per cent) and natural gas (85 per cent).[42] As per Bharat Petroleum statistics review 2014, India is the fourth largest energy consumer in the world, with oil and natural gas constituting 37.24 per cent of primary energy consumption, of which crude oil is 29.46 per cent and natural gas is 7.78 per cent, Coal constitutes around 54.51 per cent of total energy consumption in the country.[43]

According to Hydrocarbon Vision: 2025, the share of natural gas in the energy mix of India will increase to 20 per cent in 2025, as compared to 11 per cent in 2010.[44] However, given that all the plans for expansion in natural gas supply in the country with the help of additional Re-gasified Liquefied Natural Gas (RLNG) terminals, a nationwide transmission pipeline network and transnational pipelines, are expected to materialise by 2025.[45] It is envisioned, the share of natural gas in the primary energy will reach 20 per cent by 2030.

India-Myanmar Engagements in Energy Sector

Production of energy can be done on a commercial basis to be sold on some payment basis, or it can be generated through government sources for supply as public utility services. Myanmar underground oil and natural gas are yet to be fully exploited.

The present involvement of Indian companies in Myanmar's energy sector acquire the Offshore of Rakhine principally; BlockA-1/A3 (portion of the Shwe Project) of which the share owners are Daewoo International Corporation of Korea with 60 per cent shares, Oil and Natural Gas Corporation (ONGC) Videsh Ltd. of India with 20 per cent, GAIL (India) Ltd with 10 per cent and Korea Gas Corporation with 10 per cent.[46] India had revived the Thanlyin Refinery in 2006. Currently, the Thanbayakan Petrochemical Compound is under the phase of upgradation. In October 2020, India has proposed to construct a petroleum refinery in Thanlyn region near Yangon, and is planning to invest USD 6 billion in the win-win arrangement project.

An MoU on Co-operation in the Petroleum Sector between Ministry of Petroleum and Natural Gas of India and Ministry of Energy of Myanmar was signed during President's visit to Myanmar in March 2006.[47] Since then both private and public companies from India have shown interest in exploration and development activities. Following the visit of Myanmar electric power minister to India in April 2015, a working level/technical level meeting to supply 2-3 MW electricity to Tamu (Sagaing) from Manipur was held in Tamu in August 2015.[48] In 2014, OVL secured a remarkable 97 per cent participating interests in Block B-2 and EP-3, and it has strengthened India's energy interests in Myanmar. Further, India has been planning to widen their hydrocarbon linkages by introducing hydrocarbon vision 2030 and Northeast hydrocarbon vision 2030 with Bangladesh and Myanmar.

Indian Private Partners in the sector in Myanmar

India is a partner in many ventures with Myanmar through private Indian companies. One of them is ONGC Videsh Ltd. It is a branch of Oil and Natural Gas Commission of India which have entered into an agreement of production sharing contracts for two onshore blocks in Myanmar which was signed in 2010, with the Myanmar Oil and Gas

Enterprises Ltd. (MOGE), National Oil Company of Myanmar and Machine and Solutions Co. Ltd. (M and S), the local partner. There is another Southeast Asia Gas Pipeline company Ltd. (SEAGP), which got registered in Hong Kong on June 25, 2010. OVL also worked jointly with this company of Hong Kong in the Onshore Gas Pipeline Transportation project completed through joint ventures. This project was to be implemented in four phases.

SEAGP's share of investment in the mid-stream project till March 31, 2014, was about US$ 265.637 million for Block A-1 and US$ 127.63 million for Block A-3. The share-holding of the joint venture is as follows: OVL 8.34 per cent; China National Petroleum Corporation (CNPC)-50.9 per cent; Daewoo, Korea-25.04 per cent; Myanmar Oil and Gas Enterprise (MOGE) 7.36 per cent; GAIL and KOGAS (Korea Gas Corporation) 4.17 per cent each.[49] OVL has also shown interests in bidding for offshore blocks in the upcoming circle of bidding in Myanmar.

The most significant energy projects of Myanmar are mainly two: one is Shwe Natural gas project and other is China-Myanmar Oil transport project. Shwe Phyu and Mya offshore gas fields are situated in Blocks A-1 and A-3 respectively of the Bay of Bengal. Myanmar, India and China are the three countries backing this project. There is a consortium of six companies led by POSCO subsidiary Daewoo International which is also a head of the project. The project started the commercial production in August 2013 and the gas was first explored in July 2013 from its Mya field. It was in January 2014 when production from Shwe gas field started. The actual capacity of the pipeline is around 12 billion cubic meters annually, but it pumped only 25 per cent volume of its capacity in 2014 into China. A key market for the Myanmar gas was meant to be China's southern Guangxi Province, but sales have been so disappointing that Petro China is reportedly seeking to sell off its gas distribution system there, raising questions about the future ownership of its Myanmar operations.[50]

There is another Myanmar-China gas pipeline project, worth US$ 2 billion in which GAIL India has invested up to 4 per cent stake.

Separately, it is hoped that the total investment to be made by GAIL and OVL in the project in Myanmar will go to about US$ 250 million involving 870 km pipeline which is being laid in Myanmar by CNPC of the total investment of US$ 2.6 billion up to 25 per cent in the onshore and offshore blocks for the pipeline project in Myanmar is being invested by GAIL and OVL. China is likely to buy gas from Myanmar Shwe Natural gas project.

Environment Impact Assessment (EIA) of the Shwe gas project was not made public for starting the construction due to which the project attracted criticism. Hypothetically, the main charge was that the gas pipelines of the project pass through residential as well as ecologically sensitive areas including parks, rivers, marines, rainforests and sanctuary. The land belonging to the military of Myanmar was taken over by the government in order to construct the project which was opposed by Human Rights Organisations. This land fell in the area of the Gown Chewin, Thit Pate Taung, and Saba Shar areas to make way for

Map 3.9: Shwe Gas Field and Pipeline, Myanmar

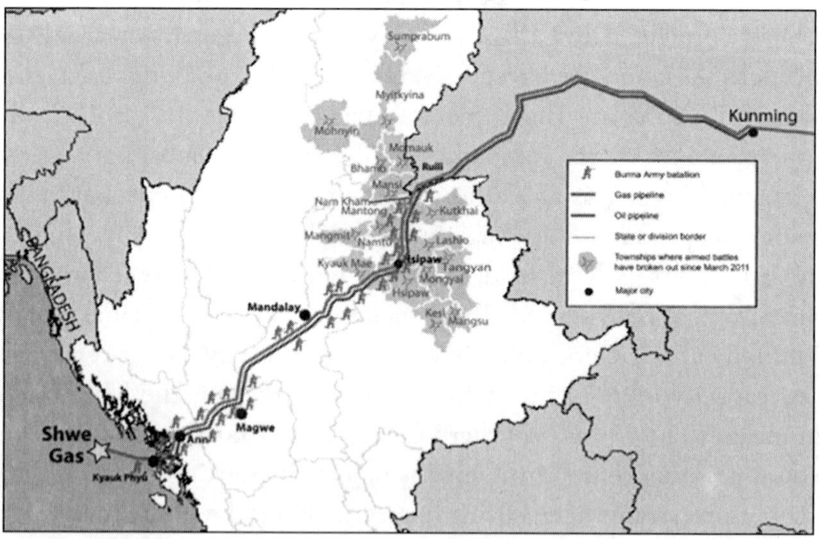

Source: Environmental Justice Atlas.

the project pipelines without giving any compensation to the natives. Myanmar Navy has prohibited the fishing in the area, as it affects bread and butter of fishers. This project has been facing criticism for providing sufficient gas for Myanmar domestic purposes.

In the last bid, Reliance Industries Ltd. (RIL) emerged as the largest private sector company who won two out of three offshore of oil and gas blocks in Myanmar, while ONGC Videsh Ltd could not grab any bid in the area. It is worthy to mention that RIL bid for three blocks in Myanmar was in the year 2013. When RIL had won shallow water block M-17 and M-18, most of the gas blocks have been won by Royal Dutch Shell, Statoil and BG Group. RIL has also signed an agreement of mutual production with state-owned MOGE for two offshore blocks which had been secured by RIL through a competitive bidding in 2013.

Eventually, RIL's participating interest percentage has become 96 per cent in the blocks. The remaining share of interest in the block will be of a company of Myanmar named United National Resources Development Services Co. Ltd (UNRDS). The location of offshore blocks is at water depth up to 3000 ft in the Tanintharyi basin of Myanmar, covering an area of 27,600 sq km. There is planning by RIL to expand its international asset base by investing in international attraction in gas and oil locations. RIL Company has the required expertise and technology and management which can create value for the exploration and procurement. RIL is going to launch the production sharing contract, work out on the program for opening work on the blocks.

The pattern of offering production sharing contract of Myanmar is similar to that of India. In India, work begins on an area of land with the exploration faith whereas in Myanmar a six months preparation period is allowed to avail to start the work after a study period of up to 12 months. It is an option thereafter to rest with the company either to quit or start exploration quickly. There is a system under which an operator can preserve a discovery for at least six years even after if it is not regarded economical as per rules of Myanmar. If the operator wants then one can be allowed some extension on year to year basis. In India, gas is sold at a cost decided by a previously approved formula, but the oil produced in India can be sold even at that very place. In Myanmar, natural gas can be sold at such a price which is realised from the market while oil can be sold at arm's length.

The National Hydroelectric Power Corporation (NHPC) signed a Memorandum of Understanding (MoU) with the Myanmar Government in 2004 for the development of the 1,200-Mega Watt (MW) Htamanthi dam on the Chindwin river, with an estimated 80 per cent of the power going to India.[51] Myanmar Hydroelectric Power Department and NHPC initiated a joint venture as per the new agreement signed in 2008 for the enhancement of the Htamanthi and Shwesayay dams (642 MW). It is indicated by a published report of NHPC titled DEALS and ALLIANCE profile (2015), that the establishment was preparing to invest nearly US$ 2.119 million. In the above project, another US$ 1.165 million invested in Shwezaye Hydro Power Project. It has been reported that the costs of these two projects have increased manifolds and there has been no progress.

India is a vast country, stands at number two in the world in the matter of population. The demands for gas in India are comparatively more than the supply of gas. The demand for gas in supply is widening with time and it would go up 35 per cent by 2030. India is looking east to get a maximum supply for natural gas and Myanmar can play a significant role in this as it has enormous untapped reserves which can solve India's energy concern. Therefore, energy market integration became a possible method for India's widening energy supply and demand gap.

Oil refining capacity of India had increased by 43 per cent to 310 million tonnes annually by March 2017. Since 2001-02, India became the leading exporter in petroleum products with the help of improving growth in refining capacity. The total oil refining capacity has been raised by the commissioning of new refineries in the country. It is the Paradip refinery on the Indian east coast which has started crude processing at 3 lakh barrels per/day. According to BP's statistical review, India has become the 4th largest refining centre after the US, China and Russia in the world. The Paradip refinery has been chosen the most worldly out of IOC's eleven plants.

The refining capacity is expected to surplus by 2030. India would also continue to have surplus in production, and with a hike in refinery capacity, production of petroleum products has expanded substantially especially during the last few years. During 2013-14, 67.864 MMT of petroleum products, valued at Rs 368,279 crore, were exported. Last year, export of these products amounted to 63.408 MMT valued at Rs 320,090 crore.[52] In 2013-14, the export of petroleum products was elevated by 7.02 per cent in terms of quantity and by 15.05 per cent regarding value as matched to 2012. India can provide the ground to Myanmar for refining crude in India's refineries, and petroleum products can be exported with the Paradip plant playing an essential role on India's eastern coast.

Border Areas Development Project

India granted assistance US$ 5 million for the Border Areas Development Project for 21 schools, 17 health centres and 8 bridges to be built in Chin State and Naga Self Administered Zone of Myanmar under the Border Region Development MoU, whereby US$ 5 million micro development assistance would be extended every year for five years by India for projects on India-Myanmar border.[53] India's Prime Minister visited Myanmar in May 2012. Both sides came on a common understanding that peace and stability must be established along the borders which are required for the development of the area and well being of people in the respective countries. Therefore, an MoU was signed between both the nations to cooperate in border areas for an overall enhancement in socio-economic development.

Table 3.1: Major projects between India and Myanmar to Promote Connectivity

S. No.	Name of Stretch	Status/Remarks
1.	KMMTTP	The sea, river, land transport system linking Indian ports and Sittwe port in Myanmar and then through riverine transport and by road to Mizoram (India). Implementation commenced in Dec 2010
2.	India-Myanmar-Thailand Trilateral Highway Project	The 1360 km cross-border transportation network would link Moreh (India) to Mae Sot (Thailand) through Bagan (Myanmar)
3.	The Tamu-Kalewa-Kalemyo Friendship Road	The 160 km cross-border road from Tamu to Kalemyo in Myanmar's Sagaing Region and forms par to the India-Myanmar Thailand Trilateral Highway
4.	Yagyi-Chaungma-Monywa	India wants Myanmar to construct the Yagyi-Chaungma-Monywa stretch. It is understood that section Yagyi-Chaungma-Monywa is under construction on a BOT basis
5.	Monywa-Mandalay	Monywa-Mandalay stretch is already developed.
6.	The Rihkhawdar-Tedim Road in Myanmar	The 80 km cross-border road from Rihkhawdar to Tedim in Myanmar's Chin State
7.	Meiktila bypass-Taungoo-Oktwin-Payagyi	The section between Meiktila and Payagyi is part of the Yangon-Mandalay highway that has been constructed
8.	The BCIM Economic Corridor	The cross-border transportation network linking China's Kunming to India's Kolkata from Myanmar and Bangladesh
9.	The Stilwell Road (the Ledo Road and the Myanmar Road)	The WW II overland road linking Ledo in Assam (India) to Kunming in Yunnan (China) through Myanmar
10.	Kawkareik-Myawaddy	It appears that the Myanmar Government shall be completing the road construction between Myawaddy-Kawkareik out of its resources soon
11.	Myawaddy-Mae Sot	Under Consideration of MEA
12.	The Delhi-Hanoi Railway Link	The Delhi-Hanoi train connectivity proposes to link India with Vietnam via Myanmar, Thailand, Malaysia, and Singapore

Source: Ministry of Development of North Eastern Region, India.

Economic Cooperation between India and Myanmar

Since independence, India has been one of the serious trading countries for Myanmar. In 1970, India and Myanmar signed a trade agreement. Since then bilateral trade between both the countries is growing with a slight slip in the 1980s. Bilateral trade rose from US$ 328 million in 1997-98 to US$ 921.19 in 2006-07 and climbed up to US$ 2.175 billion in 2016-17.[54] India perceives a vast potential in Myanmar for investments, bilateral trade and other economic cooperation. India is the 4th largest trade partner of Myanmar, 3rd largest export destination for Myanmar and 7th most significant source of imports into Myanmar.[55] After lifting sanctions, Myanmar economy is opened up to new players in the field and they have entered the country intensively for trade and investments.

Bilateral Agreements Mechanism

India and Myanmar have signed a Bilateral Investment Promotion & Protection Agreement (BIPPA) and Double Taxation Avoidance Agreement (DTAA).[56] These agreements were targeted to provide easy access and flow of bilateral investments, business profits and taxation related concerns. India and Myanmar have ratified the agreements.

Joint Trade Committee

In order to boost trade between India and Myanmar, there has been set up for Joint Committee since 2003 whose sittings are presided by respective Commerce Ministers. The main task of the committee is to review the working of JTC and fix the target for import and export of both the countries in the matter of mutual trade and commerce. The committee met five times since then. The rapid growth in commercial relations between the two countries is attributed to the JTC. India-Myanmar's fourth JTC meeting was organised in New Delhi in September 2011 and the fifth in February 2015 in Nay Pyi Taw, Myanmar. JTC has taken several important decisions, out of which there was, a decision to establish Investment Forum and Border Trade Committee, India- Myanmar Joint Trade and Border Haats, which were implemented. India and Myanmar have been organising several discussions and meetings to improve connectivity, trade and investment.

Joint Trade and Investment Forum

Following the signing of MoU, in May 2012, the Joint Trade and Investment Forum (JTIF) was established. The first meeting of the JTIF was co-chaired by Mr Sunil Mittal, Chairman Bharti Group and Mr Aung Win, President of UMFCCI and Chairman, Dagon International.[57] The first meeting was held in Yangon on June 7, 2013. At the meeting of the forum, the members made three important suggestions with a focus on mutual trade and investment so that potential available can be fully utilised. Another recommendation to achieve better connectivity between the two countries was by land, sea and air. It was also stressed that better infrastructure facility should be provided at border posts. The most significant suggestions being the starting of food processing industries and uplifting the farm production in the remote areas of Myanmar.

Border Trade Committee

The mutual concerns formed a border trade committee at joint secretary level to resolve the matters related to border trade. The first meeting of border trade committee was held in Moreh, Manipur. After that, the 2nd meeting was held at Tamu, Myanmar in November 2013 and so on. The previous decisions were reviewed in the meetings and different and innovative ways were identified to improve border trade by providing more facilitation at border posts.

Table 3.2: India-Myanmar bilateral trade Volume

(figures in US$ million)

Year	2013-2014	2014-2015	2015-2016	2016-2017	2017-2018
EXPORT	787.01	773.24	1,070.65	1,107.89	966.19
% Growth	-	-1.75	38.46	3.48	-12.79
India's Total Export	314,405.30	310,338.48	262,291.09	275,852.43	303,526.16

% Growth	-	-1.29	-15.48	5.17	10.03
% Share	0.25	0.25	0.41	0.40	0.32
IMPORT	1,395.67	1,231.54	984.27	1,067.25	639.64
% Growth	-	-11.76	-20.08	8.43	-40.07
India's Total Import	450,199.79	448,033.41	381,007.76	384,357.03	465,580.99
%Growth	-	-0.48	-14.96	0.88	21.13
%Share	0.31	0.27	0.26	0.28	0.14
TOTAL TRADE	2,182.68	2,004.78	2,054.92	2,175.14	1,605.84
%Growth	-	-8.15	2.50	5.85	-26.17
India's Total Trade	764,605.09	758,371.89	643,298.84	660,209.46	769,107.15
%Growth	-	-0.82	-15.17	2.63	16.49
%Share	0.29	0.26	0.32	0.33	0.21
TRADE BALANCE	-	-	86.38	40.64	326.55
India's Trade Balance	-135,794.49	-137,694.93	-118,716.67	-108,504.60	-162,054.83

Source: DGFT, Dept. of Commerce, India

Table 3.3: India's major Imports from Myanmar

(figures in US$ million)

	Category/Items Group	2013-14	2014-15	2015-16	2016-17	2017-18
1	Edible vegetables & certain roots & tubers (Pulses & beans)	624.13	813.85	819.91	809.45	432.27
2	Wood & articles	748.74	382.12	125.03	156.39	142.64
3	Aircraft, spacecraft & parts thereof	-	-	0.03	50.76	-
4	Lead & Articles thereof	-	-	0.09	5.46	12.24
5	Fish, meat & preparations	2.90	5.37	4.21	4.19	6.20
6	Other edible items	14.82	26.27	31.56	33.86	11.09
7	Inorganic and Organic Chemicals (Aluminium & Zinc)	0.02	0	0.73	-	9.33
8	Nuclear reactors, boilers, machinery and mechanical appliances; parts thereof	0.08	0.41	0.13	0.18	0.03
9	Electrical Machinery and Equipment and parts thereof; sound recorders & reproducers and parts thereof	0.41	0.11	0.08	0.23	0.32

10	Iron and Steel (Articles of Iron and Steel)	0.01	-	0.10	0.08	13.89
11	Raw Hide & Skins	0.38	1.31	0.67	0.52	2.58
12	Plastic and Articles thereof	-	-	0.02	0.18	0.01
13	Rubber and Articles thereof	0.15	0.45	0.18	0.73	2.60
14	Miscellaneous	0.9	2.08	1.54	5.22	6.44
	Total	1,395.67	1,231.54	984.27	1,067.25	639.64

Source: DGFT, Dept. of Commerce, India

Table 3.4: India's major Exports to Myanmar

(figures in US$ million)

	Category/Items Group	**2013-14**	**2014-15**	**2015-16**	**2016-17**	**2017-18**
1	Sugars & Sugar Confectionery	8.52	0.55	457.09	424.26	67.34
2	Pharmaceuticals	137.19	169.17	152.23	184.27	178.95
3	Electrical Machinery & Equipment	82.16	124.87	73.46	54.46	68.20
4	Nuclear reactors, Boiler, Machinery & parts	133.99	76.09	46.07	47.30	45.21
5	Iron & steel	104.27	74.74	30.43	47.55	124.00
6	Residues waste from the food industry	60.77	48.9	19.33	29.70	42.80
7	Cotton & yarn	56.19	46.91	49.50	40.91	48.01
8	Vehicles other than railway	32.55	44.39	37.52	64.35	67.44
9	Tobacco & other manufactured tobacco	-	8.26	5.67	9.81	8.21
10	Garment & textiles	15.54	30.62	39.33	32.69	23.00
11	Other metals & articles	21.61	21.02	20.43	12.43	11.88
12	Chemicals & allied products	14.99	18.27	20.43	36.56	33.66
13	Tools, implements	5.39	17.33	4.04	-	4.15
14	Edible items	17.31	17.03	15.53	15.80	18.16
15	Rubber & articles	12.89	10.54	7.65	5.89	6.96
16	Dairy Produce	13.68	10.2	0.11	-	0.08

17	Earths & stone, lime & cement	9.42	9.11	1.4	1.17	5.54
18	Plastic & articles	2.76	7.22	14.39	13.94	15.99
19	Minerals oils	8.09	3.93	2.94	-	-
20	Locomotives, rolling stock & parts	9.97	1.11	0.55	0.21	33.02
21	Ships, boats & floating structures	-	-	-	-	21.28
22	Products of animal origin	2.01	7.39	22.77	26.31	29.15
23	Mineral fuels & oils	0.22	3.27	2.84	21.68	66.96
22	Miscellaneous	39.55	24.34	44.49	41.80	46.20
	Total	787.01	773.24	1,070.65	1,111.09	966.19

Source: DGFT, Dept. of Commerce, India.

Table 3.5: India-Myanmar Border Trade Volume

(figures in US$ million)

Year	Myanmar exports	Myanmar Imports	Total trade	Balance of Trade
2010-2011	8.30	4.50	12.80	-3.80
2011-2012	8.87	6.54	15.41	-2.33
2012-2013	26.96	11.67	38.63	-15.20
2013-2014	16.46	26.12	42.58	9.66
2014-2015	17.03	39.86	56.89	22.83
2015-2016	53.02	18.62	71.64	-34.41
2016-2017	63.46	24.43	87.89	-39.02
2017-2018	68.77	21.79	90.565	-46.98

Source: Ministry of Commerce, Myanmar.

As shown in the tables, India-Myanmar trade has been dominated by agriculture products and timber wood which is heavily favouring Myanmar as it contributes nearly 1/5th of India's total timber import. It is figured out from the tables that bilateral trade has been increasing as it reached US$ 2.17 billion for 2016-17, but a clumsy decline is also noticed in 2017-18 as it dropped to US$ 1.6 billion only, due to the quantitative limitation on imports of pulses and beans by India. Myanmar is also a 2nd largest supplier of pulses and beans to India. India's major exports to Myanmar include steel and iron products, electrical machinery, pharmaceuticals products, machinery and equipment, mineral oil, rubber products and plastics.[58] India's imports growth have outpaced the growth of its exports. India and Myanmar have signed a Bilateral Investment Promotion & Protection Agreement (BIPPA) and the Double Taxation Avoidance Agreement (DTAA). These agreements were targeted to provide easy access and flow of bilateral investments, business profits and taxation related concerns. India and Myanmar have been organising several discussions and meetings to improve connectivity, trade and investment.

Indian Companies in Myanmar

India is the 9th substantial investor in Myanmar with approved investment of US$ 730.649 million by 22 Indian companies, out of the total estimated investments of US$ 58.03 billion from 41 countries by 1001 enterprises.[59] India's remarkable investments have been in the gas and oil sectors. Myanmar is under developed country but striving to reach the status of developing nations. The economy of Myanmar needs capital investments, technology and trade to meet the standards of human living index. Recently, the following companies from India have won major significant contracts and investments. Indian MNC, TATA motors have transferred the technology of truck assembly plant in Magway, Myanmar, in association with Myanmar Automobile & Diesel Industries Limited (MADI) with the GOI support.[60] These plants will cater to the requirements of the highly flexible frame and chassis assembling of Myanmar. It would also undertake trimming, painting and cab manufacturing activities with a capacity to deliver 1,000 vehicle annually. In 2013, TATA motors started its first spare, sale and service showroom in Yangon. TVS launched dealership in Mandalay and Myitkyina. New Holland Tractors, Sonalika Tractors, Escorts and their farm implements are other companies from India which are doing good business in Myanmar. In addition to the above, various Indian companies like Birla Corporation, Avantha Group, Parry Agro Industries, Amalgamated Tea Plantations Ltd., Lucky Exports, Oberoi group, Bharti Airtel, ITC Hotels, Kirloskar Pumps,

Cairn Energy India Ltd., Kanachur Industries India Ltd., Asian Oilfield Services India, Royal Solar, GMR, JK Paper and Cement, Shree Cements, etc., have shown considerable interest in investing in Myanmar.[61]

Foreign Direct Investments

Aforementioned, India is the 9th largest investor, and the significant investments have been in the oil and gas sector of Myanmar. India is an open and mixed economy and MNC's from India are investing in different countries. Similarly, Foreign MNCs are investing in India. Myanmar economy has also lifted sanctions, as a result of New Foreign Investment Law and the rules made by various respective departments. Thus, FDI is increasing in Myanmar and is ultimately allowed in particular sectors. Even in India, it has been allowed up to 100 per cent in selected sectors. There is a provision in new laws that foreign investors can get land only for 50 years, to begin with, and this contract can be extended with further 10+10 years basis. In Myanmar, the government has created a New Special Economic Zone Law, where foreign investments are invited to set up an industrial zone in industries. Myanmar has come up with reforms to take steps towards an open market for investments. Indian business companies have also shown interests in Myanmar. Largely, energy and infrastructure sectors are getting significant developments. Punj Lloyd Ltd, an Indian contractor, is executing a part of Myanmar China Oil Pipeline Project and Myanmar China Gas Pipeline Project along with South East Asia Crude Oil Pipeline Company Limited and South East of Asia Gas Pipeline Company since May 2011 with an estimated total investment of US$ 475 million.[62]

Larson and Toubro is engaged in an offshore project at M 9 & M 11 blocks in Gulf of Martaban, Myanmar, with a cost of US$ 250 million. The project involves three wellhead topsides and three jackets weight 7,000-8,000 MT installed in a water depth of 130-150 m and 21 km of 18 inches sub-sea pipelines.[63] The other project won by them was Yetagu offshore Project: Engineering procurement fabrication and installation of wellhead platforms and pipelines at Yetagu offshore field with a cost of US$ 112 million.[64]

Vihaan Networks Ltd., accomplished a project of installation of solar power telecommunication tower located on the Mandalay-Yangon highway (600 km) with a cost of US$ 5 million. Myanmar banned the export of unprocessed logs since April 2014 in the wood-based Industry sector. There are a large number of Indian companies who have set up their wood-based industries at a total estimated investment of US$ 35 million. Some of them are Century Ply, Green Ply industries, MAK plywood, B S Progressive and Fine ply. A PVC plant is being set up by Global Protek jointly with Thiha Tun Company at Monwya, Sagaing Region. George Telegraph, Kolkata, has also set up two vocational training institutes at Monwya and Mandalay as a joint venture by local firms.

An MoU was signed with the Ministry of Electric Power, Myanmar government dated April 11, 2013, by TATA Power for an imported coal-run power project in the Ayeyarwaddy region, Myanmar. This project was supposed to be in working capacity by February 2020, but it is still under development. TATA Powers also wants to enter into a partnership in the project of renewable generation of hydro gas. It also has the intention of doing business in Myanmar with the approval of India and Myanmar governments. The following are the most likely and possible areas for investments by the private players from India in various premises in Myanmar: Agri-business, Food processing, Power, Renewable Energy, hospital & Healthcare, Construction related industries, Vocational Training and Education, Mining, Pharmacy, Iron, Steel, Oil and Gas, Refinery, and Fertiliser.

Banking and Insurance Sector

Trade and investments need banking sector cooperation for strengthening the bond. Joint Secretary, Ashok Nigam headed the banking delegation to Myanmar in 2012 for expanding banking possibilities. During the visit of PM to Myanmar in May 2012, Myanmar welcomed the training of Myanmar officials in the Banking sector by Indian banks and for cooperation in the Agriculture Banking sector, and between Reserve Bank of India and the Central Bank of Myanmar.[65] In November 2015, the delegates visited Myanmar to explore the insurance field opportunities.

To facilitate quick trade transaction between the two countries, the United Bank of India has signed several banking agreements with some of the banks of Myanmar (MFTB, MICB, MEB and 9 private banks). The representative branches of UBI were also opened in November 2012 in Myanmar. UBI has also signed a MoU with MFTB, MICB and Myanmar Economic Bank (all 3 are state-owned banks) for corresponding internally. An account has been opened in the United Overseas Singapore Bank by UBI. Representative offices have got their bases in Yangon by EXIM Bank, State Bank of India, Bank of India, and UBI. Myanmar government authorised a commercial banking licence to SBI in March 2016. Approval has also been given to UBI for opening a USD *Vostro* account by Myanmar Economic Bank in UBI in Moreh branch. Moreh and Zokhawthar branches of SBI are extending facilities of ATM, Forex and duty payment in Myanmar. In June 2015, New India Assurances Limited also started its base office in Yangon.

India-Myanmar Digital Connectivity

India is a partner country with Myanmar in setting up cross-border fibre optic links including other neighbouring countries. In February 2009, India and Myanmar placed their first cross-border fibre optic links, covering the area from Moreh to Mandalay with a distance of 500 km. The long link of 640 km passed through Tamu, Monywa, Kyi Gone, Shwebo, Kampatwa and Sagaing. The above optic links are high-speed broadband links for voice and data transmission.

The project signed between the state-run Myanmar Posts and Telecommunications (MPT) and the Telecommunications Consultants India Limited (TCIL) in March 2006 during President APJ Abdul Kalam's state visit to Myanmar.[66] In the last few years, Myanmar's Information and Communications Technology (MICT) sector has shown tremendous growth and telecommunications have emerged as an essential growth sector, the link worth US$ 7 million.

Academic and Technical Training Cooperation

In 2012, Prime Minister of India visited Myanmar, committed to extending financial and technical assistance for setting up an Institute of Information Technology in Myanmar. He also supported the extension of India, Myanmar Centre of Enhancement of IT Skill in Yangon. Alternatively, it was on June 17, 2014, that Myanmar Institute of IT was opened in Mandalay. The primary purpose of opening a National Centre of Excellence in Information Technology was to conduct courses and programmes on IT and award degrees. It has been run by Myanmar government with the help of India since the past five years. Myanmar government is free to construct a permanent builiding of the Institute, presently called University of Computer Sciences, Mandalay, have started an academic session from 2015.

Moreover, Hindustan Machine Tools International Ltd. (HMTI) has started two vocational training centres at Myingyan and Pakokku in Myanmar. The equipment and other infrastructure have been supplied by HMTI while land has been given by Myanmar government and Indians conducted training facilities. Students are getting vocational training in various technical courses, such as Electronic Mechanic, Industrial Electrician, Machinist-Turner/Miller, Tools and Die Making, Machinist-Fitter, CNC machinists, Sheet Metal and Welding. India also handed over the Pakokku Centre in 2012 and the Myingyan Centre in October 2013 to the Myanmar government.

Myanmar government has also set up Language Laboratories and E-Resource Centre project for Classroom Management Software and Self-paced English, Chinese, Russian, Japanese,German and French Languages. Myanmar's Ministry of Foreign Affairs has development training skill over foreign languages. The project includes assisting with sound proofing which is established by MOFA at Yangon and Nay Pyi Taw. There is also a centre for development of advanced computing in Myanmar started with the help of India and handed over to Myanmar in April 2014.

Assistance was given to Myanmar for setting up India-Myanmar Centre for Enhancement of Information Technology Skills (IMCEITS) for short-term courses in software and programming for the eligible students of Myanmar. It was situated at the Centre for Information and Communication Technology Trainings (Hlaing) (CICTT). IMCEITS was established through C-DAC in 2010. The Centre upgraded C-DAC in 2014 through the enhancement of courses, IT equipment and training.[67] IMCEITS has been an Authorized Training Centre (ATC) of C-DAC and offers joint certification with C-DAC.

The Myanmar-India Entrepreneurship Development Centre (MIEDC) was established in February 2009 with technical assistance given by the Entrepreneurship Development Institute of India (EDII), Ahmedabad, and financial support from the Government of India and it is run by the Yangon Institute of Economics. A total of 5,115 students had passed out in the various fields of MIEDC at the end of December 2012; 3,251 students out of 5,115 have attended various training programmes conducted by MIED. Indian government is implemneting the Human Resource Development (HRD) cooperation with Myanmar under various projects, such as Technical Cooperation Scheme (TCS) under the Colombo Plan, Indian Technical and Economic Cooperation (ITEC) Programme, various scholarships are also offered by the Indian Council for Cultural Relations (ICCR) and Special Courses for ASEAN Diplomats.

In 1996, the Myanmar government launched an HRD cooperation programme. The Technical Cooperation Scheme (TCS) and Indian Technical and Economic Cooperation (ITEC) have been proven successful ventures under the Colombo Plan. These were attended by a large number of participants belonging to different ministries of Myanmar government. India is increasingly emerging as a favourite destination for education for Myanmar students who seek quality higher education, More than 12 private universities and higher education institutions participated in the two-day India Education Fair 2018 where over 48 institutes from both government and private sectors offered a choice of more than 200 courses, both short and long term.[68]

Cooperation in Agriculture Sector

India assisted Myanmar by providing agriculture machinery worth US$ 10 million on account of an agreement to cooperate with Myanmar in the agriculture sector. India is encouraging research in the agricultural sector and is assisting the setting up of the Advance Centre for Agricultural Research and Education (ACARE) as a Centre for Excellence with assistance from Indian Agricultural Research Institute, New Delhi in Yezin, Myanmar.[69] ACARE will be of utility in developing high-yield crops with the use of agriculture technology and by promoting knowledge management in the field of agriculture.

Myanmar wants to construct a Rice Bio Park in collaboration with India for imparting training and demonstrating to use biomass of rice into regular food like straw, bran, husk, roots and grain which will generate jobs for the people and sufficient income. Thus, the Rice plant will become useful to Myanmar people right from the roots to the fruits. The Park would be located in Yezin, Nay Pyi Taw. The M. S. Swaminathan Research Foundation (MSSRF) is the consultant and project manager responsible for the business plan, equipment and training. Construction work for the Rice Bio Park includes 13 different buildings and work is ongoing in full swing, including the procurement of equipment.[70]

Apart from the above, India is also likely to expand technological support for the commercial production of large Cardamom in NSA Zone of Myanmar to another project related to Cardamom Plantation project under the Spices Board of India to farmers of Myanmar. Spices board will watch the progress of plantation and monitor the plant. In 2013, the Board organised a training course in NSAZone at Lahel and Khamti. A large number of exposure visits were conducted for farmers to large cardamom flourishing areas in the Darjeeling and Sikkim under this project. The farmers from Myanmar also visited the RRS-Indian Cardamom Research Institute at Tadong, Sikkim during their tour to India. They visited India in the open season of 2014-15 after being identified as the first batch of the farmers.

An agreement between EXIM Bank and the Myanmar Foreign Trade Bank was signed in 2013 for irrigation and rehabilitation.[71] The job in irrigation canals in Myanmar is completed and the supply of farm machinery and consolidation of land has been explored.

Cooperation in Medical and Health Sector

There is a lot of potential and possibilities of cooperation between India and Myanmar in the health and medical sectors. Myanmar is constructing a hospital for children at Yangon and General Hospital at Sittwe, and India has been providing medical equipment, training to these institutions and hospital has made substantial progress. Hospital Service Consultancy Corporation India Ltd monitoring the project.

In July 2014, Sanjay Gandhi Post Graduate Institute of Medical Sciences (SGPGIMS) in Lucknow, was visited by senior doctors and administrators from Yangon General Hospital for an orientation and exposure tour. Moreover, hospitals in the Indian state of Manipur have been at the forefront of extending medical assistance to the poor communities of Myanmar's Sagaing region.[72] In 2016, Another proposal was received from Myanmar requesting improvement of the Monywa General Hospital in Sagaing, for increasing the number of hospital beds, the construction of four buildings and providing equipment such as C arm X-ray imaging equipment, MRI setups, a mini Operation Theatre, as well as the setting up of an ICU.[73] The Indian government approved the detailed project plan and the initial instalments have already been paid to Myanmar. In 2018, two hundred hospital beds have been established at Monwya under Small Development Project for US$ 2 million. Shiza Hospital, Imphal, has been organising free medical check-up camps in Monywa and Sagaing region as a friendly gesture towards the people of Myanmar in association with Monywa General Hospital and the Sagaing regional government. Shija hospital has so far organised three medical missions in Monywa meant to provide quality medical care without any cost. In 2013, the first free medical camp was conducted in Monywa General Hospital, named Mission Myanmar-I. It is notable here that the situation is generally poor in healthcare services in Myanmar. Tuberculosis and malaria-like diseases are the reasons for high mortality rates. Thus, India's role has immense value in the health sector in Myanmar.

Art and Cultural Exchanges

Exchange of cultural programmes between India and Myanmar is a regular feature since 1997 when people from both the countries come together through cultural programmes. A group of 30 students from Myanmar performed at SAARC cultural festival in 2009 in India. A popular music band from Myanmar known as 'Emperor' went to India to participate in the "South Asian Bands Festival" organised by ICCR, the band also performed in Shillong and Meghalaya. The Indian embassy in Myanmar had organised an annual "Indian Film Festival" in 2010.

Similarly, a programme was organised by ICCR and SEHER, and a group of prominent artists from Myanmar visited Puducherry to participate in "South Asian Artists Camp". The paintings drawn by various painters were exhibited in the auditorium of the embassy in November 2010 and received a wonderful response from the local community. ICCR and NSD organised a South Asian Theatre Festival in India in March 2010; a theatre group of 15 members of Myanmar arrived here to participate. The "Abiogenesis" band has also performed Mandalay and Yangon. Similarly, in January 2012, A Qawwali group had performed in Yangon and other cities in Myanmar. Birthday of Rabindranath Tagore is also celebrated in India and Myanmar. On the occasion of 150th birth anniversary of Tagore, there were commemorative activities in the calendar including dance, drama, artist camp, seminar and film festival. People and media of Myanmar enjoyed the programme performed by all artists. Indian embassy started the classes of Bharatnatyam and Yoga with the support of ICCR since December 2010.

India-Myanmar cultural ties were established during the rule of Monarch in Myanmar. These relations also strengthened by the faith of people from both the countries in Buddhism. There is a vibrant legacy of Lord Buddha in India and Myanmar. Both countries share a cultural heritage which India reinforced by the restoration of the Ananda Temple in Bagan and GOI donation of a 16-foot replica of the Sarnath Buddha Statue which has been installed at the premises of Shwedagon pagoda in Yangon. The 'Samvad-II' Interfaith dialogue was held on 6-7 August 2017, Yangon. ICCR and Sitagu International Buddhist Academy organised an

International Conference on Buddhist Cultural Heritage from December 15-17, 2012.[74] Performances on a regular basis by cultural groups have been organised. Troupes and artists of Myanmar have performed in South Asian and ASEAN cultural events are organised in India. On the request of Myanmar, India restored and renovated two historical temples in Bodh Gaya built by King Mindon and King Baygyidaw of Myanmar.[75] These temples and inscriptions will now be restored with the assistance of the Archaeological Survey of India as a bilateral friendship project.

Peace and Security Cooperation

The political transition towards a democratic system in Myanmar has acted as a catalyst and provided an opportunity for India to engage its neighbour more intimately.[76] In 2012, Prime Minister of India, Manmohan Singh, visited Myanmar after a gap of nearly 25 years. A fresh zeal and confidence was seen towards building stronger bilateral relations and agreement to increase trade to US$ 3 billion by 2015. However, it has not been achieved so far. Later, Prime Minister Narendra Modi also visited Myanmar. India has given its word to extend the loan of US$ 500 million to Myanmar for development and helping IT infrastructure schemes. India and Myanmar established a network among educational institutes such as universities and think tanks; to further enhance cooperation an agreement was signed between Institute of Defence Studies and Analysis, India, and Myanmar Institute of Strategic and International Studies.[77]

India and Myanmar recognised the urgency to generate a security mechanism for preventing instability on inland borders and an ongoing insurgency in the region. India has supplied military equipment to Myanmar for providing support to Myanmar's defence forces. Indian military is giving training to Myanmar military personnel. Myanmar Navy participated in a multilateral maritime forum, such as MILAN, because being neighbours both share maritime borders too. These initiatives are vital for India as India was also intensely pressurised to isolate Myanmar while western countries imposed various sanctions, led by the US and several EU countries.

Defence Capacity Building

Bilateral relations constitute several aspects and building defence capacity with Myanmar is one such important facet. Many military chiefs of Myanmar have visited India and similarly, many Indian military officers have visited Myanmar in the past for mutual interests. The Indian Navy has been quite proactive in this matter since Indian Naval ships have been receiving regular calls from Myanmar ports. India announced the transfer of two BN-2 'Defender' Islander maritime surveillance aircraft and deck-based air-defence guns to the Myanmar Navy, on the request made by Myanmar Navy in 2006. The first maritime security dialogue under the MoU on Maritime Security Cooperation took place in September 2019. Substantial headway was made in the field of cooperation in maritime safety, maritime domain awareness, hydrography, etc. Initiatives such as the addition of maritime patrol aircraft and increase in the frequency of coordinated patrols to twice a year has increased the efficacy of these patrols. Indian Navy has always been inviting Myanmar Navy to join MILAN meetings and the drill held at Port Blair in the Andaman and Nicobar Islands in the Bay of Bengal. During such events, senior naval officers and a naval delegation represent the occasion. Two Myanmar Navy ships were deployed at Visakhapatnam for the 2nd edition of INMEX from October 18-22, 2019. These initiatives were aimed at ensuring regional security and smooth flow of maritime trade. Both the countries discussed bilateral defence cooperation about military training. Myanmar soldiers have been offered the special warfare training by Indian Army since 2006. India offered to give training to Myanmar Army personnel as an important move during the visit of General Min Aung Hlaing, C-in-C of Defence Services of Myanmar, to India in August 2012. In the last one year, 126 trainees were deputed to various Defence establishments across India under ITEC-1 scheme. In addition to the structured courses, Indian Armed Forces Mobile Training Teams (MTT) undertook the UN Peacekeeping training courses and two courses were conducted in February and September-October 2019. Five other courses were also conducted by MTTs from

Indian Navy. Subject Matter Expert Exchange for fighter Aircrew of MiG-29 with Observer Sortie was held for pilots of Myanmar Air Force in April 2019. A Myanmar combat team was trained in October 2019. Further, training on English language, hydrography, medical has been undertaken along with cooperation on Humanitarian Assistance and Disaster Relief. Indian army transferred some of the light artillery guns and Armoured Personnel Carriers (APC) on the Myanmar government's request. An Indian Air Force Met Squadron team established two Met Squadrons of Myanmar Air Force and imparted training from August-November 2019. Indian Air Force Chief offered a counterpart generous air support in updating avionics of fighter aircraft in Myanmar's inventory during his visit to Myanmar. Installation of a Coastal Surveillance System in Myanmar is in progress.

India's foreign ministry has separate divisions for 'Bangladesh and Myanmar' and ASEAN which means the country's diplomats deal with matters relating to its relations with Myanmar as a neighbour different from those relating to Myanmar as an ASEAN.[78] Security and defence relations between the two countries focus primarily on border security and counter-terrorism. The first-ever India-Myanmar Bilateral Military Exercise (IMBEX-2017) took place over six days in November 2017 and focused on peacekeeping operations.[79] Indian army special forces launched a surgical strike in May 2015 in Myanmar in which forces killed at least 60 insurgents of NSCN-K faction in response to the killing of 18 Indian soldiers by the same.

India also plays a vital role in Myanmar's internal peace process, acting as a signatory witness to Myanmar's Nationwide Ceasefire Agreement ceremonies in February 2018 and October 2015.[80] Maritime cooperation between the two countries have also gained importance with Indian and Myanmar navies conducting their first-ever bilateral Naval Exercise; IMNEX-18 is meant to strengthen and promote stronger relations with neighbour countries' armies; the six-day training exercise also aims to train the officers of Myanmar Army in various United Nations Peacekeeping roles and tasks in March in the Bay of Bengal.[81] Multilateral MILAN naval exercise was held off the coast of the Andaman and Nicobar Island in early March. Both the countries signed an agreement in maritime security to enhance cooperation in areas of humanitarian assistance in 2017. Myanmar's army was given knowledge and skills of training curriculum challenges of peace-keeping operations according to the UNO principles, policies, guidelines, in which 15 Myanmar officers and 16 Indian army officers were engaged. Bilateral relations between two nations are heightened as both countries participate and conduct joint exercises. India and Myanmar bond would be more muscular regarding friendship and cooperation by involving themselves in such exercises which enable mutual capacity.

Humanitarian Assistance and Disaster Relief (HADR)

The Bay of Bengal is prone to natural disasters, such as tsunami, storms and cyclones which often hit the region. In recent times, Myanmar was hit by the 2004 Indian Ocean Tsunami and Cyclone Nargis in 2008 which left 78,000 people dead/missing and affected 2.4 million others.[82] Under the circumstances, many countries offered their help in providing humanitarian assistance including UK, France and the US but could not do so as their warships were denied ship-to-shore operations. However, Indian warships came for the rescue under operation named Sahayata and delivered relief items. The regional capacity to react to climate change caused a limited disaster at the operation level but Indian navy is quite effective and efficient to help under HADR, and this had been proved at the time of the Indian Ocean Tsunami in 2004. Indian navy handled responded to various HADR missions and roles since 2004. As compared to India, the capacity of the Myanmar navy is not at oar with India and would require assistance from India.

India-Myanmar Engagements Under Regional/Sub-Regional Institutions

In 1994, the two countries received a vital boost after signing a trade agreement. Since then Indian companies channelised their interest in making significant trade and economic agreements in infrastructure and other areas. Essar, GAIL and ONGC Videsh Ltd., are the companies from India who invested in Myanmar's energy sector. Tata Motors along Indian government financial assistance have established a heavy turbo-truck assembly plant. India and Myanmar are growing and coming closer to each other in strategic and economic terms. Both countries are cooperating in the sub-regional and regional context which may appear as follows:

Association of South East Asian Nations (ASEAN)

Myanmar became a member of ASEAN in July 1997. It is strategically important to India as it is the only country from ASEAN that shares land and a maritime border with India. Myanmar is India's golden gateway to Southeast Asia, and thus it has been regarded as a required impetus to realise India's Look (Act) East Policy. India's interest in Myanmar and Thailand can be realised by improving the connectivity. India would upgrade the Kalewa-Yargyi road segment to highway standard, while Myanmar would develop the Yargyi-Monywa portion. Eventually, it would connect Moreh in India to Mae Sot in Thailand via Myanmar. If India and Myanmar are to become influential regional players in Asia, it is necessary to work towards developing policies that would improve and strengthen them domestically, which in turn will encourage more confidence in their abilities to lead the region and be among the major global players.[83]

Bay of Bengal Initiative for Multi-Sectoral Technical and Economic Cooperation (BIMSTEC)

It is a regional organisation consisting of countries from South Asia and South East Asia. These are India, Nepal, Bhutan, Myanmar, Bangladesh, Thailand and Sri Lanka. Myanmar became a member of BIMSTEC in December 1997. Myanmar is a Free Trade Agreement signatory to the BIMSTEC. Myanmar is the leading country for the energy sector. Myanmar's major trade partners in the BIMSTEC are India and Thailand.

Myanmar's major exports to India are agricultural products like beans, pulses, maize and forest products such as teak and hardwoods;

import from India include chemical products, pharmaceuticals, electrical appliances and transport equipment.[84] BIMSTEC has been envisioned as a connecting bridge between two major regional groups: SAARC and ASEAN. It is an essential component in India's Look (Act) East Policy which adjoins economic cooperation between India and Myanmar.

South Asian Association for Regional Cooperation (SAARC)

The question of Myanmar joining SAARC requires to be examined from the extent it would benefit India and Myanmar to meet opportunities and challenges in the region in future. Myanmar shares a vast land and maritime border with two SAARC nations—India and Bangladesh. However, Myanmar accepted the status of observer in SAARC, given in August 2008. The member countries of SAARC are in regular touch and connected with Myanmar since then. Some SAARC countries like Sri Lanka, India and Bangladesh are enjoying their commercial and cultural links with Myanmar. As by having these relations in the region, there is a potential in receiving monetary benefits, strategic advantages and diplomatic support vis-a-vis keeping itself safe from China's assertiveness.

Bangladesh-China-India-Myanmar (BCIM) Forum for Regional Cooperation

BCIM is a sub-regional organisation of those countries that are from the Asian continent and has the objective of promoting and expanding trade and development among the member countries. The success of BCIM is linked with the ASEAN-China Free Trade Area, ASEAN-Indian Free Trade Area and the ASEAN Free Trade Area. BCIM is a sort of trade corridor which is going to combine road, rail, water and air connectivity in the region to promote and increase foreign trade and bilateral trade among the BCIM members. India and China are linked with Myanmar by common border each. India and China consider the strategic location of Myanmar as a valuable asset because Myanmar provides a massive opportunity for trade and development to all the countries in the region. Both countries do not want any disturbance in Myanmar. Therefore, any development in Myanmar is a matter of concern for them. India and Myanmar have suffered on account of a dominating attitude of China in the past, and China wants to get the benefit of Myanmar's strategic location. India and Myanmar will have to remain on guard when it comes to dealing with China. China's linkages with Myanmar are muscular in terms of strategic, economic and political than India. China strategic and economic presence in Myanmar poses a serious concern to India's maritime and economic interests, especially in the Indian Ocean. Therefore, there is an urgent need for India to play the balancing role in the region and prepare its policy to counter and overshadow the influence of China on Myanmar and in the region.

Areas of Concern between India and Myanmar

Today, unlawful activities are happening in every country. One can indulge in an unlawful deal in one country, deposit money in a different country and take shelter in another country. The widespread political, economic, social and technological changes, as well as variations in legislation, procedures and policies in different countries on mutual assistance in criminal matters, have allowed organised crime groups to become increasingly active in the international arena.[85] The present era belongs to globalisation and trade barriers are being dismantled to open up the economy. All countries have liberalised immigration policies, foreign travel policies and money transfer policies making it easy for the criminals and anti-social groups to operate. Internationally, criminals and gangs are actively into money laundering, acts of corruption, illicit manufacturing and trafficking in firearms, illicit drug trafficking, environmental crimes, women and children trafficking, credit card fraud, the use of violence and extortion, computing-related crimes, illegal trafficking of stolen vehicles, industrial espionage and sabotage, maritime piracy, etc.[86] In order to keep a check on all types of global criminal activities of the gangs, there is a need for all governments to coordinate and make national policies to track down such elements, how they are indulging in anti-national and anti-human activities and hand them over to the international police and other agencies with a view of curbing these crimes.

It has been reported that in India such criminal gangs have been working for many decades and committing organised crimes in various parts of the country. They have unknown membership and modus operandi. They keep changing their area of operations. Therefore, uncountable criminals are operating in the countryside. Their leadership pattern and working style may not be similar to the traditional Italian Mafia module. In order to hide their identities, they sometimes operate in loose form and sometimes as a well-knit group, but the depredations of such criminal gangs are too well known to be recounted. However, the only motive of this organised crime whether in India or elsewhere is to get monetary gain, and that is the only formidable force in the socio-political system.

There is no denying the fact that India-Myanmar is a forgotten border region, especially by India. India's other frontiers always get due attention, whether it is China at the North and Northeast, Pakistan at the West and South; Sri Lanka and the Indian Ocean. The tri-junction of India, China and Myanmar border is becoming more famous due to its geographical proximity. Violence has long been endemic in the region since communities and peoples were left asunder by the imposition and policing of officially demarcated borders between India and Myanmar in 1967.[87] Although, both countries were engaged in both formal and informal trade. Today, the situation is of serious concern to the government as transnational challenges in the region, such as informal trade, insurgency, drug trafficking and the spread of diseases increase.

India and Myanmar share a long land border of 1,643 km particularly sharing a land area of Indian states: Mizoram, Nagaland, Manipur and Arunachal Pradesh. The Paramilitary Force, Assam Rifles have been deployed on the border area and meant to curb the insurgency. These companies are spread over the area to keep vigil in infiltration, illegal drugs, the smuggling of arms and ammunition and counterfeit currency.

No doubt Myanmar Army has very close relations with the Indian Army for decades. However, these relations were more focused only on supplying the defence equipment. It is also acceptable in the existing dynamics in the two countries of the border areas. It has been reported many times that insurgents take safe shelters, NSCN-K, on Myanmar territory and sometimes make the place their operating base too. Besides the above group, Naga insurgents are also fighting for greater Nagaland which constitutes Indian and Myanmar territory as well. There is an agreement in place between both the armies to share their intelligence inputs against the insurgent in the border region.

Defence Operations: Surgical Strikes

The Indian Army's 18 soldiers were killed in Manipur by NSCN-K, the surgical strike was launched against the insurgents group, and the conduct of operation was in the India-Myanmar border areas. On behalf of the Indian government, a statement was released regarding "Hot Pursuit" that pushed forces to reach Myanmar border region. While these media reports in India did not corroborate the territorial incursion of the pursuit even the statement released from the office of Myanmar President denied the story regarding Indian Army operation in Myanmar territory.

The operation which followed was described as one of the worst militant attacks in India in recent years, and evoked adverse reactions in the country's Northeast and among the South Asian neighbours besides jeopardising the negotiation to end the insurgency and violent protest in pockets of India's border regions.[88] The insurgents who belonged to NSCN-K, ambushed the convoy of 6 Dogra Regiment soldiers in the Chandel district, Manipur, at Myanmar border. Another group of the same clan is NSCN-IM. This group is a recognised armed ethnic against India since 1960. The Indian government was in talks with the group; the group signed a five-point accord with the Indian government for 15 years truce in 2012. Strategists are of the view that the situation has become violent due to the absence of progress and governments dismissive look towards NSCN-IM. Over the last year or so, the Khaplang group has also collaborated with other rebel groups to form a coalition under the banner of the United Liberation Front of West South East Asia that includes the Paresh Barua faction of the United Liberation Front of Asom (ULFA) besides a faction of the National Democratic Front of Bodoland and the

Kuki Liberation Army (Jibon).[89] Myanmar border region is full of dense forests and believed to be the a haven for these groups.

India and Myanmar are working with each other to stabilise the edgy border region where irredentist waves shape secured land on both sides of the border. They often take benefit of the dense forests and challenging terrain. In 1995, a joint military operation "Operation Golden Bird" was launched along the Mizoram border following the signing of a Memorandum of Understanding for the maintenance of peace and tranquillity in the border areas.[90] In this operation, 118 rebels were captured with weapons and eight were killed. Soon after, the Myanmar army withdrew its forces to register their point on giving Nehru Award to Aung San Suu Kyi, pro-democracy leader of Myanmar, and the operation was suspended. Recently, India and Myanmar signed an agreement on security cooperation for patrol coordinating and intelligence sharing.

The North Eastern Region of India and Myanmar

The North Eastern tip of India consisting of contiguous seven states—Arunachal Pradesh, Assam, Manipur, Meghalaya, Mizoram, Nagaland, Tripura and Sikkim constitutes a single narrow passageway connecting the Indian subcontinent to Southeast Asia and East Asia and acts as a crucial corridor for human migration and development between these areas.[91] In terms of geographical size, Northeast India constitutes about 8 per cent of total India's size, Northeast India's population (including Sikkim) is approximately 44 million (2011 census). The Siliguri Corridor in West Bengal connects the NER with the central part of India. Northeast India is one of the most panoramic and strategic landscapes of India. The significance of this region has only grown over the years with its land linkages to Southeast Asia. The Northeast has been in focus for decades for its enormous potential—abundant resources, industrialisation and power generation certainly with greater focus from a security perspective in response to developments along India's northern borders in recent decades.

India's Look (Act) East Policy in its present form got initiated during 1990-91. It was only in 2008 that Northeast India appeared in related policy formulation with the launch of NER Vision Document 2020.[92] It has become an important focal point which is a robust domain in orchestrating India's Look (Act) East Policy. There are ample possibilities for Northeast India to reap benefits from India's thriving relations with South East Asia as the process of globalisation provides the countries with the opportunities to grapple with cross-market accessibility and enables them to alleviate their poverty and economic backwardness. The scenic beauty of India's Northeast serves as an attractive tourist spot, and its infrastructure is a hub of immense business potential. Consequently, the Northeast emerged as a dominant region in India's geo-economic and geopolitical calculus. Northeast is located in the cusp of Bangladesh, China and Myanmar. India has to tackle insurgency in the Northeast whose activities hurt development in the country. The porous border with Myanmar is attributed as contributing towards the insurgency problems in India's Northeast. As the International long boundary between India and Myanmar formally demarcated on March 10, 1967, and it is largely unfenced. It has now become a serious problem for both the countries as Kachin Independent Army (KIA), Chin National Front (CNF) National Socialist Council of Nagaland-Khaplang (NSCN-K), National Socialist Council of Nagaland-Isak-Muviah (NSCN-IM) and United Liberation Front of Assam (ULFA) like groups have been known to have cross-border linkages in providing shelters.

Four of India's politically sensitive North-eastern states, Arunachal Pradesh (520 km), Nagaland (215 km), Manipur (398 km) and Mizoram (510 km), share an international border. On the other side Kachin, Chin states and Sagaing region of Myanmar share a land border with India.[93] These parts have been facing insurgency-related problems. Due to their ethnic connections, insurgent groups from the northeast of India not only receive shelter in Myanmar but also have operational bases. Myanmar is a part of the Golden Triangle including Thailand, Cambodia and Laos, though, the border region has been the theatre of criminal activities such as smuggling and illegal trade in narcotics, fake currency and sources of arms supplies which have caused severe problems to India's security.[94] India shares the strategic sphere of Bay of Bengal including the strategically important area of Andaman and Nicobar Islands where the two closest Andaman and Myanmar's Coco islands are barely 30 km apart. This geographical proximity between the two countries translated into long-standing trade relations across land borders and the sea route.

The insurgency in India's Northeast is a critical factor impacting close relations with Myanmar, the 1,643 km long border passing through the Indian states Manipur, Arunachal Pradesh, Mizoram and Nagaland, having affected by the insurgency. This is not a new internal problem for India. It has been continuing since the independence of India. Presently, there are around eight active insurgent groups in India and Myanmar region. These outfits have been receiving logistic, military and financial support from Southeast Asia and South Asian countries. There is no hidden information that they have their safe bases with the connivance of sympathetic support and communities in the neighbourhood. India's security forces have been deployed and conduct counter-insurgency operations, but somehow insurgents find escape routes to neighbouring nations where enforcement agencies are either uninterested or weak. However, there are attempts to throw them out of the region or make them inactive. In 1991, the 192 insurgents were captured by Myanmar military in raids against rebel bases in Manipur including Chief Rajkumar Meghen of UNLF. Apparently, In 1994, an MoU was signed between India and Myanmar for maintaining of peace and tranquillity in border areas. As a result of the MoU between both the countries, they launched Operation Golden Bird in 1995 and captured a huge hall of arms and ammunition being transported to them from Cox Bazar, Bangladesh.

Illicit Drug Trafficking

India has been working on plans of building economic corridors between Northeast India and its neighbourhood to boost foreign trade and to give the economy the much-needed leap forward.[95] India's Look (Act) East Policy is essential in playing a complementing role in these plans to achieve the objectives.

Northeast India can develop, prosper and eventually overcome its troubles by engaging eastern foreign neighbours, especially with the recent agreement on Bangladesh, China, India, Myanmar (BCIM) economic corridor blueprint, India can access markets in China's west and southwest, through the Northeastern borders.[96] China's Yunnan province needs connectivity with the rest of the country to enhance trade activity in the area. Similarly, connectivity is an essential aspect for India's Northeast to cater to regional and sub-regional cooperation such as SAARC, ASEAN and GMC. There is also a need to understand the ethnic insurgencies in the neighbourhood (Golden Triangle Countries) that can turn into an ugly behemoth of drug trafficking. The clouds of illicit narcotic endanger the new connectivity routes and it can harm the development and growth plan in the region by disturbing human health and society's well being.

India's security strategy for the economic corridors and connectivity will have to entail watertight anti-drugs control measures and mechanisms to snuff out the possibilities of surges in narcotics trafficking that may result from better connectivity and established networks of peoples across the region.[97] India's four states: Arunachal Pradesh, Nagaland, Manipur and Mizoram share boundaries with Myanmar. National AIDS Control Organisation reports for each state, the extent of HIV and drug addiction. Western Myanmar border routes are the hideouts of insurgents from India and with dominance over the area trafficking is easy across the porous border of narcotics and contraband firearms. Recently, Manipur witnessed huge quantities of contraband high Pseudoephedrine Hydrochloride (PH)-content drugs, manufactured in India, being trafficked into Myanmar for processing narcotics especially heroin.[98] The insurgents are based in Nagaland, Manipur and Mizoram, absorbed in smuggling Pseudoephedrine to China via Guwahati and Myanmar via Delhi.[99]

Traditionally the Golden Triangle is a famous region: Thailand, Laos and Myanmar, for opium production. Opium cultivation in the GT was higher by 22 per cent as per the United Nations Office on Drugs and Crime (UNODC), Southeast Asia Opium Survey 2013 and propelled by 13 per cent of growth especially in Myanmar. A decade ago, the

Map 3.10: Major Flow of Drugs from the Golden Triangle to India's Northeast

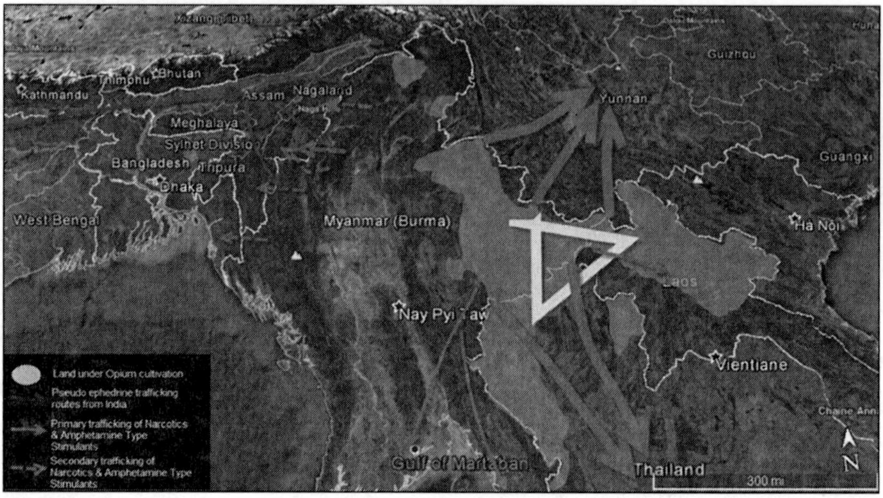

Source: Institute of Defence Studies and Analysis.

Golden Triangle supplied half the world's heroin, but drug barons backed by ethnic militias in Myanmar have turned to massive traffic quantities of amphetamines and methamphetamines—"which can be produced cheaply in small, hidden laboratories, without the need for acres of exposed land" and these narcotics now dominate the Myanmar part of the Triangle.[100] Opium production and cultivation was legal under rules in the country and has been a significant shareholder to Country's GDP. Today, Myanmar is the second largest producer in the world after Afghanistan, accounts around 25 per cent opium of the world through a vital part of the Golden Triangle. Shan and Kachin states are the concentrated areas of production in Myanmar, as it is 17 times costlier than rice there and is thus profitable.

Illicit drug trafficking is the most significant transnational organised crime which has become a serious issue confronting both developing and developed countries.[101] India has a vast land frontier of around 15,106.6 km and a coastal border of around 7,516.6 km. Its geographic location drives its many problems. Being a largest South Asian country, India has been sandwiched between Golden Crescent (Afghanistan, Pakistan and Iran) and Golden Triangle (Myanmar, Laos and Thailand). India also produces licit opium for medicinal and scientific motives, grown in Madhya Pradesh, Uttar Pradesh and Rajasthan under the guidelines of Narcotic Commissioner. In India, significant substances of the illicit drug trade are: opium, herbal cannabis, methaqualone, heroin and hashish. The most vulnerable border is India-Pakistan where it is being supplied. White heroin is being supplied from Myanmar to India. Punjab has been the worst affected by trafficking since 1980. There were reports of drug usage by students in universities of Chandigarh, Mumbai, Delhi and Kolkata. Certain Indian traditions are also responsible for this to some extent. It is customary in some places to consume Bhang (crushed leaves of the cannabis plant) on the famous festival of Holi. There is no such tolerance for charas or ganja which is also derived from the same cannabis plant.[102] India needs to have long-term strategy to curb this menace as this could impair our society from inside. There are long-term side effects of drug abuse among young people are detrimental.

Maritime Security concerns

There are a number of maritime security challenges in the Bay of Bengal for India and Myanmar, such as terrorism, drug smuggling, piracy, illegal fishing and human smuggling known as Non-Traditional Security (NTS) threats. The Indian Prime Minister also highlighted the issue during his visit to Myanmar in April 2012 and observed that both India and Myanmar need to "expand our security cooperation that is vital not only to maintain peace along our land borders but also to protect maritime trade which we hope will open up through the sea route between Kolkata and Sittwe."[103] The navy of both the countries and other sea forces are on the forefront to address climate change and sea environment related issues and must coordinate in dealing with the rescue and relief situations.

Illegal Migration

The Rohingya are one of the most persecuted minorities in the world. Their status in Myanmar is fragile. They constitute nearly 2 per cent of the total population of Myanmar.[104] Now Rohingya people are allowed to index themselves as temporary residents and were issued a temporary identification card, while they had been permitted to cast their vote in the parliamentary election in 2012. Later on, the community was disenfranchised by Myanmar government in 2015 national elections, after Buddhist hard liner pressure. The COVID-19 pandemic has brought further miseries to the community, as most of them were working in the unorganised sector. Since lockdown affected this sector quite heavily, they have lost their jobs, forcing them to live in poverty and hunger. The new citizenship law, which effectively amended India's Citizenship Act, grants citizenship rights to non-Muslim immigrants of Pakistan, Afghanistan, and Bangladesh only. Since 2017, many members of the Rohingya community in search of safe heavens have been trying to seek refuge in India.

According to Human Rights Watch, the state-sponsored violence forced full 1,25,000 Rohingyas to leave their domiciles and live in squalid refugee camps in Rakhine State in 2012, when a new Rohingya militant group, the Arakan Rohingya Salvation Army (ARSA), attacked army outposts in October 2016. State-enforced violence took on even greater ferocity.[105] A brutal crackdown by the Myanmar army caused many deaths and forced Rohingya migrants to cross over to Bangladesh, India and other countries.

As per reports, there are 98 per cent Muslims in Rakhine state and reportedly over a lakh fled to Bangladesh and forty-thousand took shelter in different parts of India such as Jammu and Kashmir, Haryana, Uttar Pradesh and Hyderabad illegally. Along with fourteen thousand immigrants are holding UN refugee cards. However, this sensitive issue poses a security threat to Indian security, and GOI is aware of it. It will tackle the issue in due course. But timely action is required here because these ethnic groups can be influenced by various insurgent groups of the Northeast, including the National Socialist Council of Nagaland (NSCN), United Liberation Front of Asom (ULFA), United National Liberation Front (UNLF) that have their camps across the border in the Kachin and Sagaing provinces of Myanmar. It is estimated that about 40 militant camps belonging to various Northeast militant groups exist on Myanmar soil.[106] Besides, there is increased trafficking of drugs along the border with far reaching security impacts. The Northeastern states of India have strong cross-border socio-cultural affinities—the outcome of a long historical process of intermingling among the people of the region.[107] As a result, insurgency movement in the Northeast has strong connections with the unrest in Myanmar. The Kuki-Chin groups migrated from Myanmar in the last century are settled along the border area. Even, the NSCN faction of Khaplang has its origins in Myanmar. The porous border between India and Myanmar and uneven terrain are the main factors which hamper Indian security operations to counter them. The role of non-state actors from Myanmar in the supply of arms to rebels in the Northeast became a severe security concern.[108] India has tagged them as illegal migrants in the country who would face deportation. India's Ministry of Home Affairs, issued instructions to concerned states to identify Rohingya and repatriate them to Myanmar. The first batch of Rohingyas was sent back to Myanmar in 2018.

Notes

1. Salman Haider and Ruhee Neog (2017), "Three Years of the Modi Government," *Institute of Peace and Conflict Studies,* p. 19. Available at http://www.jstor.org/stable/resrep09416 (Accessed on January 17, 2018).
2. Television Interview of U Kyaw Lwin, the Union Minister, Ministry of Construction, Government of the Republic of Union of Myanmar, on June 25, 2015. Available at https://www.youtube.com/watch?v=IjA-56qvPjA (Accessed on March 11, 2016).
3. Soe Myint (2003), *Burma file: A question for Democracy*, India Research Press, Delhi, p. 31.
4. Ministry of External Affairs, India, India-Myanmar Relation, May 2016. Available at http://www.enterpriseindiamyanmar.in/pdf/BILATERAL-RELATIONS.pdf (Accessed on October 22, 2016).
5. Ibid.
6. A Sundaram (2013), "Look (Act) East Policy," *International Journal of Advancements in Research and Technology*, Vol. (2)5, p. 1.
7. Prabir De and Jayanta Kumar Ray (2013), *India-Myanmar Connectivity: Current Status and Future Prospects*, KW Publishers, New Delhi.
8. Embassy of India, Yangon, Myanmar, Indian Projects." Available at http://www.indiaembassyyangon.net/index.php?option=com_content&view=article&id=54:major-indianprojects&catid=20&Itemid=183&lang=en (Accessed on May 12, 2015).
9. Press Information Bureau, Government of India, "Joint Statement on the occasion of the visit of PM of India to Myanmar," Prime Minister's Office, 28 May, 2012

Available at http://pib.nic.in/newsite/ erelease.aspx?relid=84517 (Accessed on June 23, 2015).

10. *The New Light of Myanmar*, "President U Thein Sein welcome Indian Prime Minister Dr. Manmohan Singh," Vol. 20 No. 39, May 29, 2012. Available online at http://www.Myanmarlibrary.org/ docs13/NLM2012-05-29.pdf (Accessed on June 18, 2015).
11. Based on Personal Interaction with Dr. Rahul Mishra, Senior Lecturer, University of Malaya at JNV University, Jodhpur, Rajasthan on March 22, 2015.
12. A Conference Report (September 28-29, 2015), "India-Myanmar Relations: Looking from the Borders," *Institute of Social Science: Burma Centre Delhi*, New Delhi.
13. Anurag Singh Thakur, Question No. 6280 in Lok Sabha on April 12, 2017 & its Answer by M. J. Akbar, Minister of State MEA, India. Available at http://mea.gov.in/lokabha.htm?dtl/28382/QUESTION_NO6280_KALADAN_MULTIMODAL_TRANSIT_TRANSPORT (Accessed on December 15, 2017).
14. Ibid.
15. See Annexure C.
16. A Report by the Kaladan Movement (2013), "One Cannot Step into the Same River Twice: Making the Kaladan River People Centred." Available at https://aippnet.org/wpontent/uploads/2013/06/KM_Report_Eng-20130612093417.pdf (Accessed on June 23, 2016).
17. Ibid.
18. Ibid.
19. Prabir De and Jayanta Kumar Ray (2013), "India-Myanmar Connectivity: Current Status and Future Prospects," KW Publishers, New Delhi, p. 121.
20. Swapna Bhattacharya (2015), *The Rakhine State (Arakan) of Myanmar: Interrogating History, Culture and Conflict*, Manohar Publication, New Delhi, p. 85.
21. Rajeev Jayaswal (2010), "Indian Oil: Oil India in talks to buy into Essar's Myanmar Block," *The Economic Times*. Available at https://economictimes.indiatimes.com/industry/energy/oil-gas/indian-oil-oil-india-in-talks-to-buy-into-essars-myanmar-gas-block/articleshow/6423763.cms (Accessed on November 11, 2016).
22. Joint Statement During the visit of Chairman, State Peace and Development Council of Myanmar, July 27, 2010. Available at http://mea.gov.in/bilateraldocuments.htm?dtl/4283/Joint+Statement+during+the+visit+of+Chairman+State+Peace+and+Development+Council+of+Myanmar (Accessed on May 5, 2016).
23. India-Myanmar pact on combating terror hailed in NE, *The Assam Tribune*, July 29, 2010. Available at http://www.assamtribune.com/scripts/mdetails.asp?id=jul2910/at03 (Accessed on August 30, 2017).
24. V. S. Seshadri (2014), "Transforming Connectivity Corridors between India and Myanmar into Development Corridors," *Research and Information System for Developing Countries*. Available at http://www.ris.org.in/transforming-connectivity-corridors-between-india-and-myanmar-development-corridors (Accessed on July 10, 2016).
25. Amit Baruah (2001), "India, Myanmar Road Opened," *The Hindu*, February 13. Available at https://www.thehindu.com/thehindu/2001/02/14/stories/01140004.htm (Accessed on June 26, 2015).

26. V. S. Seshadri (2014), "Transforming Connectivity Corridors between India and Myanmar into Development Corridors," *Research and Information System for Developing Countries*. Available at http://www.ris.org.in/transforming-connectivity-corridors-between-india-and-myanmar-development-corridors (Accessed on March 21, 2017).
27. Ministry of Development of North Eastern Region, Bi-Lateral Projects with Myanmar & Indian Projects to Promote Connectivity & Trade with NER. Available at http://mdoner.gov.in/myanmar (Accessed on September 12, 2017).
28. "Survey on for Imphal-Mandalay bus service," *The Times of India*, January 13, 2015. Available at https://timesofindia.indiatimes.com/city/guwahati/Survey-on-for-Imphal-Mandalay-bus-service/articleshow/45859613.cms (Accessed on February 5, 2016).
29. Feasibility Report (2017), "Construction of 69 Bridges including approach Roads on the Tamu-Kyigone-Kalewa Road Section from 0.00 km to 149.70 km of the Trilateral Highway in Myanmar on Engineering, Procurement and Construction Mode," Ministry of External Affairs, New Delhi. Available at http://www.mea.gov.in/Images/attach/4_RFP_Vol_III_Feasibility_Report_Part_I.pdf (Accessed on January 19, 2018).
30. Htaung Sian Kan (2017), "Current Status and Challenges to Facilitation of International Railway Transport in Myanmar," *Working Group on the Trans-Asian Railway Network and Global Smart Rail Conference,* Ministry of Transport and Communication, Myanmar. Available at https://www.unescap.org/sites/default/files/Myanmar%20country%20report-TAR%20WGM-5.pdf (Accessed on January 18, 2018).
31. Pranjal Kumar Phukan (2016), "Trade Imbalance due to Connectivity Issues between India and Southeast Asia," *Society for Policy Studies,* No. 3, pp. 1-12.
32. Peter Hodgkinson (1999), "Development of the Trans-Asian Railway" , Economic and Social Commission for Asia and the Pacific of United Nations Organisation Report. Available at https://www.unescap.org/sites/default/files/tarsc-fulltext_1980.pdf (Accessed on July 14, 2016).
33. Prabir De and Jayanta Kumar Ray (2013), *India-Myanmar Connectivity: Current Status and Future Prospects,* KW Publishers, New Delhi, p. 148.
34. Adarsh Vijay (2018), "India and Myanmar: Prospects of Maritime Reciprocity," *National Maritime Foundation*. Available at http://www.maritimeindia.org/View%20Profile/ 636540793561642770.pdf (Accessed on October 15, 2018).
35. Prabir De and Jayanta Kumar Ray (2013), "India-Myanmar Connectivity: Current Status and Future Prospects," KW Publishers, New Delhi, p. 151.
36. Prabir De (2016), "ASEAN-India Air Connectivity Report," *Research and Information System for Developing Countries*. Available at http://ris.org.in/newasiaforum/sites/default/files/ Publication%20File/Air_ Connectivity_Report.pdf (Accessed on June 22, 2017).
37. Ibid.
38. Ranjit Bhartakur (2014), "Gateway to the ASEAN: India's Northeast Frontier", *Northeast Advisory Council of FICCI Report*. Available at https://www.pwc.in/assets/pdfs/publications/ 2014/gateway-to-the-asean.pdf (Accessed on June 16, 2017).
39. Fatih Birol (2015), "India's Energy Outlook," World Energy Outlook Special Report. Available at https://www.iea.org/publications/freepublications/publication/IndiaEnergyOutlook_WEO2015.pdf (Accessed on June 10, 2017).

40. Srinjoy Bose (2007), "Energy Politics: India-Bangladesh-Myanmar Relations," *IPCS Special Report,* No. 45, p. 4.
41. Energising Growth of the Nation, Annual Report 2014-15, Ministry of Petroleum and Natural Gas, India. Available at http://petroleum.nic.in/sites/default/files/AR14-15.pdf (Accessed on August 21, 2016).
42. Marie Lall (2008), "India-Myanmar Relations: Geo-politics and Energy in Light of the New Balance of Power in Asia," *Institute of South Asian Studies Working Paper,* No. 29, p. 17.
43. Marie Lall (2006), "Indo-Myanmar Relations in the Era of Pipeline Diplomacy," *Contemporary Southeast Asia: A Journal of International and Strategic Affairs,* Vol. (28) No. 3, pp. 424-446.
44. As per the "Hydocarbon Vision 2025" Report of Government of India. Available at http://petroleum.nic.in/ sites/default/files/vision.pdf (Accessed on June 14, 2016).
45. Akhil Mehrotra (2013), Industry Group Report for Petroleum and Natural Gas Regulatory Board, "Vision 2030," Natural Gas Infrastructure in India. Available at http://www.pngrb.gov.in/Hindi-Website/pdf/vision-NGPV-2030-06092013.pdf (Accessed on June 30, 2016).
46. Pakistan Defence Forum, "India offers $150 million Investment in Myanmar," June 9, 2013. Available at https://defence.pk/pdf/threads/india-offers-150-million-investment-in-myanmar. 257397/ (Accessed on August 20, 2016).
47. Bilateral Economic and Commercial Relations, Embassy of India, Yangon, Myanmar. Available at https://www.embassyofindiayangon.gov.in/pages (Accessed on January 14, 2018).
48. Fatih Birol (2015), "India's Energy Outlook," World Energy Outlook Special Report. Available at https://www.iea.org/publications/freepublications/publication/IndiaEnergyOutlook_WEO2015.pdf (Accessed on July 11, 2017).
49. Anasua Basu Ray Chaudhary and Pratnashree Basu (2015), "India-Myanmar Connectivity: Possibility and Challenges," Observer Research Foundation. Available at https://www.orfonline.org/wp-content/uploads/2015/12/IndiaMyanmar.pdf (Accessed on November 25, 2017).
50. Gordon Brown (2015), "Chinese Market for Myanmar's Shwe Gas Stalls," *Mizzima News,* May 2, 2015. Available at http://www.mizzima.com/business-features/chinese-market-yanmar%E2%80%99s-shwe-gas-stalls (Accessed on October 17, 2016).
51. Baseline Assessment Report Hydropower (2017), "Strategic Environmental Assessment of the Hydropower Sector in Myanmar," *International Finance Cooperation: World Bank Group*. Available at https://www.ifc.org/wps/wcm/connect/3f136d35-74fe-4601-90f8-4a03c4d22a2b/Chapter+2_SEA+Baseline+Assessment_Hydropower.pdf?MOD=AJPERES (Accessed on July 19, 2018).
52. Nidhi Verma and Aditya Kalra (2018), "India plans to raise refining capacity by 77 percent by 2030,"The Economic Times, February 08. Available at https://energy.economictimes.indiatimes.com/news/ oil-and-gas/india-plans-to-raise-refining-capacity-by-77-pct-by-2030-govt-report/62835748 (Accessed on November 15, 2018).
53. Fukunari Kimura & So Umezaki, "ASEAN-India Connectivity: The Comprehensive Asia Development Plan, Phase II," ERIA Research Project Report 2010, No. 7. Available at http://www.eria.org/ RPR-2010-7.pdf (Accessed on March 8, 2016).

54. David Sinate (2017), "India's Engagement with CLMV: Gateway to ASEAN Markets," *Export-Import Bank of India*, Occasional Paper No. 180. Available at https://www.eximbankindia.in/Assets/Dynamic/PDF/PublicationResources/ResearchPapers/Hindi/69file.pdf (Accessed on January 13, 2018).
55. Embassy of India, Yangon, Myanmar, "Bilateral and Economic Relations." Available at http://www.indiaembassyyangon.net/index.php?option=com_content&view=article&id=60&Itemid=189&lang=en (Accessed on March 15, 2018).
56. See Annexure D.
57. Embassy of India, Yangon, Myanmar, "Bilateral and Economic Relations." Available online at http://www.indiaembassyyangon.net/index.php?option=com_content&view=article&id=60&Itemid=189&lang=en (Accessed on 1March 15, 2018)
58. Ibid.
59. Michael O'Kane (2014), "Doing Business in Myanmar," Andalus Publishing, Chicago, p. 54.
60. Tata Motors to construct heavy truck plant in Myanmar under Government of India Line of Credit, Tata Motors, March 22, 2010. Available at https://www.tatamotors.com/press/tata-motors-to-construct-heavy-truck-plant-in-myanmar-under-government-of-indias-line-of-credit/ (Accessed on April 16, 2016).
61. Anasua Basu Ray Chaudhary and Pratnashree Basu (2015), "India-Myanmar Connectivity: Possibility and Challenges," Observer Research Foundation. Available at https://www.orfonline.org/wp-content/uploads/2015/12/IndiaMyanmar.pdf (Accessed on April 14, 2016).
62. Zhao, Hong (2011), "China–Myanmar Energy Cooperation and Its Regional Implications," *Journal of Current Southeast Asian Affairs,* 30 (4), pp. 89-109.
63. S Nallayarasu (2015), "Engineering for Oil and Gas Exploration," *Indian Institute of Technology of Madras*. Available at http://www.drnallay.com/pdf/Engineering%20for%20Oil%20 and%20Gas.pdf (Accessed on May 28, 2017).
64. Baker Mckenzie (2017), "Doing Business in Myanmar for Indian Companies." Available at https://www.bakermckenzie.com//media/files/insight/publications/2017/08/br_myanmar_dbimyanmarforindiancompanies_aug17_2.pdf?la=en (Accessed on May 9, 2017).
65. *The Economic Times,* "Indian Companies, Banks plan to Invest in Myanmar," June 6, 2013. Available at https://economictimes.indiatimes.com/news/economy/foreign-trade/indian-companies-banks-plan-to-invest-in-myanmar/articleshow/20465778.cms (Accessed on July 19, 2017).
66. Myanmar-India optical fibre link project to complete in next March, Ayerwaddy, December 17, 2008. Available at http://ayerawaddy.blogspot.com/2008/12/myanmar-india-optical-fiber-link.html (Accessed on October 18, 2016).
67. Annual Report 2015-16, Centre for Development of Advanced Computing. Available at https://www.cdac.in/index.aspx?id=pdf_annualreport_15-16 (Accessed on December 31, 2017).
68. *The New Light of Myanmar*, "President U Thein Sein welcome Indian Prime Minister Dr. Manmohan Singh," Vol.20 No. 39, May 29, 2012. Available at http://www.Myanmarlibrary.org/ docs13/ NLM2012-05-29.pdf (Accessed on April 24, 2016).
69. See Annexure E.

70. Shristi Pukhrem (2012), "The Significance of Connectivity in India-Myanmar Relations," *IDSA Comment*. Available at https://idsa.in/idsacomments/TheSignificanceofConnectivityinIndia MyanmarRelations_spukhrem_230512 (Accessed on April 12, 2016).
71. *The Economic Times*, "EXIM Bank extends $354 million to Myanmar Foreign Trade Bank," December 30, 2013. Available at https://economictimes.indiatimes.com/industry/banking/finance/banking/ exim-bank-extends-354-million-to-myanma-foreign-trade-bank/articleshow/28148390.cms (Accessed on August 21, 2016).
72. *The Tribune*, "India signs 8 MOU's with Myanmar," September 6, 2017. Available at https://www.tribuneindia.com/news/nation/india-signs-8-mous-with-myanmar/462993.html (Accessed on March 20, 2018).
73. Ibid.
74. India-Myanmar Relations (2017), Ministry of External Affairs, India. Available at https://www.mea.gov.in/Portal/ForeignRelation/MYANMAR_August_2017_new.pdf (Accessed on March 22, 2018).
75. Vivasvan Shastri and Yesha Bhatt (2018), *Dynamic Diplomacy and Foreign Policy*, Prabhat Prakashan Publishers, New Delhi, p. 95.
76. Vijay Sakhuja (2012), "India and Myanmar: Choice for Military Cooperation," *ICWA Issue Brief*. Available at https://icwa.in/icwa_hindi/pdfs/IBindiamyanmar.pdf (Accessed on September 2, 2016).
77. See Annexure F.
78. Viraaj Solanki (2018), "India boosts relations with Myanmar, where Chinese influence is growing," *International Institute of Security Studies*. Available at https://www.iiss.org/blogs/analysis/2018/05/india-myanmar-china-relations (Accessed on October 11, 2018).
79. Naresh Mitra, "India-Myanmar Joint Military Exercise to begin on 20 November in Meghalaya," *The Times of India*, November 18, 2017. Available at https://timesofindia.indiatimes.com/india/india-myanmar-joint-military-exercise-to-begin-on-nov-20-in-meghalaya/articleshow/61703643.cms (Accessed on February 15, 2018).
80. Viraaj Solanki (2018), "India boosts relations with Myanmar, where Chinese influence is growing," *International Institute of Security Studies*. Available at https://www.iiss.org/blogs/analysis/ 2018/05/india-myanmar-china-relations (Accessed on October 11, 2018).
81. Prashantha Parameswaran, "What's Behind the New India-Myanmar Naval Exercise?," *The Diplomat,* March 29, 2018. Available at https://thediplomat.com/2018/03/whats-behind-the-new-india-myanmar-naval-exercise/ (Accessed on August 15, 2018).

820 Howard L Berman (2008), "Burma in the Aftermath of Cyclone Nargis: Death, Displacement and Humanitarian Aid," Subcommittee on Asia, The Pacific and The Global Environment, Sr. No. 110229. Available at https://www.gpo.gov/fdsys/pkg/CHRG-110hhrg42477/pdf/CHRG-110hhrg42477.pdf (Accessed on July 14, 2017).

83. Sridhar Ramaswamy and Tridivesh Singh Maini (2014), "The strategic importance of Myanmar for India," The Diplomat. Available at https://thediplomat.com/2014/08/the-strategic-importance-of-myanmar-for-india/ (Accessed on March 16, 2017).

84. Cooperation between India and Myanmar in regional milieu, Youth Forum on Foreign Policy, February 2015. Available at https://yffpindia.wordpress.com/2015/02/01/cooperation-between-india-and-myanmar-in-regional-milieu/ (Accessed on November 1, 2017).
85. Shankar Pratap Singh, "Transnational Organised Crimes: Indian Perspective," 119th International Training Course, Participant Paper, Resource Material Series No. 59. Available at https://www.unafei.or.jp/publications/pdf/RS_No59/No59_38PA_Singh.pdf (Accessed on June 13, 2018).
86. Based on Personal Interaction with Dr. Udai Bhanu Singh, Senior Associate Fellow at IDSA, New Delhi on October 14, 2015 and Electronic Media Interaction. Available at https://idsa.in/askanexpert/what-is-the-politico-strategic-impact on April 12, 2019.
87. Anasua Basu Ray Chaudhary and Pratnashree Basu (2015), "India-Myanmar Connectivity: Possibility and Challenges," Observer Research Foundation. Available at https://www.orfonline.org/wp-content/uploads/2015/12/IndiaMyanmar.pdf (Accessed on October 23, 2017).
88. Laldinkima Salio (2015), "Blending Force and Consent: India's Counter Insurgency Dilemma in Northeast," *Institute of Southeast Asian Studies*, ISAS Brief No. 379, p. 2
89. Tenshubam Hemo Singh (2016), *Terrorism in Indo-Myanmar Region*, Akansha Publishing House, New Delhi, p. 135.
90. Laldinkima Sailo (2015), "Blending Force and Consent: India's Counter Insurgency Dilemma in the Northeast," *Institute of South Asian Studies Brief*, No. 379, p. 4.
91. Ashok Kumar (2017), "India-Myanmar Relations: Economic and Security issues," *KAAV International Journal of Arts, Humanities and Social Sciences*, Vol. 4 (1) pp. 37-45.
92. A Sundaram (2013), "Look (Act) East Policy," *International Journal of Advancements in Research and Technology*, Vol. (2)5, p. 3.
93. Ashok Kumar (2017), "Chinese Angle in India-Myanmar Relations," *IOSR Journal of Humanities and Social Sciences*, Vol (22)8, Ver. 16, pp. 5-9.
94. Ibid., p. 8.
95. Namarta Goswami (2014), "Drugs and Golden Triangle: Renewed concerns for Northeast India," IDSA Comment. Available at https://idsa.in/idsacomments/DrugsandtheGolden Triangle_ngoswami_100214 (Accessed on March 12, 2017).
96. Mohd Aminul Karim & Faria Islam (2018), "Bangladesh-China-India-Myanmar Economic Corridor: Challenges and Prospects," *The Korean Journal of Defence Analysis,* Vol. (30)2, pp. 283-302.
97. Pushpita Das (2012), "Drug Trafficking in India: A case Study of Border Security," IDSA Occasional Paper No. 24. Available at https://idsa.in/system/files/OP_DrugTraffickinginIndia.pdf (Accessed on August 21, 2017).
98. Namarta Goswami (2014), "Drugs and Golden Triangle: Renewed concerns for Northeast India," IDSA Comment. Available at https://idsa.in/idsacomments/DrugsandtheGoldenTriangle_ ngoswami_100214 (Accessed on July 15, 2017).
99. Based on Personal Interaction with Dr. Pushpita Das, Research Fellow at IDSA, New Delhi on January 17, 2017 and Electronic Media Interaction. Available online at https://idsa.in/askanexpert/ myanmar-part-of-the-golden-triangle-india (Accessed on April 25, 2019).

100. Namarta Goswami (2014), "Drugs and Golden Triangle: Renewed concerns for Northeast India," IDSA Comment. Available at https://idsa.in/idsacomments/DrugsandtheGoldenTriangle_ ngoswami_100214 (Accessed on July 15, 2017).
101. Vinod Kumar (2014), "Drugs and The Golden Triangle: Renewed Concerns for NE India," *Indian Review of Global Affairs*. Available at http://irga.in/article.php?id=506 (Accessed on September 17, 2017).
102. Pushpita Das (2012), "Drug Trafficking in India: A case Study of Border Security," IDSA Occasional Paper No. 24. Available at https://idsa.in/system/files/OP_DrugTraffickinginIndia.pdf (Accessed on March 27, 2017).
103. Vinod Anand (2013), "The Evolving Indo-Myanmar Defence relationship: An Analytical Perspective," *Vivekananda International Foundation* Available at https://www.vifindia.org/article/2013/february/11/the-evolving-indo-myanmar-defence-relationship-an-analytical-perspective (Accessed on August 8, 2018).
104. Niranjan Sahoo (2017), "India's Rohingya Realpolitik," Observer Research Foundation Comment. Available at https://www.orfonline.org/research/indias-rohingya-realpolitik/ (Accessed on September 16, 2018).
105. Ibid.
106. B.B Sharma (2011), "Myanmar's impact On NE insurgency." Available at http://www.burmacentredelhi.org/indoburma-relation/relevant-reports/921-myanmars-impact-on-ne-insurgency-articles.html (Accessed on August 19, 2017).
107. S P Sinha (2008), *Lost opportunities: 50 years of insurgency in the North-east and India's response*, Lancer Publication, New Delhi, p. 58.
108. Hlaing Kyaw Yin and Talor Robert H (2005), "Myanmar: beyond politics to societal imperatives," Institute of Southeast Asian Studies publication, Singapore, p. 89.

4
Role of China in Myanmar and its Impact on Indian Security

Introduction

China shares a huge land border (2,185 km) with Myanmar. This strengthens their relations as they call themselves pauk-phaw which means siblings in Myanmar language.[1] Due to China's pragmatic foreign policy, it is one of the major supplier and investor in Myanmar from the last two decades. Myanmar's significant geographic situation is perceived as a connecting bridge between China and the Indian Ocean which further allows China to have an approach in this region. Myanmar is believed to be the solution to the Malacca problem of China.[2] China's energy resources needs are mainly met through the Strait of Malacca in the IO. Under the One Belt One Road Initiative China is constructing ports and other facilities in Pakistan, Myanmar, Maldives and Sri Lanka to provide a platform for China to secure its shipment interests in the region.

The influence of China over Myanmar government has been in the limelight of international politics after the democratic shift in Myanmar. After the boycott of Western countries from the agricultural and industrial sectors, China has emerged as an essential foreign player in Myanmar. China's extensive presence in Myanmar and its influence over Myanmar bear two different aspects. It is a matter of the fact that no foreign player or an international group may influence all the top leaders of the regime at the same time. This holds for China and Myanmar as well. China's influence in Myanmar depends upon both the opinions within China itself and reluctance of Myanmar to trust China too much. Nevertheless, government-to-government cooperation between Myanmar and China is substantial, and China repeatedly blocked UN Security Council Resolutions against Myanmar.[3] China has been forming linkages with Myanmar on significant issues like the economy and national security. However, there are also some issues such as anti-Chinese riots in Myanmar and President Thein Sein's decision to block the China-backed Myitsone Dam and the Chinese links to various minorities.[4] The political and official visits from Europe and the US have shaken the position of China in Myanmar.

In the light of Myanmar-China security relations in the past few years, the relations have improved but with some limitations due to China's tough dealing with the government of Myanmar given the non-uniformity and centralisation of Chinese strategy. Myanmar's relationship with China has started responding on a similar track. In reality, it has become increasingly apparent that the differences in China's strategy towards Myanmar are seen between Beijing, the People's Liberation Army (PLA), the regional government in Yunnan, private business interests, and a multitude of other factions.[5] China's strategy appears to be formed and centrally driven. However, it is arguably inconsistent and in dissonance with the centrally directed policies. In the case of Myanmar due to geographical closeness to China, Chinese minority groups have substantial influence in Myanmar. This allows firm stand of business interests at local levels for developing Yunnan province which is not as developed as other regions in China. The influence of China on the leadership in Myanmar especially after the recent elections should not be exaggerated; regional leaders in Yunnan could have a greater impact in Myanmar than Beijing in many cases. Nevertheless, there is no doubt that China has increased its influence at all levels in Myanmar, often to such an extent that both Myanmar and other international actors are uncomfortable.[6]

At present, China and India are competing with each other for constructing bridges and roads, upgrading ports and oil extraction in Myanmar. The interests of both the nations lie in gaining access to

Myanmar's natural resources and making strategic corridors in Myanmar. However, India's investments are underneath as compared to China. While India invested over US$ 763.56 million in Myanmar by the end of August 2018 which accounts only .99 per cent of Myanmar's total FDI, China's investment has reached up to US$ 20.97 billion in Myanmar in for the same period which holds 26 per cent of total FDI of Myanmar.[7] Therefore, regarding investments, China has been able to surpass India in Myanmar. However, there have been some issues that have come up in China's infrastructural projects as primarily the Myitsone Dam has been stopped by Myanmar. This Work on the US$ 3.6 billion mega hydropower project began in 2009 but was suspended in September 2011 due to protests by residents over possible detrimental impacts of such a project on the local environ.[8]

On the contrary, India also marked its presence in various infrastructural projects in Myanmar that includes the India-Myanmar Friendship Road of 160-km long connecting Moreh with Kalemyo and Kalewa in Myanmar. India is also engaged in building India-Myanmar-Thailand trilateral highway and Kaladan Project. Unfortunately, India has not been able to complete any of its commitment on time, thereby raising concerns being a trustworthy partner to rely on in such cases. The growth-oriented relationships are built upon the basis of securing their economic and strategic interests in the region.

Geo-strategic Significance of Myanmar to China and China to Myanmar

Geographically, Myanmar shares its Northeastern part of the border with China. China has a long land border of 2,185 km in its Southwestern province which makes a corridor for China to connect itself to Bay of Bengal and the Indian Ocean. China's primary strategy in Myanmar is to adhere to a win-win principle of peaceful cooperation between sovereign countries to provide support for domestic reformist steps, placing emphasis on political stability in Myanmar, and to pursue core strategic and economic goals which envisage Myanmar as a strategic outlet for China to the Indian Ocean thus freeing it from the strategic passiveness of a one-ocean policy.[9] China's prominent interests in Myanmar can be interpreted in the briefs that follow.

First strategically, China has been viewing Myanmar as a buffer and security wall in the region. China is of the view that Myanmar's strategic position may be exploited by foreign aggression causing a security challenge to China. For instance, during the per-Independence phase, Japan and Britain used Myanmar as a theatre of aggression and posed a threat to China's Southwest. After having Westerns sanctions and embargoes. China used Myanmar's strategic channel to siege the outside forces to safeguard its interests. China was also using Myanmar as a transport corridor during World War II to block the Japanese in Southwest China. Over the period, Japan and US intentionally exploited Myanmar as a bait between India and China to trigger the scuffle for their gains. The United States also stepped up its efforts to build a "C-shaped ring of encirclement" against China.[10] Therefore, China intends to maintain good and sustainable bilateral relations with Myanmar which can ensure stability and security in China's Southwest frontier as well as a smooth passage to the Indian Ocean critical for the successful implementation of the BCIM Economic Corridor initiative and its two-ocean strategy.[11] China through its economic and military expansion is establishing a position that strengthens it both in India and Southeast Asia, and this even improves its access to the Indian Ocean channel.[12] Accordingly, China is interested in utilising Myanmar as a future springboard to the Indian Ocean.[13] As such, China's predominant security concern is to keep Myanmar from becoming part of the "encirclement of China" policy of the US.[14]

Second politically, China has always been playing in favour of Myanmar at the international level. Myanmar and China have adopted different politico-social development patterns from Western world societies. The Western world has been criticising Myanmar and China on democracy, freedom and human rights among other issues, which may bring both countries together to support each other. They are connected by many ethnic minorities who live across the Myanmar-China border. Thus, peace, stability and harmony have become more significant on borders for both countries. This region has also become prone to cross-border crimes. As an epicentre for drug production and trafficking, this has a serious impact on both social stability and economic development of China's Southwest region.[15] Therefore, both central governments and local bodies need to cooperate effectively to counter this phenomenon.

Third, economically, China sees Myanmar as a relevant field for the development of its Southwest region. This safeguards its interests regarding energy security and vital source for natural resources. China requires a safe and stable environment in its Southwest for prosperity in the region. Moreover, Myanmar's Northeast region is in a poor and backward state which is wrecked with ethnic disputes making it unfavourable for China's economic development. As some political analysts point out, "China wants what Myanmar has – Indian Ocean access and abundant natural resources to support its rise."[16] China's 80 per cent oil imports come through the Malacca Strait, and its maritime energy deliveries from the Persian Gulf to SCS are not sufficient and further have their security applications in the sea. To address these concerns, China has to approach the Indian Ocean to make a direct passage from its Southwest frontier through Myanmar. Consequently, in June 2013, the China-Myanmar oil and gas pipeline was completed with gas starting to flow to China in October 2013.[17] Furthermore, large market size and precious natural resources produce a boost for economic growth to the Chinese and it provides an essential field for industrial transfer and Chinese exports as well.

Therefore, China efficiently occupied the vacuum which was built by Western sanctions and provided a platform to Myanmar for its economic and trade cooperation needs. China largely focused on infrastructure development concerning businesses and economic cooperation with Myanmar. For instance, the Myitsone dam and Letpadaung copper mines are the infrastructure projects constructed and financed by Chinese enterprises and government.

China's foreign policy and strategic considerations are by and large regarded on the geographic position of Myanmar. As already stated, Myanmar is strategically an essential spot for China to approach both the

Indian Ocean and the Pacific Ocean under its two-ocean strategy. China has an objective to upgrade its naval into a 'Blue Water Navy' by 2030 to safeguard its primary interests in the Indian Ocean Region. This region has vital importance for China as it connects to the Indian Ocean through the Coco Islands of Myanmar. Due to this access, the PLAN would be able to reach the Bay of Bengal by shortening 3,000 km distance and also reducing the five to six days voyage by not crossing the Strait of Malacca. China has set a possible target in its strategic ambition to transform this region into a regional trade zone with Laos, Thailand, Myanmar and Yunnan. Besides, the alleged Chinese station at the Zadetkyi Island on Myanmar's southern end showed China's intuitions about its subsequent maritime aspirations in the Indian Ocean.

Myanmar is perceived to be a game changer in energy prospects in the sphere. It is a comparatively unexplored natural resources-rich country which has 50 million barrels proven reserves of Crude oil and 283 billion cubic meters proven reserves of Natural Gas accounting for 0.1 per cent of the total world gas reserves.[18] Although it does not contribute enough for regional energy security; Myanmar's gas reserves have utmost significance. Myanmar is also well aware of its strategic location between China and India. Both desire to be superpowers in Asia continent. Also, China's thirst for natural wealth in Myanmar has made these resources monetary worth. Thus, Myanmar attracted greater income sources. Myanmar sees China as a reliable partner who will implicitly support Myanmar trade and government which is again crucial for political and economic sustainability.

Further, Myanmar has always been manipulating China. Myanmar takes a number of services from China in terms of financial assistance to infrastructure construction in the country. China and Myanmar share an asymmetrical relationship, and their capability and potentials are unmatchable. Myanmar still has the advantage in this relationship. Myanmar has been utilising China's political influence in the international domain, by and large, when interacting with international and regional entities especially concerning resources exploitation. Myanmar played over its critical geographic situation and natural resources with India,

Japan, US, China and ASEAN members. The regional actors surrounding Myanmar are aligning with the current government of Myanmar. Myanmar knows the importance of Realpolitik and understands that it is more influential than other political credences. Hence, this situation revolves around the simple term of economic supply and demand. As surrounding countries of Myanmar are developing countries, who need access to Myanmar's natural resources, especially energy quest countries. On the other side, Myanmar manipulates its strategic advantage to achieve political and economic interests. Myanmar has been utilising this supply and demand formula with powerful countries such as India and China. Myanmar has been successful so far to manage Southeast Asian and South Asian nations to secure its interests in the region.

Historical Relations between China and Myanmar

The visit of the Pyu delegation in 802 AD to Changan, the capital of the Tang dynasty was regarded as the first confirmed diplomatic contact with China by Myanmar historians.[19] There were some other official connections after that event. That developed harmonious relation by the independent kings of two independent states. China came under the Yuan Dynasty of the Mongols from 1271 to 1368; relations turned sour between them. Bagan was invaded in 1287 by China ruled by the Mongols that fragmented Bagan and ruled till 1303. They also attacked in the 14th century, but the matter was amicably resolved. Enmity between the Ming emperor and the Manchus increased in the late 17th century and got distributed into the territory of Myanmar. The ultimate conflict occurred between 1765 and 1769. During this period forces of the Konbaung dynasty repulsed four Chinese incursions resulting in a treaty of peace and friendship that was signed in December 1769.[20] Chinese rulers treated Myanmar kingdom equally using regular visits and exchange of letters till 1874 when Britishers made Myanmar a colony. Myanmar subsequently had intermittent tributary relations with Chinese empires in the long sweep of history, but this situation could not hold under the impact of Western imperialism.[21] It was 1885 that last king of Myanmar had fallen. In China, the last dynasty of the

Qing came to an end in 1911. The trade of Myanmar with China was set up in the 18th century and also grew up during the British rule whereas small-scale inter-border trade with Yunnan had started several Centuries back.

China-Myanmar Relations since Independence

The People's Republic of China came into being in 1949 whereas Myanmar became free from British rule in 1948. As a matter of co-incidence, Myanmar and China suffered from the attack by Japanese forces during the expansionist policies of Japan. From the Myanmar perspective, it seems that China has always regarded Myanmar as essential to its security and the latter stands high in the degree of importance China attaches to its peripheral areas.[22] Both countries slowly and steadily started developing by lateral relations and came close to each other. Zhou Enlai of China visited Myanmar in June 1954, and thereafter U Nu of Myanmar paid a visit to China in November 1954. Despite taking steps to develop a closer relationship with each other, there have been many fluctuations since 1950. In the meantime, the instance of Panchsheel agreement was signed by China, India and Myanmar to maintain the five Principles of Peaceful Co-existence in 1954.[23] These five principles are as under:

- Mutual respect for territorial integrity and sovereignty
- Non-aggression
- Non-interference in each other's internal affairs
- Equality and mutual benefits
- Peaceful co-existence and peaceful settlement of disputes.

These principles, later on, became the foundation of NAM for maintaining international relations.

In the 1960s, there were anti-China protests and agitations in Myanmar. It was a challenging phase for their relations, thousands of people died, and there was the destruction of houses, shops and looting of markets. There was heavy fighting between the army and Communist party of Myanmar. The diplomatic relations between China and Myanmar remained suspended from 1967 to 1970. China is a powerful country, and the Myanmar government has been cultivating fear and apprehensions from China. China has the attitude of snubbing small countries in its neighbourhood. In this background, the aggressive, expansionist, revolutionary rhetoric emanating from the rulers of the new People's Republic of China made the leaders of the newly independent Myanmar particularly wary of China. Prime Minister U Nu sounded India more than once about a possible defence pact, but Nehru not only turned down such suggestions but also actively assisted in bringing Myanmar and China closer to each other.[24]

Bertil Lintner, the Thailand based strategic analyst, spent a lifetime studying Myanmar asserts, "... regardless of the political nature of the government in power (in Myanmar) China has always considered Myanmar to be a vassal state."[25]

Thus, China's attitude reflected in its relations with Myanmar and Myanmar had to cope up with China unwillingly. The Communist Party of Burma (CPB) was the central element of China's Myanmar policy until the late seventies irrespective of whether the official relationship between the governments of the two countries was a mixture of bad, good or indifferent.[26] In a smart move, China continued its supply of economic aid and military power to Myanmar so that China may influence Myanmar. The puppet master calibrated the extent and levels of violent revolts depending upon its agenda at any given point of time. China was involved in Myanmar through the CPB. The CPB, however, was only a communist party in name and was projecting Chinese interests.[27]

There was a spate of pro-democracy demonstrations in Myanmar in 1988, but these were dealt with heavy hands with assistance from China. They paved the way for more scope of China's role. China facilitated the disbandment of the Myanmar Communist Party in 1989. China later also facilitated ceasefire agreements between the government and most ethnic groups. Eventually, the context and contours of the China-Myanmar relationship changed dramatically as China emerged Myanmar's pre-eminent partner. The development of their multi-pronged relations can be explained based on the following instances:

- Myanmar's economy is primarily integrated with China; the Northern Myanmar's economy especially connected more with Yunnan than with rest of the country.
- Official Myanmar statistics indicate that China became the leading investor in Myanmar, with a total investment of US$ 18.53 billion as of January 2017 since 1988.[28] A total of 69 Multinational Corporations (MNCs) of China were identified by Earth Rights International (ERI), which were engaged in a minimum of 90 projects in Myanmar from China. The projects undertaken by companies of China has been going up since then in all sectors. The performance of all the investing companies in China has been found satisfactory. These were involved in the infrastructure and hydropower projects and dominating in the oil and gas exploration. Another big task which is being handled by China is related to the development of seaports at Hanggyi, Mergui and Zadetyeki in the south, and the excellent deep water at Kyaukphu from where Myanmar is going to supply gas to Yunnan by the source of pipelines. It will also be used to get oil from the Persian Gulf region. There is big storage of oil at Yunnan. Large multi-purpose SEZs have also been set up by China there. China is also building rail and road links between Myanmar and Yunnan. Myanmar is dependent on China for developing economic, transport infrastructure, connectivity to the Bay of Bengal and the Indian Ocean.
- Since 1988, China has been Myanmar's pre-eminent international patron providing it with diplomatic protection from international punitive actions, inter alia, by vetoing a US-sponsored resolution in the United Nations Security Council in 2007.[29]
- It is also by far the main weapons supplier to Myanmar and has supplied almost US$ 2.5 billion worth of arms since 1988 in a continuing strong defence relationship. This relationship has overseen the expansion of the Tatmadaw, the armed forces, from about 150,000 in 1988 to over 516,000 in 2018.[30]
- It has been estimated that people of Chinese origin account for more than 2 million, all are settled in Mandalay having become a virtual city of China where even small businesses are flourishing by Chinese.

China has by and large acquired capabilities in Myanmar for having a significant role in internal affairs which brings strategic consequences especially in the discourse of overall factors affecting security and national interests of India. There is a threat to India of trapping itself into the web of Chinese strategic plans. Therefore, it has become critical for India to forbid Myanmar of being an instrument in China's strategic policies. These overarching imperatives have to be considered by Indian policy makers towards Myanmar.

The US imposed sanctions including a prohibition on Myanmar-made commodities in July 2003. China came to the rescue of Myanmar and compensated it with trade and economic cooperation. EXIM Bank of China gave a loan of US$ 200 million at preferential interest rates to Myanmar in August 2003. The China International Trust and Investment Corporation (CITIC) signed an agreement to supply generators and other goods and low-priced machinery to Myanmar. Apart from this, it also supplied equipment and services, low-interest rate loans for a more extended period and export credits by local monetary institutions to make Myanmar an active player in the field. It is quite apparent that Yunnan region of China wishes to have a direct entry route via Myanmar to Bay of Bengal seaports which enable China to export its products to Europe, the Middle East and South Asia. It increased the export of China manifold at the cost of Myanmar's exploitation. China desires to avail Myanmar as an alternate to avoid the Malacca Strait route if a conflicting situation arises in the South China Sea. Thus, China is considered in a positive way, especially when it comes to the stability of Myanmar-China relations.

China's economic cooperation with Myanmar for developing roadway-railway links and other projects started with Chinese investments such as power generation from hydro sources. There is quite a shortage of electricity in Myanmar since the 1990s. It has constructed many hydro power plants and thermal power stations with the assistance of Chinese companies from 1996 to 2005 which measures one-third of the whole domestic capacity. As such, China is playing a measurable role in the generation of hydroelectricity in Myanmar. The Paunglaung hydro power project is an apt example of financial, managerial and technical ability utilised by Chinese companies who are engaged in power generation. In March 2005, this project was completed by the Yunnan Machinery Import and Export Corporation (YMIEC). It was the largest dam project of Myanmar and was estimated at the cost of US$ 160 million. The Chinese EXIM bank funded this project.

There were 11 major hydro power projects under construction in 2006 to increase Myanmar's total generating capacity of 1,734 MW. All these projects were given to Chinese companies for completion. There was Yeywa hydropower plant which was the largest among all with a capacity of 790 MW, and the total cost was US$ 700 million.

China is the largest trading partner as well as one of the most important sources of investment for Myanmar. China's Ministry of Commerce Official data shows that as of July in 2019, China's cumulative investment in Myanmar accounted for over 25 per cent of Myanmar's total foreign investment. There are complexity and multiplicity in the relation between China and Myanmar. China has historical relations with Myanmar which developed speedily after 1988. In 1988, State Law and Order Restoration Council (SLORC 1988-97) was formed and renamed as State Peace and Development Council (SPDC 1997-2011). There was a phase when Myanmar was aloof and could not share anything with the rest of the world. There was a military dictatorship in Myanmar from 1988 to 2011 which could not allow any political party to raise its voice and there were no civil liberties. Furthermore, the military Junta was mainly accused of human rights violations which was condemned by several countries. It also imposed economic sanctions on the state especially the United States.

China focused on economic development cooperation with Myanmar, especially Thilawa Port, Yangon, in the construction sector. China also supported construction in textile mills, pulp and paper mills, rice mills, plywood plants, agriculture equipment factories and other manufacturing factories through economic cooperation projects. Myanmar fulfils China's demand for energy in a significant way. With the rise of China's economy, its demand for energy has widely increased. The gas and oil reserves of Myanmar have attracted the attention of China significantly. However, the Chinese presence in the gas and oil fields of Myanmar have been observed. China's National Offshore Oil Corporation (CNOOC) signed six agreements on output allocation with the Myanmar Oil and Gas Enterprise (MOGE) of the Ministry of Energy from October 2004 to January 2005. The China Petroleum and Chemical Corporation and its subsidiary Dian Qiangui Petroleum Exploration also operate on the inland fields. The four old oil fields in central Myanmar are also being upgraded by China National Petroleum Corporation (CNPC) whom contracts have been awarded. The companies have invested US$ 163 million which is rather small as compared to the US$ 2,635 million total of foreign investment in Myanmar's oil and gas sector.[31] In 2017, Chinese companies vigorous investments highlighted in Myanmar. Out of 26 Chinese foreign investments, 16 projects were made either in 2004 and 2005, occupying nearly 70 per cent in terms of investment value, mostly in the mining and energy sector.[32]

In 2007, contracts on products sharing basis were finalised by CNPC with MOGE for crude oil and natural exploration projects off the Rakhine coast. Petro China attained sole purchasing rights at an estimated cost of 6 trillion cubic feet of natural gas in the Shwe offshore field. China understands the importance of energy sources of Myanmar not only as an accessible alternative to gas and oil supplies from the Middle East, but it also addresses the country's Malacca dilemma. The Middle East facilitate China's 58 per cent of oil requirements through the Malacca Strait. Thus, the Malacca Strait has been an important shipping passage for oil imports from the Middle East to China. However, China's energy security concerns are facing two major threats due to its over-reliance on the strait. The first threat is the penetration of strong nations in the Strait of Malacca region to control the navigations, and the other threat is concerned with the maritime terrorism and piracy. China is also involved in constructing gas and oil pipelines overland from the Kyaukphyu port in Rakhine to Kunming in Yunnan Province to bypass the Malacca Strait.

In 2010, Chinese Premier Wen Jiabao visited Myanmar to commemorate the 60th anniversary of China-Myanmar relations.

During his visit, Wen also witnessed the signing of 15 MoUs and agreements for cooperation in economic development and technology sectors, rail transportation, trade, hydropower, energy and mining.[33] The year 2010 beholds several high-level visits between China and Myanmar for increasing multi-dimensional cooperation. Both the sides decided to enhance mutual relations and developed high-level cooperation. However, Myanmar is also conscious about its sovereignty and is endeavouring to minimise its over-dependence on China especially reforming its foreign relations with ASEAN, India and Russia.

The Impacts of Political Reforms on Myanmar and the Reactions of Other Powers

In 2011, a period of reforms and political changes started in Myanmar. These political reforms brought positive changes in external as well as internal affairs. President U Thein Sein started several reform procedures, held a meeting with Aung San Suu Kyi, providing amnesty to political prisoners, relaxed censorship of press and internet and brought new labour laws in the country which allow labour unions and protests. The general elections were held in 2012 in which NLD secured a big victory; it was an important event in the political reform process of Myanmar. Moreover, the new government achieved a ceasefire agreement with the Karen National Union that ended the world's longest-running civil conflicts.[34] These reforms have proved useful that ASEAN members accepted the bid of Myanmar for ASEAN Chair for 2014. Moreover, relations between Myanmar and the US became warm as after a long period the Secretary of State Hillary Clinton paid a visit to Myanmar in December 2011. The US lifted the sanctions and restrictions on IMF and World Bank for Myanmar. Both nations' relations were also restored at the ambassadorial level. Furthermore, the EU allowed top Myanmar officials to travel in any of EU country. Similarly, the Australian and Japanese government also lifted travel restrictions and started economic exchanges in terms of investments, aid and trade.

The Impact of reforms on China-Myanmar Relations

There was indeed an impact of political reforms on the strategic, political and economic relations of Myanmar and China. Leaders in Myanmar knew that China was dominating in Myanmar in the economic and political domain. Thus, adopting political reforms in Myanmar was one of the factors that reduced over-dependence on China.

When president U Thein Sein suspended the Myitsone Dam project of China, it was not only a shock, but this move alerted China to take Myanmar's foreign policy shift. Thein Sein government wanted to follow the public view and tried to pacify the demands of the Western countries for democratic reforms in the country. There was widespread resentment against Chinese projects inclusive of CNPC oil and gas pipeline projects and NORIKO copper mine project. Moreover, the US, EU, Korean and Japanese companies arrived in the field to challenge Chinese companies because it was considered one of the least underdeveloped market of Southeast Asia. In July 2011, there was an unfortunate collision of high-speed trains which forced Myanmar to turn to a more technologically advanced nation for such projects. China lost the high-speed railway contract to Japanese companies from Yangoon to Nay Pyi Taw.

China's strategic interest in Myanmar comprised Nay Pyi Taw's support for China at the ASEAN plus three meetings and the Greater Mekong Sub-regional economic cooperation, as well as for its national bridgehead strategy that would turn Myanmar into China's outlet into the Indian Ocean with a potential for naval cooperation.[35] Although China has earned maximum throttle in Myanmar especially due to the Western sanctions and international isolation in the past. It is also true that Myanmar is trying to have viable alternatives to scale China. Today, China is also aware of the fact that it cannot impose its policy on other countries to add an unconditional associate to enhance its dominance in the region. Myanmar's recent engagements with the US have challenged the strategic interests of China and its regional influence of China. In early 2009, Southeast Asian analysts in China reminded that the normalisation of US-Myanmar relations could threaten China's security, damage the existing China-Myanmar cooperation and indirectly hurt the security of the Chinese border and energy transportation route.[36] Many scholars in China considered it as a Zero-sum game and believe that it is the result of the US manipulation to isolate China and Myanmar in the international field. Meanwhile, possible military cooperation between the United States and Myanmar alerted China more than anything else. Additionally, both the invitation of Myanmar to observe the US-led Cobra Gold joint military exercise and the potential intelligence sharing between the CIA and Myanmar are seen to be serious challenges to China's national security.[37] The position of Myanmar stands changed now to a great extent, and Myanmar is not so much dependent on China as before. There was a time when Myanmar supported China at the forum of ASEAN, but Myanmar has now set itself free from China's liability. Myanmar is active in playing its cards for its own identity in ASEAN and the international platform. According to President Thein Sein's advisor, Myanmar determines its position on the South China Sea by its national interest and solidarity with ASEAN as the regional organisation, implying that Myanmar has no intention to back up China's position.[38] In 2000, the foreign minister of China and Myanmar signed a mutual statement to maintain bilateral cooperation in future. The agreement contained a future course of relations between both the countries by five principles of Panchsheel and strengthened the relations to the extent of broader regional stability and development. Both countries have positive responses from each other. However, serious endeavours are required to make it a reality. Today China needs energy because it has to meet its industrial requirements and for this China is little dependent on Myanmar for its oil and gas supplies. Therefore, China wants to have cordial relations with Myanmar and China does not want that Myanmar has good relations with its counter rivals such as the US and India.

China's Policy with NLD Government

China was uncertain whether Myanmar would bow under the US pressure or thwart the pressure. China intends to continue having harmonious relations with ASEAN members and Myanmar. China's growing engagements in the economic field would increase its stake in Myanmar. China is also willing to maintain customary and cultural relations with Myanmar in the long run. There is internal and external pressure on the Myanmar government to have good relations with China because the US has a hard-line policy which is not suitable to Myanmar. Despite this, Myanmar is also under pressure from member countries of ASEAN such as the Philippines and Thailand. It has been observed that close engagements with China will certainly be beneficial for all ASEAN members from the economic, political and military angle, especially during isolation period when sanctions were imposed by the Western countries. China is the only country on which Myanmar can rely on in the worst situation of sanctions and isolation from the Western world.

The general elections were held in Myanmar on November 8, 2015, which brought large-scale changes in the political set up of Myanmar. It was a fresh beginning for NLD which won the elections in Myanmar. China has also drafted its policy of relations with Myanmar under the new government which took over in March 2016. Aung San Suu Kyi is facing many problems borrowed from the previous government which are yet to be settled with China. Myanmar wants to develop relations with all the neighbouring countries and also to reduce dependence over China. The change of government in Myanmar does not amend China's strategic pursuits to have its connectivity and infrastructure projects which would go through the country to the Bay of Bengal. China needs a stable and tranquil border and does not want the US influence especially with the new government of Myanmar by providing financial and military assistance. China is also aware of the fact that Myanmar has merged into a democracy and their government already suspended the China's Myitsone dam. China is all set to offer the new government fresh aid projects, financial capital and assist the peace making pacts with the ethnic groups, which is Myanmar's priority objective too. However, China is actively engaged with Myanmar to address its concerns especially the suspended Myitsone dam project, clarity on the construction of the Kyaukphyu special economic zone, a series of agreement on OBOR projects. China is further interested in the peace negotiations with the ethnic groups especially with those along the China-Myanmar border. Aung San Suu Kyi vowed to lead the peace process; many argue that her unique background and popular strength might bring more confidence to the ethnic minorities in the process and therefore break the impasse.[39]

On the other hand, China understands efficiently that her interests would be best served if there would be peace and integrity in Myanmar. A disturbed Myanmar will also cause problems for China because both share common borders in northern Myanmar, and conflict in this area would raise an immediate obstacle in strategic and economic programmes of China. It is hoped that Suu Kyi will be able to bring round the conflicting ethnic groups on the table for peace talks and China will not sabotage the process. China can play a major role in Myanmar to establish peace. China desires to demand Myanmar's cooperation with its projects, and at the same time, China wants that Myanmar should respect their national interests when it is dealing with the Western world, especially the US. China assured Myanmar of its full cooperation for its economic development. Whenever Aung San Suu Kyi wants to have smooth relations with the West, there is always a strong reaction from China. This creates a sense of doubt and suspicion in the matter of her relations with China and the Western countries at the same time. The situation is probably to continue till things get settled in due course of time. The NLD government has a mindset of this perception. Aung San Suu Kyi and NLD should not expect that China will abandon its relationship with other political forces in Myanmar, including the USDP, the military and the cronies.[40] No country is certain about its political future, and China is making sense by having good connections with all potential players.

Ethnic Conflicts between China-Myanmar

There are 135 ethnic groups living in Myanmar, some on the shared border with China. Several ethnic groups have signed agreements with the governments of both the countries and are enjoying some degree of semi-autonomy in their regions and also in the border area between China and Myanmar. Although, the ceasefire agreements are no guarantee of the finale of the long civil war. Although the ethnic groups are under a ceasefire agreement with the government, they remain subjugated and suppressed under the draconian rule and have struggled for their fundamental rights.[41] These ethnic groups are struggling for the equal rights which have encountered a series of hindrances with the Myanmar government and especially to China and its security of border region. China made a substantial economic investment in the border areas of Myanmar where the situation remains tense as the ethnic groups are engaged in conflicts with the government over the demands for a federal union and reconciliation process. The Myitsone dam and other oil and gas pipelines to Kunming, Yunnan, run through these disturbed ethnic areas which are under control of this ethnic insurgence. These situations are a matter of serious concern as huge investments are involved from both sides.

China-Myanmar Equation: A Strategic Framework

The People's Republic of China was recognised in 1949 by Myanmar as a first-known communist country. This gesture paved the way for strong bilateral relations between the two countries. Myanmar leadership opted for a more neutral foreign policy in the Asian region with a little tilt towards China. Since the military junta took over Myanmar, it has assumed a greater significance in the Asia-Pacific strategic environment.[42] This was strengthened by the higher amount of Chinese arms selling to the junta. Since 1988, the capability of the Tatmadaw, the Myanmar armed forces, has been vastly enhanced with the assistance of China's PLA (People's Liberation Army).[43] According to the SIPRI report, from 2011 to 2018, China's maximum defence exports were to the nations surrounding India. Its biggest client was Pakistan, which received 35 per cent (US$ 2,988 million) of China's arms exports followed by Bangladesh at 20 per cent (US$ 1,650 million) and Myanmar came third with 16 per cent (US$ 1,338 million).[44] Therefore, the above figures show the dependence on Chinese military equipment in the region.

China is the fastest growing economy of the world with an approximate GDP of US$ 14.14 trillion in the year (2019).[45] China is interested in energy sources of Myanmar. This tempted China to enter into strategic cooperation with the countries who are rich in terms of natural resources, including its immediate neighbour Myanmar. Subsequently, China has been proving itself as the reliable partner of Myanmar in this century. China's strategic model in respect to Myanmar attaches on its realistic external policy and Myanmar's geographical location. It has been discussed in the following major segments: political and security consideration, energy resources, and economic considerations.

Political and Security Considerations

Myanmar geographically is in the Southwestern region of China. It is beneficial for China to reach the Indian Ocean through Myanmar-controlled islands which are just 30 km away from islands controlled by India. China hopes of world-class Blue Water Navy status by 2050. For China, Myanmar is crucial for getting multi-directional access to both the Indian Ocean and the Pacific Ocean and this route through the Strait of Malacca to reach the Bay of Bengal reduces the voyage considerably by five to six days.[46] China would be able to shorten the distance by 3000 km. A deep water port of Kyaukpyu on Ramree islands in the Bay of Bengal is proposed to be built jointly by China and Myanmar. The Nicobar Islands are 18 km away from the Great Coco Island where Myanmar is building an 85-metre jetty with the help of China. China has already set up a modern observer and intelligence system on the Coco Island. Similarly, it has observance facilities to monitor Indian forces' movements including missile testing in the Ocean around Alexandra Channel. All these facilities provided by Myanmar to China are against the security interests of India. Thus, China's strategic advantages in strengthening relations with Myanmar have long-term security implications.

China and Myanmar are getting closer to each other in the field of defence cooperation after 1988. A military delegation from Myanmar visited China in 1989 to buy arms worth US$ 1.4 billion. Besides the supply of arms (inclusive of jet fighters, armoured vehicles, and naval vessels) China also agreed to train Myanmar's air force and army personnel; the motivation for the purchase was to upgrade Myanmar's military capability to suppress minority separatist insurgencies.[47] China also offered favourable terms for Myanmar's arms purchases by offering free loans and granting credit to the military regime, as well as economic aid and investments for the construction of Myanmar's necessary infrastructure, such as dams, bridges, roads, ports as well as for industrial projects.[48] There is also a road on the side of Irrawaddy River to connect Yunnan province with the Bay of Bengal. China's purpose of having a strong strategic alliance and economic collaboration with Myanmar could be observed from the regular high-level meetings from both sides to upgrade multi-pronged cooperation, and many agreements have been signed in the areas of economic, environment, forestry, agriculture, education, culture, science and for combating illicit drugs.

Energy Resources

Fast-paced industrial development of China is creating a demand for more and more energy, and China is in search of the abundant sources where it can get the required energy to meet its domestic demands. Myanmar has an abundance of oil and gas reserves in its soil and China pays special attention to Myanmar for getting these benefits. China is also helping Myanmar to produce electricity from its hydro sources, like reserves by constructing dams and other projects. China's National Offshore Oil Corporation (CNOOC) has entered into six agreements with the Myanmar Oil and Gas Enterprise (MOGE) to explore oil and natural gas in Myanmar. The China Petroleum and Chemical Corporation (CPEC) and its subsidiary Dian Qiangui Petroleum Exploration also operate on the inland fields.[49] Moreover, the China National Petroleum Corporation (CNPC) and its subsidiary Chinnery Assets are operating in the fields of central Myanmar to upgrade the four old oilfields. The investment of these companies cost US$ 163 million, rather little as compared to the US$ 2,635 million total foreign investment in Myanmar's oil and gas sector.[50] However, it is only in the recent years that Chinese companies have vigorously invested in Myanmar. Out of 26 Chinese foreign investments, 16 projects were done in FY 2016-2017, which accounts a colossal portion of investment value. Most of those were invested in the energy and mining sector.[51]

Figure 4.1: South and Southeast Asian Countries Investments in Myanmar

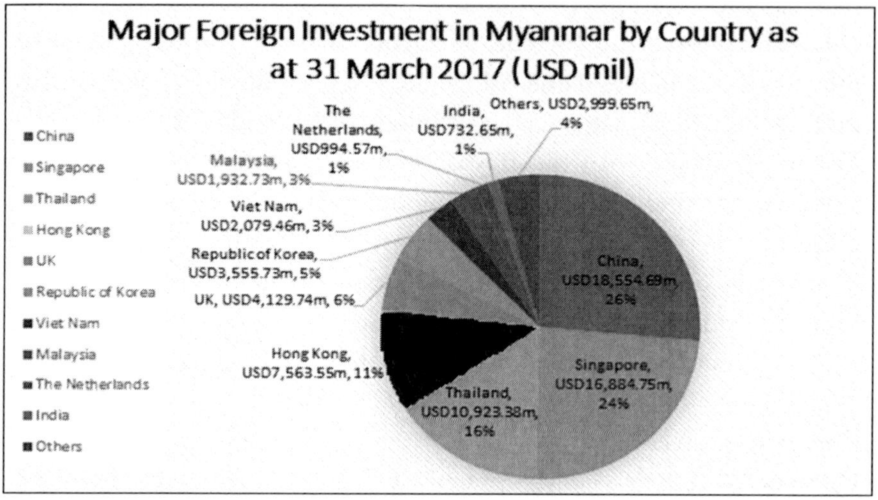

Source: Malaysia External Trade Development Corporation

Petro China is also considering another big project of laying a gas pipeline from A-1 block of Shwe gas field near to the coast of Rakhine state to Yunnan province. The Shwe field is containing 200 billion cubic meter of gas. Petro China signed a Memorandum of Understanding with the Myanmar Oil and Gas Enterprise (MOGE) to buy gas from the block for 30 years starting from 2009.[52] The sale of gas by exporting to India is also a huge source of foreign exchange earning for Myanmar. Moreover, Myanmar also gets a strategic advantage by exporting oil and gas to the neighbouring countries. Although there are several importers of gas from Myanmar India managed to enter in the contract to buy gas from block A-1 with great efforts but on very favourable conditions of taking payment. India has undertaken the guarantee to make the payment every year to Myanmar even if it does not access the gas field due to any reason. It also appears that in the tug-of-war competition between Indian and China, Myanmar has emerged a winner.

Economic Considerations

China and Myanmar had historical and economic relations since Bagan dynasty in the 11th century. There have been people-to-people interaction among upper Myanmar, Shan and Kachin state of Myanmar and the border region of Yunnan province. Yunnan province of China with a population of 44 million was once a Southwest Silk Road trade route between the two countries connecting Myanmar with Southwest Asia. It has now emerged as a potential target for China's long-term strategic ambition, transforming the whole region as part of a golden 'Quadrangle' trade zone involving Yunnan, Myanmar, Thailand and Laos.[53] China and ASEAN have declared the Free Trade Area Agreement for Yunnan province which is open to the whole of Southeast Asian region. Many of the corporations of China have invested mostly in the industry and energy development of Myanmar. China increased its economic cooperation with Myanmar during the period of economic sanctions by the western world especially the US.

Several infrastructure projects are financially supported and constructed by the Chinese public and private sectors with preference to power generation. There is also a huge shortage of electricity in Myanmar since 1990. China has entered into many contracts for power generation from thermal and hydropower stations in Myanmar from 1996 to 2005, and Chinese companies have been able to produce electricity, accounting for one-third of the entire national capacity. The Paunglaung hydropower project is the best power project from technical, financial and managerial aspects run by the Chinese companies. It was completed in March 2005 by Yunnan Machinery Import and Export Corporation (YMIEC). It has installed the capacity of 280 MW of power generation. The previous biggest power plant was the Baluchaung (168 MW) constructed by the Japanese firms. The Paunglaung dam project is one of the largest hydropower plant supporting Southeast Asia. China financed this project with a cost of US$ 160 million from EXIM bank of China. Out of the under-construction hydro power plants, the largest is Yeywa plant which has a generation capacity of 790 MW and is being built by EXIM Bank of China at the cost of US$ 700 million. Apart from the above, the China International Trust and Investment Corporation (CITIC) also got the contract to supply generators and all the related equipment for the project to Myanmar. In addition to low-priced machinery, equipment and services, long-term and low-interest loans and export credits offered by public financial institutions made it possible for Chinese enterprises to become major players in this field.[54] There is a direct route from Yunnan province to South Asia through seaports of Myanmar which further goes to the Middle East and Europe. This is going to reduce the transport costs and time for China greatly and can also skip the Malacca Strait in the case of a clash in the South China Sea. It would certainly cater to the aim of China's maritime silk route policy.

China's Investment in Myanmar

There are some major sectors of the economy of Myanmar in which China has made investments through public and private players, like the hydropower, mining, oil and gas sectors. As per Myanmar embassy statistics, 63 per cent of China's investments in Myanmar were in power sector, while investment in oil and gas and mining sectors occupied 36 per cent. The total of the three make up 99 per cent of all Chinese investments in Myanmar, 1 per cent investment was in infrastructure and construction including transportation like roads, railways and ports facilities.[55]

Figure 4.2: Sector-wise Chinese Investments in Myanmar

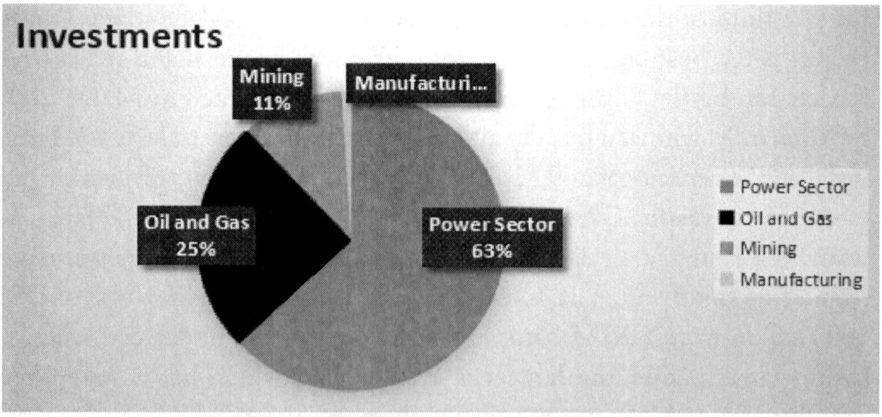

These sectors are important sectors of Myanmar for boosting the economy investments in these sectors are preferable. No doubt China has also invested in the agriculture sector but minimally. There is opium substitution on the China-Myanmar border in the Shan state and

Kachin state where the main focus on rubber, sugarcane, fruit plantation and horticulture are done by private companies of Yunnan province. Government is also providing training in agriculture plantation projects at the national level and state level. China has not been invested in the tourism sector of Myanmar.

According to Myanmar's new Foreign Investment Law, an investment may be carried out in either of the following two ways:

- As a 100 per cent foreign-owned entity
- By way of a joint venture with a Myanmar citizen or the Myanmar Government.

China made investments in Myanmar in both. There are some joint ventures with the share of Myanmar in power, oil and gas, mining and manufacturing companies. Some private companies of China have invested solely or jointly with the collaboration of local companies of Myanmar.

Map 4.1: Chinese Investments in the Major Cities of Myanmar

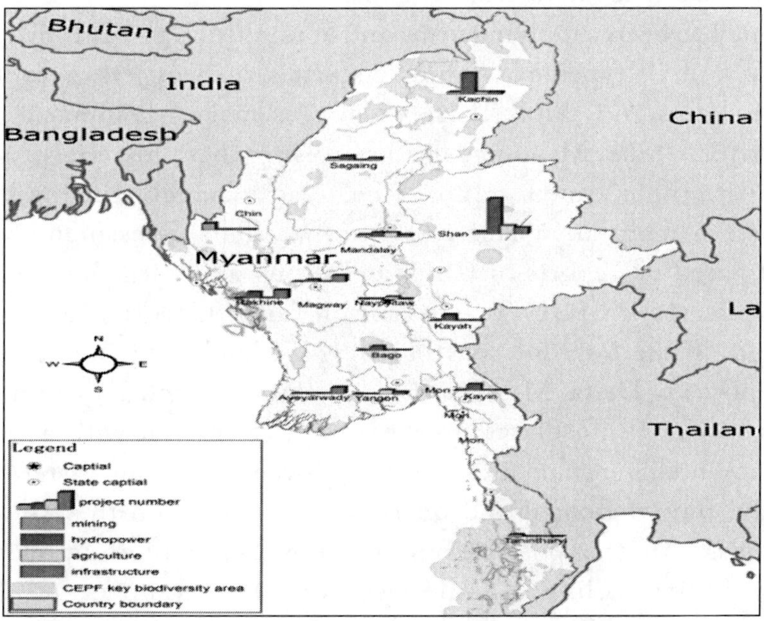

Source: Global Environmental Initiatives

Table 4.1: Top Trading Partners of Myanmar

(figures in US$ million)

	Country	2016-2017			2017-2018		
		Export	Import	Trade	Export	Import	Trade
1.	China	5,055.487	5,749.286	10,804.773	725.588	4,290.105	5,015.693
2.	Thailand	2,202.234	2,085.938	4,288.172	2,412.666	1,033.975	3,446.642
3.	Singapore	472.764	2,494.315	2,967.079	753.495	3,084.631	3,838.126
4.	India	1,107.89	1,067.25	2,178.44	966.19	639.64	1,605.84

Source: Ministry of Commerce, Myanmar

According to the figures from a government agency of Myanmar, for the financial year 2017-18 Myanmar's trade with China was worth US$ 5.015 billion; with Thailand US$ 3.446 billion; with Singapore US$ 3.838 billion; and, with India in spite of a long border and relatively good relations only US$ 1.377 billion, which is somewhat less comparatively.[56]

China's Defence Interests in Myanmar

China has been supplying arms and ammunition to Myanmar since 1954 and all types of warfare materials such as jets, aeroplanes, boats, guns and ships. These exchanges make Myanmar a client state for China. Myanmar has been using these materials to fight against ethnic armed groups, rebels and insurgents in the border states to maintain peace in Myanmar. This assessment was in part based on reports of China delivering and allegedly operating equipment for SIGINT activities on Great Coco Island, Ramree Island off the Rakhine coast, Hainggyi Island at the mouth of the Ayeyarwady Delta, Monkey Point in Rangoon and Zadetkgi Kyun off the Kra Peninsula along the Tanintharyi coast with a view to collect intelligence on air and naval movements in the eastern parts of the Bay of Bengal and on Indian's facilities on the Andaman Islands.[57] Another possible objective was also to intercept telemetry from Indian ballistic missile test launches. Myanmar and China negotiated a military cooperation agreement in 1996 containing provisions for intelligence exchanges.[58]

Economic relations continued to flourish, despite changing political attitudes. According to Myanmar's Directorate of Investment and Company Administration, China was Myanmar's largest trade partner. China's cumulative investment in Myanmar reached the level of US$ 20 billion by August 31, 2019.[59] The view of Myanmar as China's client state was also based on claims of Chinese involvement in massive civil and military development projects including the upgrading of airstrips and ports. It was believed it could potentially serve as forwarding operating basis for the People's Liberation Army Navy [PLAN] and even support a permanent Chinese military presence in future.[60]

Indeed, at a certain level, Myanmar hinted that it wanted to avoid a political and economic alliance with China because it affected the sovereignty of Myanmar at the international level. Myanmar started purchasing helicopters and gunships in 1955 from Russia and used MIG-29s in 2001. It also got a supply of arms and ammunition from India, Serbia, North Korea and Ukraine. While they continued purchases, Chinese military equipment was no longer bought as was seen in the early 1990s. Although observers in 2004 speculated that a further significant arms deal was being negotiated.[61]

Relations of Myanmar and China are based on Panchsheel principles as they also share paukphaw and China is considered the elder one. However, China's over indulgence created suspicions and it alerted Myanmar. Myanmar at the same time wants to have close bilateral relations with India, Russia, Thailand and other ASEAN members. Myanmar may get some free hand from China, in turn, China wants to use Myanmar for the fulfilment of its national interests in the Indian Ocean by approaching ports in this region to expand its businesses.

Strategically, China aspires to get approach to the Andaman seaports not just for trade but also as an attainable storage ground and base emplacement for troops, warships and aircraft. China has a plan to build railway and road network alongside pipeline to base its troops and to supply the same to naval vessels by using west coast ports of Myanmar. This potential increase in China's ability to project power in the region was a key concern for Southeast Asian countries and in Singapore's long-term strategic thinking. Besides, China also adopted the strategy of expanding its trade in goods and investment in developing capacity in areas of importance to China's interests. The areas of concentrated efforts had been mining, energy (oil and natural gas) and hydropower sectors. The investment in infrastructure had been largely linked to the areas that had served China's strategic interests.[62]

Myanmar is considered a bridge to reach the waters in and beyond the Bay of Bengal. However, this approach of China was dangerous for India because China is using Myanmar to encircle India. Other factors are influencing China's planning. China considers Myanmar as an important nation crucial in its energy security. Another factor impacting China's strategy towards Myanmar was the US Administration's engagement policy.[63] Myanmar is located at the junction which connects India, China and ASEAN members, a possible short route to the Indian Ocean for China. China has the intention to adopt strategic route from Gunnison province in Southwest China through Myanmar up to the Indian Ocean. According to Voon Phin Keong, the director of the Centre of Malaysian-Chinese Studies in Kuala Lumpur, an outlet to the Indian Ocean would add a new dimension to China's spatial relations with the world. It would enable China to overcome its 'single-ocean strategy' and to realise what would constitute a highly significant plan for a two-ocean strategy.[64]

China-India Linkages: Historical Background

This is a fact that India and China are the oldest living civilisations of the world—the great powers of Asia. Both are neighbouring countries and have old trade relations with each other. Historically, there has been a two-way interaction in the exchange of trade and cultural relations between them. The four routes of communications facilitated the exchange, namely the Central Asian Route or the so-called Silk Route; Assam-Myanmar and Yunnan Route or the famous Southern Silk Route; Tibet Nepal Route; and the Sea Route or the so-called Maritime Silk Route.[65]

The initial believable data regarding the India-China connection is supplied by Si Maqian (145-90 BC). He was an outstanding Chinese historian in his accomplished records of a Historian: Foreigners in Southwest. The record recites that when Zhang Qian, a Han diplomat in the western neighbourhood, came back to the court in 122 BC, he informed Han Emperor Wu Di (140-87 BC) that while in Bactria or Bactriana in Central Asia (later variedly called as Tukharistan, Tokharistan, and Tocharistan) he saw Sichuan silk and bamboo walking sticks there. He came to know from the local merchants that they were procuring these and other Chinese products from the Indian markets thus establishing the fact that India and China were already having trade relations in the 2nd century BC.[66] Pearls, corals and lapis lazuli were the primary products India traded with China, whereas silk appears to be the major item transported from China to India. Ban Gu's book also mentions the sea route connecting southern India and China, and certain states such as Huangzhi (identified as Kanchipuram) having brisk diplomatic and trade relations with China.[67]

During those times, there were exchanges of material goods as well as the spiritual connectivity which changed the relationship altogether. It was a period when Buddhism was adopted as a religion by the Chinese people and most common version the dream of the Golden Buddha by Ham Emperor Ming Di (AD 58-75). As a result of these dreams, Emperor Ming Di dispatched his scholar to India to search for Buddhist scholars, and two of them namely monk Kashyapa Matanga and monk Dharmaraksha were taken to China. The monastery, White Horse Monastery, which was built to accommodate them in Luoyang attracts thousands of devotees and tourists even today. In May 2010, during her visit to China the Indian President Pratibha Patil inaugurated a Buddhist complex, built with an Indian investment of 4 million US dollars next to this monastery.[68] India has been sending scholar-monk to China till the 3rd century AD. During the 4th and the 7th centuries, the influence of Buddhism in China broadened, and thousands of scholar monks from China to India and from India to China visited each other.[69]

On the other hand, Hinduism also made inroads to China. It was discovered that people of China were impressed with the Hinduism culture. It was followed at the sites such as Dali in Yunnan, Kizil and Dunhuang grottoes in Gansu, Lopnor in Xinjiang and Quanzhou in Guangdong provinces of China. The statues of many Hindu lords were unearthed from Dali and Quanzhou in China. This proves that a large number of people from India also settled there since then. Indian art, fables, dramas, stories and medicines reached China. Above all, the cultural diplomats from China to India and India to China increased and reinforced mutual perspectives which act as an activator in the modern history of India and China for performing mutual assistance and understanding by the Chinese and Indians during their national freedom struggle.

Both Countries Interaction in Modern Era

From Ming and Yuan dynasties onwards until India and China initiated their freedom struggles, the cross-cultural currents between them virtually went unnoticed. The interactions were intervened by the domestic changes and more importantly by the gradual eastward expansion of Western colonialism. Following this, India was colonised entirely by the British, and China gradually changed into a semi-feudal and semi-colonial society. The anti-imperialist efflorescence of the Indian and Chinese people manifested a significant challenge to the colonial system for the first time during the First War of Indian Independence (1857-59) in India and the Taiping Uprising (1850-64) in China. It was for the first time Indian soldiers stationed in China changed over to the Taipings and fought shoulder to shoulder against the imperialists and the Qing government. This rapprochement continued when the Indian and Chinese people launched a more organised struggle for national independence. The reports of Indian soldiers joining the Taiping could be found in the memorials of the Qing army generals or other officials of the throne and with the foreigners who were directly involved in this peasant uprising.

It was due to the synergy between the cultures and the plight of India and China that the nationalists and revolutionaries of India and China developed deep mutual contacts and friendship amidst their anti-imperialist struggle. They became natural allies and sought various ways to extricate the imperialists out of their countries. The supporters of

Tilak, the leader of militant nationalists carried out activities like Shivaji's commemorative meetings as far as Tokyo in order to make the Indian voice of anti-imperialism reach outside India. These activities had the positive support of the Chinese nationalists such as Zhang Taiyan and Sun Yat-sen. Sun Yat-sen developed strong links with various Indian nationalists and revolutionaries. This introduced them to the leading Japanese personages thus enabling them to carry out their anti-British activities unobstructed. Nationalists like Surendermohan Bose, Rash Behari Bose, M.N. Roy, Barakatullah, Lala Lajpat Rai and many other outstanding pioneers of Indian freedom movement maintained good contacts and friendship with Sun Yat-sen.

Apart from operating from Japan, the Indian revolutionaries also made China as one of their centres to carry out anti-British activities. Except few, most of them were the members of Ghadar Party. Much of the activities centred around Hankou, being the centre of Kuomintang (KMT) government and Shanghai and Hong Kong being the space where Indian settlers including police officers and troops numbered maximum. Their post-Siam-Myanmar Plan activities found a link with the Kuomintang (KMT) and the Communist Party of China (CPC). Ghadar support to the Chinese nationalist government and in turn enlisting latter's support was the direct outcome of the formation of First United Front in China between the KMT and CPC. Their activities came to an abrupt end with the collapse of the United Front in 1927 though some individuals continued to be active unto 1931 and 1932.

Gandhi's arrival in the Indian political scene and his movement of satyagraha and ahimsa generated heated debates in China. The Chinese people pronounced him as a symbol of 'eastern civilisation.' The Chinese media paid utmost attention and widely covered the Indian freedom struggle in various newspapers and journals. Eastern Miscellany took the lead and introduced Gandhi and Gandhian movement to the Chinese people. It covered the Non-cooperation Movement of 1920-22 and Civil Disobedience Movement of 1931-34 extensively. The Chinese people showered both encomiums and criticism on Gandhi when he led the Non-Cooperation and Civil Disobedience Movements. Sun Yat-sen, however never approved of his weapon of non-violence, for he was of the view that an armed struggle was indispensable for national liberation.[70] Nevertheless, Sun Yat-sen accepted Gandhi's pacifist techniques such as non-cooperation and civil disobedience. Gandhi even suggested these techniques and principle of non-violence to the Chinese people but came round to the Chinese viewpoint that it cannot be applied to China's national situation, especially when it was engaged in an armed struggle with the Japanese.[71]

During the War of Resistance and the Second World War, as long as China suffered at the hands of the Japanese, the reverberations were felt in India too. India dispatched a medical operation to China in 1938. Dr Kotnis, a doctor of this operation, became a martyr when he died while serving the wounded soldiers of Eighth Route Army and other Chinese people. Nehru made the bonds of friendship even stronger when he visited China in 1939. The Chinese people at first supported the Indian viewpoint in not joining the war unless it was acknowledged free. Later, they asked support from India for the war effort of allied powers, as the whole situation had changed with the formation of India-China-Myanmar War theatre. President Chiang Kai-Shek visited India in 1940 especially to break the ongoing deadlock between the British and the Congress, and they met Gandhi afterwards.

In retrospect, the civilisational cross-cultural currents between India and China went unhindered for many millennia. Especially the colonial period was the period when both the people of India and China rendered support and sympathy to each other in their common struggle. It was Nehru's vision that in future India and China would necessarily come closer to each other for the vast and tremendous potentials of economic cooperation in a New World after the War. India was the first country in the non-communist bloc to recognise China and established diplomatic relations.

India-China Relationship since Independence

China came into existence in October 1949, whereas India got independence on August 15, 1947, although both countries have a history of old cultural and economic relationship for thousands of years. Both countries have seen distinct challenges especially in the era of the nuclear age. The two nations are the most populous, yet speedily developing economies in the world. China is posing a serious challenge to the US uni-polarity in the context of global power.

India recognised the People's Republic of China on April 1, 1950, against the Taiwan-led Republic of China and also set up diplomatic relations with China. The famous Hindi expression of "Hindi-Chini Bhai Bhai" was public during comparatively friendly relations between the two. It is also covered in international relations literature that India under Nehru, refused offers from USA and Union of Soviet Socialist Republics (USSR) to be a permanent seat at the United Nations (UN) Security Council to encourage greater integration of China in the international community.[72] Eventually, however, ties between the two nations began to sour.

In 1954, both the countries signed an agreement on trade and Panchsheel. The Five Principles of Peaceful Coexistence (Panchsheel) and the Bandung Conference were in the limelight of India-China cooperation. However, the cooperation did not last. By the late 1950s, relations started straining between both countries due to the border issues which led to the war of 1962.

The India-Pakistan conflict eventually reached to its disenchantment with the UN, for its incapability and sensed partiality in resolving the Kashmir dispute. Moreover, the USA sided with Pakistan instead of India inviting it to be a part of its security alliances as early as 1954, due to its explicit anti-communist stand, whereas India was perceived to be equivocal about its stand on communism.[73] India became a common enemy of China-Pakistan-US from 1970 onwards. Thereafter, the relations between China and the USSR got disturbed due to ideological, economic and security concern from the period of 1960 to 1980. China came with economic reforms post-1978 to expand its economy, branching away from India regarding economic potential, and from USSR in terms of ideology. Instead, this period saw warming of relationships between India and USSR culminating in a friendship treaty between both nations in 1971.[74] This stood for an implicit military security backing by USSR, for India. At the time, both the US and China had nuclear weapons, and India was yet to run its first nuclear test, which came in 1974.[75] India left its NAM approach and established friendly relations with USSR; soon it became the largest supplier of military equipment to India. The friendship of India and USSR continued up to the disintegration of USSR and end of the Cold War in 1991. Later, different Indian governments in their reign attempted to improve relations with the US and with China after Mao Zedong. However, the growing nuclear power of India and dispute with Pakistan, China and other situations kept India more or less same until 1991 in terms of foreign policy of India.

India in the post-Cold War period lost its strategic backing from the USSR after the disintegration of the USSR. The world converted into the unipolar world, and the US emerged as the only superpower. The economic power of China increased considerably, and it became the most powerful country in Asia posing a threat to India and the US at a global platform. India also underwent rapid economic development due to the first phase of economic reforms in 1991, and joined China as the fastest growing economy of the world. The rapid hop was seen in the GDP of India which created the ground work for economic cooperation between India and the US. India gained more recognition in the geopolitics at the international level. This created the right platform for a new beginning between India and the US relations of this era. China is a threat to India as well as the US at the global and regional level. Thus, the India-US Nuclear deal was signed in 2008 as recognition for India to be a strong regional power in Asia and a reliable associate against the threat of China in the area. China and Pakistan developed their reliable strategic partner, with China assisting Pakistan; increasing its defence and nuclear potentials thereby becoming active partners in economic terms. India is now facing a threat from two fronts, one from the Pakistan and other from China. However, economic liberalisation in India also led to an enlargement of economic relations between China and India which transformed into warming of tensions due to border challenges and the nuclearisation of India. Bilateral agreements and expansion of investments and trade have been a result of no major conflict between both the countries since 1987. Both countries are competing with each other for becoming a regional power and having multilateral partnerships to expand their influence. China has veto power as a member UNSC, and it has blocked the resolution several times against India, such as Jaish-e-Mohammad (JeM) chief Masood Azhar, being declared as an international terrorist by UN and India's NSG membership bid.

Economic Relations

After the death of Mao Zedong, China began opening up its economy and implementing reform in 1978. This lead to a divergence in economic development between India and China where China was growing into a much larger economy.[76] China started on those projects which led to the export of goods because there was cheap labour available in there. Moreover, China opened up its economy by doing economic reforms. Foreign investors started investing in China by bringing foreign currency because the economy was under development and with much scope for investments in the diversified fields in China. India had the economic reforms much later in 1991 that led to economic liberalisation, privatisation and gave free space to the foreign investors for their business. Both the countries have open economies, and both have accumulated large stocks of foreign exchange reserves. Although political relations between the two countries were not so good due to the 1962 war, yet economic relations developed steadily between them. The bilateral trade between India and China has grown from US$ 1.99 billion in 1999 to a massive US$ 71.8 billion in 2016. India's trade deficit with China fell to US$ 48.66 billion in 2019-20 on account of decline in imports from the neighbouring country, according to government data. Exports to China in the last financial year stood at US$ 17.97 billion, while imports aggregated at US$ 74.92 billion. India faces a substantial trade deficit in trade relations with China (US$ 56.95 billion in 2018-19) considering the current trade mix to be unsustainable.[77] China mainly imports commodity goods like cotton, gems, copper and iron ore from India, while India imports manufactured capital goods from China because it is a low-cost manufacturing hub.[78] The reason for trade deficit is that India is unable to export manufactured goods to China.

As far as Chinese investment in India is concerned, it was only US$ 1.35 billion from 2000 to 2016. However, when India increased its efforts through make in India projects, a good number of Chinese companies started production units in India. Since June 2016, Chinese companies have pumped in almost twice the money they invested in the country in the decade and a half before that. Tensions between India and China have been brewing for the past few months, due to India placing higher restrictions on Chinese FDI and its public turn to '*Aatmanirbharta*', a clarion call for Indian consumers and businesses to use domestic products, and lower India's significant dependence on Chinese imports. However, the immediate catalyst for the Blocking Order seems to be the spurt in clashes across the Indo-China border, which have resulted in martyrdom of several Indian soldiers, such as at Galwan valley. These clashes have also had other fallouts, such as Indian and Chinese customs authorities delaying each other's exports by invoking extremely stringent customs inspections. The railways have reportedly cancelled a signalling project that was given to a Chinese company in 2016. And, according to reports, the government has also asked e-commerce companies to display the country of origin for the products they sell. The eastern state of Bihar has cancelled a contract for a US$ 390 million bridge over the Ganges River due to the involvement of Chinese companies, according to local media. The state of Maharashtra has frozen three Chinese investments, including the planned purchase of a General Motors plant there by privately run Great Wall Motor. India has also tightened scrutiny of shipments from China, leaving products such as mobile phones stuck at ports. A tariff hike on solar cells may be considered as well. India has been adding solar capacity to address electricity shortages and make its power supply greener. The country imports about 80 per cent of its cells from China. India aims to reduce its reliance on imported solar equipment, and the government is expected to impose import restrictions of some sort aimed at Beijing. Bilateral trade between the countries, already down by 15 per cent since the 2018 financial year, could take a further hit as India mulls extra tariffs and anti-dumping duties on Chinese imports. The government, which has been aggressively banning several Chinese applications, is believed to be mulling import curbs on over categories of goods which are largely imported from China, items such as toys, steel tubes, steel bars, consumer electronics, telecom items, heavy machinery, paper, rubber articles and glass will be brought under mandatory Indian Standards (IS) regime by next year. Procurement regulations revised last week now require businesses in countries that share a land border with India to register with the relevant authorities and receive permission from the external affairs and home affairs ministries before bidding for contracts. This applies to a broad range of public-sector business, including state governments, state-run businesses and banks, and public-private partnerships. Though India borders China, Nepal, Bhutan, Pakistan, Bangladesh and Myanmar, exemptions in effect limit the scope of the rules to China and Pakistan. India's measures aim to "strengthen the defense and national security" of the country. The apparent goal is to freeze Chinese companies out of India's public sector entirely.

In 2010, a Strategic Economic Dialogue Mechanism was started on a macroeconomic basis. A Financial Dialogue forum has existed since 2005 to enable greater bilateral financial cooperation. In a Five Year Trade and Economic Development Plan signed in September 2014, key sectors like Pharmaceuticals, IT, Tourism, Textiles and Agro-Products were recognised to exploit complementaries within.[79] At the Strategic Economic Dialogue in 2016, both countries agreed to strengthen economic ties through cooperating on sourcing energy from international markets, construction of high-speed railways and the development of coastal manufacturing zones, looking towards the future of the global economic system.[80] Today both governments have signed 24 new agreements on a bilateral basis covering the fields of health, tourism, skill development, a sister cities programme, railways and the establishment of consulates amongst other things. These signals are the future trajectory of economic relations between India and China.

Economic Engagements in Regional Organisations

India and China are the two prominent players in the region of South Asia. Both are engaged in multilateral economic partnership and cooperation for the benefit of each. India is aware of interference by China in the Indian Ocean Region and the South China Sea which is the cause of concern for India. India wants to maintain cooperation with China on multilateral forums such as the G-20, the East Asia Summit and BRICS (Brazil, Russia, India, China, South Africa). The BRICS members have started the New Development Bank in 2014. China is also seeking greater economic cooperation with India on the Bangladesh-China-India-Myanmar corridor and the New Silk Route programme. India and China are part of the 21 countries that have signed on to the Asian Infrastructure Investment Bank (AIIB), that aims to form an Asian counterpoint to the World Bank and the IMF.[81] ASEAN has also formed RCEP with the help of India and China for free trade in the region. China has initiated One Belt One Road (OBOR) which would cover more than 60 countries. It started in May 2017, but India has not Joined this project. The China-Pakistan Economic Corridor (CPEC) is also linked with OBOR. India has not disclosed its stance, whether to join or not. However, India would not hold back from being a partner in the gigantic program that is capable of increasing Chinese influence internationally. The Shanghai Cooperation Organisation (SCO) formed by China along with Russia and other Central Asian countries have been seen as one of the few countervailing forces to the US unipolarity, through a political, economic and military function of the organisation.[82] India was acknowledged as a full member of SCO with Pakistan in 2016. With Pakistan and China formed a sort of bloc in the area, India needs to have strong relations with countries in South Asia. China has not been made a member of South Asian Association for Regional Cooperation (SAARC) despite a proposal by Pakistan. China accepted the status of a dialogue partner in the Indian Ocean Rim Association, started by other nations and India. The Bangladesh, Bhutan, India,

Nepal (BBIN) initiative and the Bay of Bengal Initiative for Multi-Sectoral Technical and Economic Cooperation (BIMSTEC) are the regional startups being nourished by India. India also made its relations strong with Japan to counterbalance Chinese power in Asia.

Border Disputes between India and China

There is a common border of 4,056 km long between India and China, but most of it is disputed because it has not been appropriately demarcated so far, only a cut as the edge by Line of Actual Control (LAC). The demarcation existed as the informal cease-fire line between India and China after the 1962 conflict until 1993, when its existence was officially accepted as the 'Line of Actual Control' in a bilateral agreement.[83]

Arunachal Pradesh

When China illegally captured the Tibet and forced the Dalai Lama (permanent exile in India) in 1959, the India-China border became complicated. The border between Arunachal Pradesh region with Tibet was controlled by North East Frontier Province (NEFP) which is now claimed by China as South Tibet. Chinese believes that many years ago, this area was part of Tibet, but it was given to India by the Britishers as per Simla Agreement of 1913-14, where the famous Mac Mahon Line is drawn. In the 1950s, India believed this dispute could be resolved with all parties jointly recognising the validity of the Mac Mahon Line. However, the border got further confrontational with time, and in the 1962 war, China claimed Arunachal Pradesh as part of its territory through military intervention.[84] However, China withdrew its forces from the region after winning the war. China negotiated the matter of Arunachal Pradesh region with India and tried to put an offer in exchange for control over Aksai Chin. China again tried to claim over the territory in 2006, but India registered and refused the proposal and sent back their soldiers by increasing military presence in this area. It is clearly understood that China only uses border dispute as leverage in international relations with India to influence.

Aksai Chin

This area falls in the eastern part of Ladakh in Jammu and Kashmir and it is a disputed region between China and India. The responsible party for this dispute goes to the British government who demarcated it before the independence of India. India considers the Johnson Line drawn up in 1865 and advocated by the British post-1940s, which puts Aksai Chin as part of India, as the official border in this region. On the other hand, China considers the Macartney-Mac Donald Line, which left the Aksai Chin within Chinese borders, as the official border.[85] In 1958, the area of Aksai Chin was abundant space without any population but it was treated as Indian territory. China made illegal encroachment in this area. The Chinese had been building a highway from Tibet to the autonomous Chinese region of Xinjiang, through the region, within a few months Chinese maps began to display the region as part of their territory.[86] It was a matter of open provocation by China to India. Thereafter, India granted asylum to Dalai Lama and his followers in 1959 which complicated the matter further. Many letters were written by Indian Prime Minister to Chinese Premier and vice versa, but the tension went on increasing ultimately leading to Chinese aggression on India in 1962.

Today, China administers the area of Aksai Chin though India still claims it. There is National Highway 219 of China which goes from Yecheng in Xinjiang to Lhatse in Tibet. This highway is strategically vital to the Chinese because it provides essential North-South transportation and logistics link between its two most western territories—Xinjiang Province and Tibet.[87]

In 2013, Chinese troops entered the Daulat Beg Oldi region, close to Aksai Chin, into Indian territory, causing a three-week standoff that was later resolved through bilateral negotiations.[88]

Map 4.2: Disputed Area between India and China

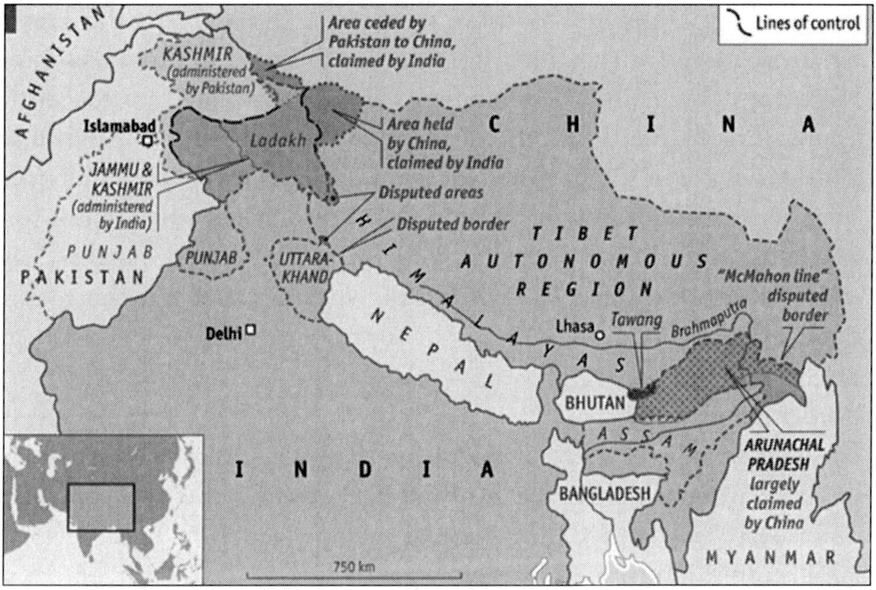

Source: Kashmir International Research Centre

Sikkim

There is a border dispute between India and China over Sikkim. It began with the incident of 1967 which took place at Nathu La and Cho La as Chinese forces infiltrated Sikkim which was not a part of India at that time. Later in 1975, by way of unanimous referendum people of Sikkim decided to merge with India. However, it was unacceptable to China at that time. Later in 2003, China agreed to accept Sikkim as an Indian state, on condition of recognising Tibet as an autonomous region of China by India. This was already recognised by India in 1953.[89]

Shaksgam Valley

The Shaksgam valley also known as Trans-Karakoram tract has an area of 9,900 sq. km. It is part of the Xinjiang region of China. The area was controlled by Pakistan until it ceded the region to China in 1963 under the Sino-Pak Frontier Agreement, an important step in the growing China and Pakistan relations.[90] India claims this area as a part of its territory. China has built in this region Hotan-Golmud Highway which links Xinjiang to Qinghai province up to central China. This road reduced the distance to Golmud, and it is useful for a military base in China. The Siachen Glacier is easily accessible from Shaksgam Valley through this road, and it is also a very crucial road for Pakistan during any conflict with India. China and Pakistan have a close strategic alliance and China allows Pakistan to use this road in times of emergency.

Border Agreements

China started its economic reforms in 1978 while India had it reforms in 1991 with the opening up of the economy. The economic and diplomatic ties with China were also improved. The LAC received legal recognition through bilateral agreements, with the Agreement on the Maintenance of Peace and Tranquillity along the Line of Actual Control (LAC) being signed during a diplomatic visit in 1993, and with an agreement on Confidence Building Measures in the Military Field along the LAC signed in 1996.[91] The Border Defence Cooperation agreement was entered into by both the countries in October 2013 for cutting possibilities of military conflict on account of the border patrol. However, China blocked specific resolution against Indian interests in UN since the present NDA government came into power in 2014. The Indian government wants to have peaceful mutual acceptance for the border disputes between high-level ministerial meetings that often take place in this regard.

Military Encounters between India and China

There have been chiefly three direct encounters over the territorial disputes between India and China, since 1949.

Map 4.3: Geographic Positions of LOC (Pakistan) and LAC (China)

Source: *Indian Defence Review*

India-China War of 1962

People's Liberation Army of China attacked Aksai Chin across the Mac Mahon line in Arunachal Pradesh on October 20, 1962. India was caught unaware by China and India was not at all prepared for war with China. India had an insufficient military to compete with the Chinese Army, and as a result, there was a huge loss of Indian soldiers. Chinese attack on India came as rude. It shocked the Prime Minister of India, Jawahar Lal Nehru, as it was unexpected. China was secure with the US posing a neutral stand in the event of China-Indian conflict in the early 1960s, along with USSR's offer of restitution of China-Soviet alliance in mid-October 1962 and mitigating its pro-India tilt due to the Cuban Missile Crisis. This removed all hurdles in the way of China's attack on India.[92] India requested for help from both the US and USSR, but none turned to the rescue. It was an intense threat situation for India to shun the policy of neutralism. This event caused a change in India's foreign policy to take a pragmatic stance from being an idealist nation. It was the time when India realised the importance of international cooperation and not depending on others to resolve the conflicts. The Chinese are claimed to have declared a unilateral ceasefire and withdrawn out of the war.[93] Some of the defence experts say that China withdrew from the war because its capacity to prolong the war beyond Tawang region in Arunachal Pradesh was over, and another possibility was the interference of US in the issue if escalated.

1967 Skirmish

The Indian-China battle of 1967 is by and large not widely known of, and referred as the Nathu La and Cho La skirmish which continued from September 11-14 and October 1-10 respectively. At this time Chinese forces infiltrated into the Sikkim territory because Sikkim was not part of India. However, it was a protectorate by India, so India had to come to the rescue of Sikkim. On October 1, 1967, the Chinese People's Liberation Army invaded the parts of Sikkim but was pushed back by the Indian forces by October 10. However, in the battle of Nathu La and Cho La, 88 Indian soldiers were martyred and 163 were wounded. While on the Chinese side, 340 soldiers were martyred and 450 were wounded in action.[94] Indian forces compelled the Chinese military to withdraw from Sikkim. In 1975, Sikkim became an integral part of India. China also recognised Sikkim as an integral state of India in 2003 and in return India would consider Tibet Autonomous Region as a part of China where India had already recognised it in 1953. There is no denial in the fact that China has a fat military budget compared to India but what ultimately matters is the courage in the man behind the machine.[95]

Doklam Stand-Off

In 2017, there was again a stand-off between the Chinese army and Indian army which continued for more than two months which falls in the territory of Bhutan. Chinese army tried to infiltrate Bhutan in mid-June through Doklam area, and it requested India to interfere. China was constructing a road in the disputed territory in the Doklam plateau to which Royal Bhutanese Army objected. Doklam is situated as a tri-junction between India, Bhutan and China. At the intervention of India, China stopped the construction work in Doklam but claimed Doklam as its territory while both armies were sending reinforcements at the border. The Kailash Mansarovar pilgrimage was cancelled due to this standoff, situated at an altitude of 15,160 feet. This yatra is holy to Jains, Buddhists and Hindus. Bhutan is an ally of India. Indian army had to face PLA expecting Siliguri corridor as a major concern for India. China was threatening the Indian army for another 1962 Indo-China war to which the Indian army gave a stern response that India was ready for "two-and-a-half war." Despite some diplomatic talks, China was not interested in disengaging its forces. However, an official press release came out by Ministry of External Affairs from India on August 28, 2017, where both countries agreed to withdraw their soldiers back. Indian troops withdrew in the afternoon followed by Chinese troops with their road construction machinery. There was no other detail leakage regarding peace and diplomatic talks which resulted in this bilateral solution.

After just 5-6 days of the withdrawal, a statement came out from the China that they will continue building more roads in the disputed land and Indian army should get accustomed to such situations. The tensions in the Doklam plateau is over but no one can rely on Chinese intentions, and they may create disturbance any time in the disputed land. Currently, Indian forces are deployed in the disputed area to monitor their movements. India is clear that if such a situation is created in the future by China, then a similar deadlock reaction is the possibility all over again.

Ladakh Stand-Off

Indian and Chinese troops had a face-off in the Galwan river sector in the first week of May 2020. Chinese troops, travelling along the Galwan river from their rear base(s), are supposed to have crossed the LAC in this sector. And they were confronted at a point known as Patrol Point 14 (PP14), which on Indian side but very close to the LAC. Post the engagement, the Chinese troops are supposed to have gone back to their side of the LAC. Satellite images shared by some analysts on social media platforms that there is some troop built-up on either side of the LAC by both the countries. However, there is no evidence so far of the Chinese having squatted on Indian side of LAC or captured any territory. The LAC runs very close to the alignment of the Shyok River in this sector and by extension, to the new DS-DBO road. The confluence of Shyok and Galwan river is ~8 km from the LAC and hence, the added sensitivity.

The supposed trigger for the Chinese aggression in this area is an attempt by the Indian Army to build a feeder road emanating from DS-DBO road and which comes till PP-14. Such a road will improve India's ability to patrol this area and to respond to any exigency. The Indian government has already communicated that infrastructure work in the entire Ladakh sector, including Galwan River area, will continue and be completed as per the original requirement. Galwan Sector remains a sensitive area because of the proximity of DS-DBO road to LAC and threat of interdiction by the Chinese. However, this would have been known to Indian planners from the beginning itself. Further, this is not the only segment of DS-DBO road which faces this threat from the Chinese, there are other segments as well. In addition to this, during any conflict, the road will also come under long-distance artillery fire as well. But this does not reduce the significance of the road. It will continue to serve the army in peacetime and help in building up troops and materials before any shooting match starts. Further, you can expect the army to take adequate measures to protect the road. At the same time, the army is also working on developing an alternate route to DBO sector which lies in depth within Ladakh and does not suffer from same threat as DS-DBO road. As for the current stand-off, since there is no differing perception of opinion in this sector, nor is there any evidence of the Chinese having come into India side of LAC, it should be easiest to settle. However, at this stage, there is no clarity as to when this is likely to happen.

Nuclear Capabilities

India and China are part of the nine nuclear weapon powers of the world. China officially became part of the nuclear club with its nuclear test on October 1, 1964, making it the fifth nuclear power.[96] When China conducted nuclear test US was greatly disturbed because it tilted the balance of power in Asia and the world. The stakes for non-proliferation of nuclear weapons rose, signified by the Non-Proliferation Treaty (NPT) of 1970, where the horizontal proliferation of nuclear power was banned, conferring nuclear status only upon US, USSR, UK, France and China.[97] When China attempted a nuclear test in 1964, it gave an alarming call to India as India had already suffered defeat from China in 1962. India also wanted to acquire the nuclear power because India was left unattended by the US and USSR without any support against China. Thus, India decided to pursue nuclear power on its own, to develop a nuclear deterrent and stayed out of the NPT in 1970. India ran its first nuclear test in Pokhran, in 1974, during the Indira Gandhi government.[98] India got a big boost with this test. India continued its nuclear development along Ballistic Missile Development (BMD) as a part of the delivery system of the weapon. In 1998, India tested 5 nuclear weapons as part of the Pokhran-II Test, bringing its nuclear program out of the shadows, and onto a global scale. This deteriorated India's relations with the US, and the non-proliferation community at the time, and instigated Pakistan as well.[99] Thereafter, Pakistan started its nuclear programme secretly within a span of a few weeks. It is suspected that China played a major role in the development of Pakistan's nuclear capabilities, training its scientists and even sharing weapons designs and tests.[100] China wanted to create a counter balance force against India, a common enemy in the region.

The North side of India being blocked by two strategically allied nuclear weapon states is one of the major constraints faced by India, in its quest for power. As per current estimated nuclear warhead inventories, China stands at 280 warheads, with Pakistan and India being at around 145 and 135, respectively.[101] India and China have no first use policy of nuclear weapon, and both would not like to engage in a war with each other. However, hostility with Pakistan has triggered talk within India, to have a modification in the policy vis-à-vis Pakistan. Currently, India is working on its nuclear potentiality, which is less developed than Chinese potentials. The Indo-US nuclear deal allowed India to use its uranium for weapon making and import material for nuclear power. China called it a breach of the Non-Proliferation Treaty. India has not signed the Comprehensive Test Ban Treaty till now. India is continuing its test series in the missile development and has achieved numerous milestones in it, intercontinental missiles are one of them, which is a cause of concern for China and Pakistan.

India-China in the Indian Ocean

China has the intention to expand its geopolitical presence in the region, especially in the South China Sea by creating artificial islands to use them for military future and economic gains. China is also increasing its naval capabilities, covering nuclear-based submarines and wants to convert its navy as Blue Water Navy. China's policy of String of Pearls is meant to encircle India by military and commercial bases with the help of Sri Lanka, Pakistan, Bangladesh, Myanmar and Maldives in the Indian Ocean, where India historically influences the region.

Whereas, India identifies the challenges from a string of pearl strategy of China, India has actively improved relations with its maritime neighbour countries. India's Look (Act) East Policy emphasises on developing closer ties with Myanmar, Maldives, Sri Lanka and Bangladesh to improve its connectivity with East Asian countries. India is also striving hard to counter China by developing friendly relations with neighbour countries of China. Further, India has signed multiple agreements with countries such as Iran, Uzbekistan, Turkmenistan, Kazakhstan, Mongolia and

Kyrgyzstan. Besides, India maintains cordial relations with South Korea, Russia and Japan. India's outreach has increased largely with steady and silent steps.

Map 4.4: Chinese Encirclement: String of Pearls and India's Counter Responses

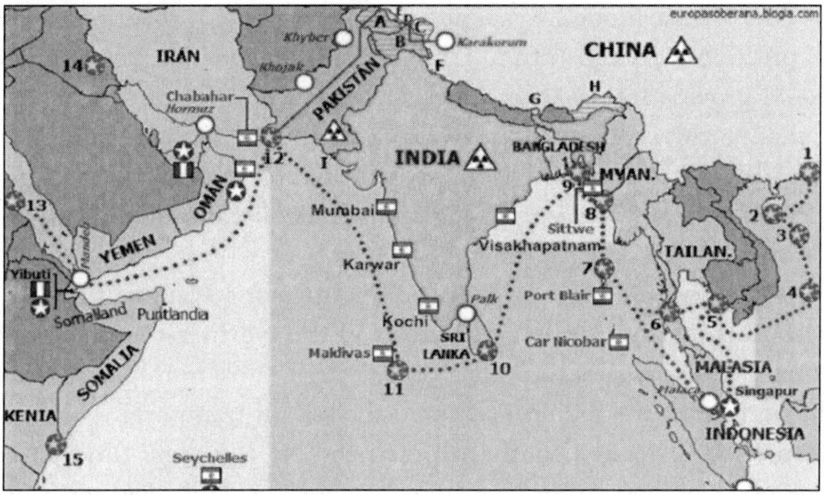

Source: www.gisreportsonline.com

India-Myanmar-China Triangle

As already stated, Myanmar is of great strategic significance to both India and China. China's increasing presence and its role in Myanmar is an issue of worry for India. In the early years of the military regime, India pushed hard that a democratic system should be established in Myanmar. Meanwhile, China has become an increasingly attractive source of low-interest loans, grants, development projects, technical assistance to Myanmar. India has already realised that the primary beneficiary of strained India-Myanmar relations was China, for access to all important hydrocarbon energy sources and transport corridors.[102] China is investing heavily in infrastructure, mining projects, hydropower dams and oil-gas pipelines to help southern China's growing energy needs and gaining greater access to the Indian Ocean through Myanmar. China is Myanmar's biggest investor with some US$ 14.251 billion spanning 65 projects as of June 2016. Bilateral trade between the two countries stood at US$ 5.015 billion for 2017-18, making up 38.89 per cent of Myanmar's total foreign trade value. In the fiscal year 2017-18, over 60 per cent of Myanmar's total border trade (over US$ 3 billion) poured in from China via Muse, making it the highest border trade transaction between the two countries.[103]

The China-funded Kyaukphyu port project with road link, gas and oil pipelines to Yunnan from China was to be completed by 2015. This would provide China with direct strategic access to the Indian Ocean bypassing the choke point at Malacca Strait.[104] China's presence in the Coco Islands of Myanmar is in the name to ensure the security of piracy affected Strait of Malacca through which its oil-carrying tankers pass is also a cause of worry for India.[105]

India and China are openly competing for Myanmar's favour for strengthening their strategic interests in the Northeast areas of Indian Ocean. China wishes to protect its southern flank from possible future Indian threats and requires access to the sea for transportation of goods from its land-locked southern provinces. At the same time, India is looking at an inland transportation route for the landlocked states of the Northeastern region through the Kaladan river that flows from Myanmar into Mizoram and further southwards into the Bay of Bengal.[106] Besides India fears encirclement by China due to its influence with Myanmar and Pakistan. This strategic competition also worries the members of ASEAN that a weak and vulnerable country like Myanmar will fall into China's orbit and become a Chinese pawn in the region.[107] Nevertheless, China's bilateral relation with Myanmar is further strengthened with the supply of arms, logistic equipment and infrastructure development that is primarily meant for military purposes. However, India is already exporting rocket launchers, mortars, rifles, radars, night-vision devices, Gypsies, bailey bridges, communication and Inmarsat sets as well as road construction equipment like bulldozers, tippers and soil compactors to the Myanmar armed forces. India is trying to have strong defence cooperation with Myanmar and this will benefit India to reduce the over-dependence of Myanmar over China. Recently, India increased its high-level delegation visits to Yangon, with the primary objective of moving Myanmar away from close ties with China. Besides playing on security and strategic issues, India also used religion in fostering closer India-Myanmar relations. The Indian leadership depicts Buddhism and Hinduism as 'branches of the same tree'. Thus, India's main objective is to remove Myanmar from China's orbit or sphere of influence.

India with regard to the increase of China's presence in Myanmar relates to its possible implications on the cross-border security cooperation along India's Northeast and Myanmar's role as a gateway to the realisation of the goals under India's Act East Policy. Rapid completion of ongoing Indian infrastructural projects in Myanmar would be instrumental in sharing strong relations between the two countries ensuring cooperation in the realms of security, economy and culture. India needs to give sincere attention to the Rohingya crisis in Myanmar as our ongoing projects are placed in this area as well. This may also hamper India's Northeast and internal security, so India needs to safeguard its interest to be an influential power in the region.

Myanmar faced the period of sanctions and internal crisis and due to these sanctions and unrest in the country, it could not accelerate the multi-dimensional development of Myanmar in the region even when Myanmar has the potential. After uplifting all the sanctions from state and by forming a new democratic government, a state should invite all world powers to her land to invest via FDI and trade. Myanmar also considers the fact of over-dependence on China. Myanmar's engagement with the US, EU ASEAN, India and Japan may help in decreasing the influence of China in Myanmar, East Asia and Southeast Asia region.

Support has been shown by the leaders of Myanmar to China's One Belt One Road (OBOR) initiative which intends to boost connectivity and cooperation between China and the rest of Eurasia. It includes the land-based "Silk Road Economic Belt" (SREB) and oceanic "Maritime Silk Road" (MSR). India should involve itself in OBOR initiatives by safeguarding its national interests in this project because the what is worrisome for India in this project is the China-Pakistan Economic Corridor (CPEC) which proposes to connect China's Northwestern Xinjiang region and Gwadar in Southwestern Pakistan. The CPEC also passes through Pakistan-occupied Kashmir thereby intruding on India's territory and causing serious concern for India.

Notes

1. Speech at the Second "China-Myanmar Pauk-Phaw Friendship Day," by H. E. Mr. Hong Liang, Ambassador of the People's Republic of China to the Republic of the Union of Myanmar on 12/06/2017. Available at http://mm.china-embassy.org/eng/xwdt/t1469543.htm (Accessed on March 8, 2018).
2. Sampa Kundu (2017), "China-Myanmar Relations: New Challenges Unfolding," *Institute of Chinese Studies*, Delhi. Available at http://www.icsin.org/uploads/2017/04/21/ 4edad1cdb533433cc652f084cf85fbd8.pdf (Accessed on September 19, 2018).
3. Security Council fails to adopt draft resolution on Myanmar, owing to Negative votes by China, Russian Federation, Security Council, United Nations, January 12, 2007. Available at https://www.un.org/ press/en/2007/sc8939.doc.htm (Accessed on September 15, 2018).
4. Xinhua News, "China, Myanmar to enhance military ties," English.news.cn, November 28, 2011. Available at http://news.xinhuanet.com/english2010/china/2011-11/28/c_131275049.htm (Accessed on March 10, 2018).
5. Niklas Swanstrom (2012), "Sino-Myanmar Relations: Security and Beyond," *Institute for Security and Development Policy*, Asia Paper. Available at http://isdp.eu/content/uploads/images/stories/ isdp-main-pdf/2012_swanstrom_sino-myanmar-relations.pdf (Accessed on July 4, 2018).
6. Ian Storey (2010), "China's Charm Offensive loses momentum in Southeast Asia (Part-II)," The Jamestown Foundation, *The China Brief*, Vol.10 (9). Available at https://jamestown.org/program/chinas-charm-offensive-loses-momentum-in-southeast-asia-part-ii (Accessed on August 11, 2018).
7. Directorate of Investment and Company Administration, The Republic of the Union of Myanmar, Foreign Direct Investment Data August 201. Available at www.dica.gov.mm/sites/dica.gov.mm/files/document-files/bycountrycomplete.pdf (Accessed on September 6, 2018).
8. Niluksi Koswanage (2011), "Analysis: No Stopping Big Hydro Project, Despite Lao Veto," *Reuters*. Available at http://www.reuters.com/article/us-dams/analysis-no-stopping-big-hydro-projects-despite-laoeto-idUSTRE7BD0GN20111214 (Accessed on August 12, 2017).
9. Balazs Szalontai (2014), "Modern China-Myanmar Relations: Dilemmas of Mutual Dependence," *Journal of Cold War Studies*, Vol. 16(4), pp. 245-246.
10. Dai Yonghong (2014), "Rivalry and Cooperation: A New Great Game in Myanmar," *Institute for Security and Development Policy*, Asia Paper. Available at https://docplayer.net/65906094-Rivalry-and-cooperation-a-new-great-game-in-myanmar-dai-yonghong.html (Accessed on September 9, 2017).
11. The *BCIM Economic Corridor* is an initiative that seeks to promote sub-regional cooperation within the BCIM countries. The multi modal corridor will be the first "express way" between India and China through Myanmar and Bangladesh.

12. Wayne Bert (2004), "Myanmar, China and USA," *Pacific Affairs*, Vol. 77 (2) p. 263.
13. Niklas Swanstrom (2012), "China-Myanmar Relations: Security and Beyond," *Asian Paper of Stockholm, Institute for Security and Development Policy*, p. 15.
14. Loreen Tsin (2014), "China and Myanmar: Bejing's Conflicting Role in the Kachin Peace Process," China Monitor, *Mercator Institute for China Studies*, No. 9, p. 2.
15. Chen Lijun (2012), "SWOT Framework Analysis on Current India-Myanmar Relations," *South Asian Studies*, No. 4, p. 14.
16. Asia Sentimental, "Unrest in Kachin: China's Mixed Blessing," March 6, 2013. Available at https://www.asiasentinel.com/politics/unrest-in-kachin-chinas-mixed-blessing/ (Accessed on March 14, 2018).
17. Aswini Sriniwas (2014), "Sino-Myanmar Oil and Gas Pipeline and their Implication for India," *Global Journal of Finance and Management*, Vol. 6(9), pp. 951-956.
18. Ashwini Sriniwas (2014), "China-Myanmar Oil and Gas Pipelines and Its Implication for India," *Global Journal of Finance and Management*, Vol. 6(9), p. 952.
19. Daljit Singh and Chin Kin Wah (2003), *Southeast Asian Affairs 2003,* ISEAS Publishing, Singapore, p. 148.
20. Tin Maung, Maung Than. "Myanmar and China: A Special Relationship?" *Southeast Asian Affairs*. Available at https://muse.jhu.edu/article/400084/summary (Accessed on October 18, 2018).
21. Robert H Taylor (1987), "The State in Myanmar," University of Hawai'i Press, Hawaii, p. 13.
22. Tin Maung, Maung Than, "Myanmar and China: A Special Relationship?," *Southeast Asian Affairs*. Available at https://muse.jhu.edu/article/400084/summary (Accessed on October 18, 2018).
23. See Annexure H.
24. Gilles Bouquerat (2001), "India's confrontation with Chinese interests in Myanmar," in Amitabh Mattoo and Fredric Grare, (eds.), *India and ASEAN: The Politics of India's Look (Act) East Policy*, Manohar Publishers & Distributors, New Delhi, p. 92.
25. Bertil Linter (1992), "Myanmar and Its Neighbours," in Surjeet Maan Singh (ed.), *Indian and Chinese Foreign Policies in Comparative Perspective*, Radiant Publishers, New Delhi, p. 135.
26. Ibid., p. 137.
27. Marie Lall (2008), "India-Myanmar Relations- GeoPolitics and Energy in Light of the New Balance of Power in Asia," *Institute of South Asian Studies*, SAS Working Paper 29 (2), p. 25.
28. Feng Yengqui (2018), "Myanmar takes new measures to promote Foreign Investment", *Asia and Pacific Edition,* 01 July. Available at http://www.xinhuanet.com/english/2018-07/01/ c_137293050.htm (Accessed on October 22, 2018).
29. Satish Kumar (2014), *India's National Security: Annual Review 2013*, Routledge Publisher, New Delhi, p. 352.
30. Myanmar's Military Active strength of 2018 data, Global Fire Power. Available at https://www.globalfirepower.com/country-military-strength-detail.asp?country_id=myanmar#manpower (Accessed on October 19, 2018).
31. Tenzing Chopel Sherpa (2016), "Importance of Myanmar in China's Strategic Interests: A case study of Sino-Myanmar Gas and Oil Pipeline," M.Phil Dissertation, International Relations, Sikkim University, Gangtok, p. 54.

32. Ken Davies (2013), "China Investment Policy: An Update," OECD Working Paper on International Investment 2013/01. Available at https://www.oecd.org/china/WP-2013_1.pdf (Accessed on June 17, 2017).
33. Hnin Yi (2013), "Myanmar's Policy towards rising China since 1989," Ritsumelkan Center for Asia Pacific Studies, Working Paper Series "Dojo." Available at http://www.apu.ac.jp/rcaps/uploads/fckeditor/publications/workingPapers/RPD-13002.pdf (Accessed on June 11, 2017).
34. Alexander Dukalskis (2017), "Myanmar's Double Transition: Political Liberalization and the Peace Process," *Asian Survey*, Vol. 57 (4), pp. 716-17.
35. Yun Sun (2013), "Chinese Investment in Myanmar: What lies Ahead?," *Stimson Centre*, Issue Brief No. 3, p. 6.
36. Yun Sun (2012), "China's strategic misjudgement on Myanmar," *Current Southeast Asian Affair,* Vol. 31 (1), p. 82.
37. Divya Dwivedi (2018), "China-Myanmar Relations trends and its Implication for India," *International Journal of Advance Research and Development,* Vol. 3(1), p. 51.
38. Ibid., p. 53.
39. *Asia Times* (2015), "China's Relations with Myanmar: Does an NLD Government mark an new Era," December 8. Available at http://www.atimes.com/article/chinas-relations-with-myanmar- does-an-nld-government-mark-a-new-era/ (Accessed on November 15, 2018).
40. Ibid.
41. P T Lachungpa (2015), "Problems in Kachin and Shan States of Myanmar and its impact on China", M.Phil Dissertation, Department of International Relations, Sikkim University, Gangtok, p. 82.
42. Poon Shee Kim (2002), "The Political Economy of China-Myanmar Relations: Strategic and Economic Dimensions," *Ritsumeikan Annual Review of International Studies*, Vol.1 p. 42.
43. H Shivananda, (2002), "Asia-Pacific Defence report," *Asia-Pacific Defence Publication*, Vol. 28, p. 4.
44. Charles Clover (2016), "China Arms Export continue to Surge," *Financial Time.* Available at https://www.ft.com/content/8fb5af60-d921-11e5-98fd-06d75973fe09 (Accessed on May 21, 2018).
45. Sanjay Baru (2017), "Comparing the Economies of China and its impact on India's Strategic and Security Studies," *The United Service Institution of India*, Journal No. 607. Available at http://usiofindia.org/Article/?pub=Journal&pubno=607&ano=2927 (Accessed on December 25, 2017).
46. Teshu Singh (2013), "China and Myanmar: The Great game of Gas Pipe line," *Institute of Peach and Conflict Studies*, Article No. 4102. Available at http://www.ipcs.org/article/india/ china-and-myanmar-the-great-game-of-the-gas-pipeline-4102.html (Accessed on October 13, 2018).
47. Lexin Geng (2006), "China-Myanmar Relations: Analysis and Prospects," *The Cultural Mandala*, Vol.7 No.2. Available at http://www.international-relations.com/CM7-2WB/China-Myanmar.htm (Accessed on July 12, 2018).
48. Ibid.
49. Maung Aung Myoe (2007), "China-Myanmar Economic Relations since 1988," *Asian Research Institute,* Working Paper No.86, p. 35.
50. Ibid., p. 36.

51. Michael O'Kane (2014), *Doing Business in Myanmar*, Andalus Publication, New York, p. 78.
52. Lexin Geng (2006), "China-Myanmar Relations: Analysis and Prospects," *The Cultural Mandala*, Vol. 7, No. 2. Available at http://www.international-relations.com/CM7-2WB/China-Myanmar.htm (Accessed on July 12, 2018).
53. Teshu Singh (2013), "China and Myanmar: The Great game of the Gas Pipeline," *Institute of Peace and Conflict Studies*, Working paper 4102. Available at *http://www.ipcs.org/ comm_select.php? articleNo=4102* (Accessed on October 13, 2018).
54. Ibid.
55. Christopher Dunn (2016), "Chinese Investment in Myanmar: A Scoping Study," *Global Environmental Institute,* p.7. Available at https://myanmarbiodiversity.org/portfolio-items/chinese-investments-in-myanmar-a-scoping-study/ (Accessed on November 15, 2018).
56. Embassy of India, Yangoon, Myanmar, "Bilateral and Economic Relations." Available at http://www.indiaembassyyangon.net/index.php?option=com_content&view=article&id=60&Itemid=189&lang=en (Accessed on March 15, 2018).
57. Jurgen Haacke (2006), *Myanmar's Foreign Policy: Domestic Influences and International Implications*, Routledge Publications, New York, p. 113.
58. Ibid., p. 138.
59. Rajiv Bhatia (2016), *India-Myanmar Relation: Changing Contours*, Routledge Publication, New York, p. 55.
60. Jurgen Haacke (2006), *Myanmar's Foreign Policy : Domestic Influences and International Implications*, Routledge Publications, New York, p. 156.
61. Ibid., p. 158.
62. Preet Malik (2016), *My Myanmar Years*, Sage Publications, New Delhi, p. 95.
63. Rajiv Bhatia (2016), *India-Myanmar Relation: Changing Contours*, Routledge Publication, New York, p. 74.
64. Wai Moe (2008), "China Signs Burmese Gas Deal for 30 years Supply," *The Irrawaddy*, December 26. Available at http://www2.irrawaddy.com/article.php?art_id=14849 (Accessed on May 12, 2017).
65. B R Deepak (2016), *India and China: Foreign Policy Approaches and Responses*, Vij Books Publication, New Delhi, p. 202.
66. Ibid., p. 210.
67. Ibid., p. 211.
68. Ibid., p. 212.
69. Ibid., p. 213.
70. S.P. Sinha (2008), *Lost opportunities: 50 years of insurgency in the North-east and India's response*, Lancer Publication, New Delhi, p. 156.
71. Ibid., p. 158.
72. Anton Harder (2016), "When Nehru Refused American bait on a Permanent seat for India at the UN," The Wire. Available at https://thewire.in/diplomacy/when-nehru-refused-american-bait-on-a-permanent-seat-for-india-at-the-un (Accessed on October 13, 2017).
73. T.V. Paul (2005), *The India-Pakistan Conflict: An Enduring Rivalry*, Cambridge University Press, UK, p. 82.
74. James Heitzman and Robert L Worden (1995), "India: A Country Study," Federal Research Division, Library of Congress. Available at https://www.loc.gov/resource/

frdcstdy.indiacountrystud00heit/?sp=5&r=-0.675,0.303,2.35,0.889,0 (Accessed on October 25, 2017).

75. The NPT and the Aftermath of India's Nuclear Test-May 1974, Association for Diplomatic Studies and Training. Available at https://adst.org/2015/05/the-npt-and-the-aftermath-of-indias-nuclear-test-may-1974/ (Accessed on November 1, 2017).
76. Sudha Ramachandran (2016),"The Trouble with India's Project in Myanmar," *The Diplomat*. Available at http://thediplomat.com/2016/09/the-trouble-with-indias-projects-in-myanmar/ (Accessed on May 23, 2018).
77. India-China Bilateral Relations, Ministry of External Affairs, India. Available at https://www.mea.gov.in/Portal/ForeignRelation/China_October_2017.pdf (Accessed on October 15, 2018).
78. R S Kalha (2016), "$56 Billion and Growing, It's time India address the Trade Deficit with China," The Wire, December 12. Available at https://thewire.in/external-affairs/indias-china-trade-deficit (Accessed on October 16, 2018).
79. Joint Statement between India and China during Prime Minister's visit to China, Ministry of External Affairs, May 15, 2015. Available at https://www.mea.gov.in/bilateral-documents.htm?dtl/25240/Joint_Statement_between_the_India_and_China_during_Prime_Ministers_visit_toChina (Accessed on February 5, 2018).
80. Ibid.
81. Neeta Lal (2016), "India and China, a New era of Strategic Partner," Inter Press Agency, September 8. Available at http://www.ipsnews.net/2016/09/india-and-china-a-new-era-of -strategic-partners/ (Accessed on August 17, 2018).
82. Andrei Volodin (2011), "America's Unipolar World and the Counter vailing Powers of the Eurasian SCO Military Alliance," *Centre for Research on Globalisation*. Available at https://www.globalresearch.ca/america-s-unipolar-world-and-the-countervailing-powers-of-the-eurasian-sco-military-alliance/25176 (Accessed on September 14, 2018).
83. India-China Border Dispute, The Global Security. Available at https://www.globalsecurity.org/military/world/war/india-china_conflicts.htm (Accessed on March 18, 2018).
84. Brahma Chellaney (2012), "A War China won only to lose," *LiveMint*, October 17. Available at https://www.livemint.com/Opinion/fINQNMSls85qPWbI0WjSDL/A-war-China-won-only-to-lose.html (Accessed on March 16, 2018).
85. The Great India-China Game, The Rediff, June 23, 2003. Available at http://www.rediff.com/news/ 2003/jun/20spec.htm (Accessed on May 9, 2018).
86. John W Garver (2006), "China's Decision for War with India in 1962" in A I Johnston and Robert S Ross Edited book, "New Directions in the study of China's Foreign Policy," Stanford University Press, California, p. 69.
87. Peter Navarro (2015), "How China and India May come to Blows," *The Globalist*, November 4. Available at https://www.theglobalist.com/china-india-south-asia-war-politics/ (Accessed on June 27, 2018).
88. Sandeep Dikshit (2013), "China ends stand off, pulls out troops from Daulat Beg Oldi Sector," *The Hindu*, May 5. Available at https://www.thehindu.com/news/national/china-ends-standoff-pulls-out-troops-from-daulat-beg-oldi-sector/article4686606.ece (Accessed on August 23, 2018).

89. "India and China agree over Tibet", BBC News, June 24, 2003 Available at http://news.bbc.co.uk/2/hi/south_ asia/3015840.stm (Accessed on August 21, 2018).
90. Senge H Sering (2013), "China's Interests in Shaksgam Valley," Indian Defence Review, October 11. Available at http://www.indiandefencereview.com/news/chinas-interests-in-shaksgam-valley/ (Accessed on October 24, 2018).
91. "India-China Border Dispute", *The Global Security*. Available at https://www.globalsecurity.org/military/ world/war/india-china_conflicts.htm (Accessed on June 18, 2018).
92. Sunil Khatri (2017), "Events leading to Sino-Indian Conflict of 1962," IDSA Monograph Series 58. Available at https://idsa.in/system/files/monograph/monograph58.pdf (Accessed on October 19, 2018).
93. Hong Yuan (2012), "China Won, but never wanted, Sino-Indian War," *Global Times*, June 28. Available at http://www.globaltimes.cn/content/717710.shtml (Accessed on September 17, 2018).
94. Taurgo (2015), "Second Sino-Indian War of 1967: Decisive Victory for India and Defeat of China," Active Defence, April 21. Available at http://activedefence.blogspot.com/2015/04/ second-sino-indian-war-of-1967-decisive.html (Accessed on August 15, 2018).
95. Darshil Patel (2016), "India decisively won the 1967 Indo-China war: killed 340 Chinese Soldier," Indian Defence News, October 20. Available at http://defencenews.in/article/India-decisively-won-the-1967-Indo-China-War--Killed-340-Chinese-Soldiers-18840 (Accessed on July 2, 2018).
96. 16 October, 1964 - First Chinese Nuclear Test, CTBTO Preparatory Commission. Available at https://www.ctbto.org/specials/testing-times/16-october-1964-first-chinese-nuclear-test (Accessed on September 8, 2018)
97. Daryl Kimball (2012), "The Nuclear Non-Proliferation Treaty at a Glance," Arms Control Association. Available at https://www.armscontrol.org/factsheets/nptfact (Accessed on May 5, 2018).
98. First Nuclear Test at Pokhran in 1974, Federation of American Scientists, July 4, 2000. Available at https://fas.org/nuke/guide/india/nuke/first-pix.htm (Accessed on August, 13, 2018).
99. Robert Farley (2015), "India's mighty Nuclear Weapons programme: Aimed at China and Pakistan?," *The National Interest*, January 3. Available at https://nationalinterest.org/feature/indias-mighty-nuclear-weapons-program-aimed-china-pakistan-11956 (Accessed on August 12, 2018).
100. Alex Kingsbury (2009), "Why China helped Countries like Pakistan and North Korea build Nuclear Weapons," US News, January 2. Available at https://www.usnews.com/news/world/articles/2009/01/02/why-china-helped-countries-like-pakistan-north-korea-build-nuclear-bombs (Accessed on August 12, 2018).
101. Kelsey Davenport(2017), "Nuclear Weapons: Who Has What at a Glance," Arms Control Association. Available https://www.armscontrol.org/factsheets/Nuclearweaponswhohaswhat (Accessed on August 28, 2018).
102. Ashok Kumar (2017), "Chinese Angle in India-Myanmar Relations," *IOSR Journal of Humanities and Social Sciences*, Vol. 22 (8), pp. 5-9.
103. "Myanmar implements new special economic zone to boost trade china," Asia Briefing, Business Intelligence from Dezan Shira & Associates, August 26, 2014.

Available at http://www.asiabriefing.com/news/2014/08/myanmar-implements-new-special-economic-zone-boost-trade-china/ (Accessed on August 19, 2016).

104. R Hariharan (2013), "Sustaining change in Myanmar," *South Asia Analysis Group*, paper 5439. Available at http://www.southasiaanalysis.org/node/1218 (Accessed on July 18, 2018).
105. Zhiquen Zhu (2010), *China's New Diplomacy: Rational, Strategies and Significance*, Ashgate Publishing Ltd., United Kingdom, p. 92.
106. "Kaladan Multi Modal Transit Transport Project," *Ministry of Development of North Eastern Region*, GOI. Available at http://mdoner.gov.in/index3.asp?ssid=232 (Accessed on September 3, 2018).
107. Andrew Selth."Myanmar, China and the Myth of Military Bases," *Asian Security*, Vol. 3, No. 3, p. 238.

5
Significance of India's Look (Act) East Policy with Special Reference to BIMSTEC

Introduction

International politics was subsequently transformed by the world-shaking events in the early 1990s which changed the vision of each nation in the 20th century. The two military blocs were brought to an end of the bipolar world. It was the period when the cold war ended which was the confrontation of two military and economic-political impressions. It also brought an end to the stability of the world based on mutual deterrence. The high-risk and high-stability situation has been replaced by a low-risk and low-stability situation.[1] The cold war that ended also brought the Soviet Union reorientation of friendly states, especially the third world countries and entered in market economies. These global changes have precipitated two consequences in the prevailing international relations. First, there is a growing interdependence between countries, and second, economic and trade issues are gaining vital precedence over the political and military ones.[2] International politics have revolved around the economic aspects especially due to shifting in a geopolitical and geo-strategic vision to geo-economic vision. The world quickly turned into economic blocs from an ideological bloc.

In 1990, the evolution of India's Look (Act) East Policy was derived from the changed discourse of the international system. This policy was initiated in 1991 and has its origin at the end of the Cold War, followed by the Soviet Union disintegration. A fundamental change in the international system was noticed with the end of the cold war that led to the birth of regional and sub-regional economic organisations. The economy has become a dynamic variable in international politics. Eventually, externalities and issues of transnational aspects have become prominent in most of the areas. This phase witnessed the transformation in values and vision in the specific regions. Perception of the policy makers was changed, and it brought success stories of economies in East Asia which pushed India strategically and economically to focus its attention towards the fast-growing economies of Southeast Asia and East Asia. It was the emerging trend of regional integration in Asia that the indispensableness in the equation of India's Northeast, Myanmar with Bay of Bengal Initiative for Multi-Sectoral Technical and Economic Cooperation (BIMSTEC) came up as the decisive factor. Emerging India's Northeast-BIMSTEC-Myanmar equation is an outcome of these new developments in international systems.

Two supplementary prongs of India's 'Look (Act) East Policy' are Bay of Bengal Initiative for Multi-Sectoral Technical and Economic Cooperation (BIMSTEC) and the Mekong-Ganga Co-operation (MGC).[3] BIMSTEC member countries are from around the Bay of Bengal—Bangladesh, Bhutan, India, Nepal, Thailand and Myanmar. Unlike SAARC, BIMSTEC is a geographically rational group with an improved equilibrium of power since India's Northeast region relies on Myanmar and Bangladesh. Simultaneously, India received another forum and exposure to dealing its relation with Bangladesh in BIMSTEC. India gets an upper edge in developing its relations with Myanmar which is strategically important to India and countering China's presence in every aspect in Myanmar. Therefore, BIMSTEC becomes a desirable mechanism for bridging South Asian nations with Eastern Northeast neighbours.

On the other track, Mekong-Ganga Co-operation (MGC) is a sub-regional organisation with tremendous potential for co-operation in the area of tourism, culture, education and transport communication. India and ASEAN are connected due to this organisation especially with Thailand, Laos, Myanmar, Cambodia and Vietnam. The MGC has become a vital framework where India can make its relations stronger with ASEAN as India shares geographical and cultural proximity with these nations. From a strategic standpoint, a number of realist political commentators pointed out that the end of the Cold War and the beginning of the Gulf War (1990-91) created unprecedented opportunities for India.[4]

India's Internal and Regional Environment during 1990-91

In the international system, no nation can survive in isolation internally as well as externally. The impact of outer situations on foreign policy cannot be washed away as both have rapid response mechanism, external opportunities and challenges and foreign policy are complementary to each other. Consequently, variation in the state of affairs requires alteration in the behaviour of nations. Hence, all states were affected by the developments from 1989 to 1991. Even India was not untouched by this wave and had a significant impact on its foreign policy as well as at the national level.

There was a turbulent phase at the beginning of the 1990s. India witnessed a shaky national environment featured by growing political instability, insurgency and terrorism, financial crisis and economic doldrums. The trembling national environment was compounded by the unsupportable regional atmosphere. Although insurgency in Punjab declined by the end of 1992, there was an increase in a number of violent incidents perpetrated by insurgents in Jammu and Kashmir and Northeast India.[5] The militant outfits in Jammu and Kashmir became violent and had acquired radical religious ideology in order to legitimise their actions. Most of these militants managed to get logistic support from Pakistan in terms of training, sophisticated arms and ammunition and even finance which in a way gave them some clout to demonstrate their power.[6] In the early 1990s Pakistan became more strident against India and encouraged and provided aid to militants in Jammu and Kashmir, make J&K topic internationalise. The resurgence of Sindhi and Baluchi movements in Pakistan, Nepalis in Bhutan, Terai versus hill people in Nepal, Chakmas in Bangladesh, Tamils in Sri Lanka and various tribal communities in Northeast India are all representing sub-nationalist or ethnic-centric tendencies threatening the existing state structure.[7] The trouble was combined by the appearance of India's Northeast insurgent's safe haven in Sagaing division of Myanmar; the undercover smuggler's industry of Cambodia as a vital base of ammunition and arms and the smugglers market drugs in the Golden Triangle Laos, Myanmar, Thailand and Cambodia. India's national security was endangered by these activities which could come from the east, so cooperation with these countries was required in dealing with such threats.

Despite reforms during the Rajiv Gandhi led Congress government in the mid-1980s and throughout the latter part of the decade, the percentage of trade to Gross National Product had fallen from 12.4 per cent in 1984-85 to 11 per cent in1988-89.[8] There was a minimal percentage of trade involved in the economy and had a little hope for adjusting any jump in the cost of oil within overall trade balance. The small rise in the price of oil, due to the 1990-91 Gulf Crisis, was translated into a 21.9 per cent increase in the import bill in rupee term.[9]

The degree of the rising problem is discernible from the reality in 1965. India's energy importation imposed only about 8 per cent of its commodity exports, whereas energy importation imposed around 25 percent of the worth of exports in 1990.

In 1990, the Indian economy was stricken by the Gulf crisis as its dependency was huge on the West Asian nations for trade and oil. During this time, political turmoil and economic recession were knocking India's door. In the Gulf Crisis, India lost remittances of US$ 205 million from Indians employed in Iraq and Kuwait. It lost an amount of US$ 500 million owing it from Iraq at the start of the crisis and lost about US$ 112 million in a trade with Iraq and Kuwait.[10] In that same period, India suffered severely from trade with European nations with the collapse of the communist system. Eventually, in mid-1990, India was pushed to take International Monetary Fund assistance as foreign exchange reserves have dropped hardly to revive two weak imports. An agreement was reached by the then Indian government with the IMF in January 1991 on loan for US$ 1.8 billion partly out of the compensatory financing Facility (to offset increased oil imports) and partly as a first credit tranche standby.[11]

The political turmoil was on its heights as three successive governments were replaced by each other within two years. The developing economic crisis at the end of the 1980s coincided with the electoral cycle in 1989 in which Indian electorate chose to express its dissatisfaction by opting for political weakness and instability at the centre by electing a parliament with no party in the majority.[12]

BJP pulled out its support from National Front government which resulted in the crash of the National Front government by the end of 1990. This crash resulted in a split in the Janata Dal which was the major party of the national front government. It was the moment when Chandrasekhar left the Janata Dal and created a party named the Samajwadi Janata Party. After the fall of the National Front government led by P. Singh, a minority government with Chandrashekhar as Prime Minister, was installed with the support of the Congress party with 195 although his party had only 58 members out of 473 in the Lok Sabha.[13] They had a small number in parliament that could not survive, but they did because the government could not bear another election. Chandrashekhar government's biggest hurdle was non-existence of financial reserves which led to an inability to form any firm economic policy even a budget. In June 1991, the Congress withdrew their support from Chandrasekhar government and a fresh election was ignited. Congress appeared a single largest party with 232 seats. Subsequently, a Congress supported by some regional parties made the government led by PV Narasimha Rao as Prime Minister in June 1991.

Prime Minister PV Narasimha Rao encountered a number of challenges ahead of his government; topmost priority was to bring back the derailed economy on track, maintaining political stability in the country, exploring new opportunities and challenges which emerged with the arrival of globalisation and the new world order concept. During that time, the non-productive expenditure was enormously increased. Defence expenditure rose from 15.9 per cent of central government spending in 1980-81 to 16.9 per cent in 1987-88 to nearly 19 per cent in 1990-91. Subsidies grew from 8.5 per cent in 1980-81 to 11.4 per cent in 1989-90.[14] The new government main focus was on restructuring the economic activity and boost international trade and market. India faced a tough balance of payment crisis, a sudden decrease of competitiveness of Indian products in the international market and acknowledging the significance of external capital in a nation's financial development. In June 1991, economic liberalisation system was initiated with a vision to attract foreign investments, both direct and portfolio and then to encourage exports. The primary motive of such a reform programme was to connect India's economy with the world economy. Sandy Gordon summarises a few of the steps taken by the government to revive the economy which was mentioned in the budgets of 1991-92 and they are as follows:

- Falling value of the rupee by about 30 per cent against the US dollar, aiming full convertibility.
- Increasing the ceiling of external ownership to 51 per cent and giving high at few instances, with partly repatriation of wealth at the market price on a 40:60 basis (40 per cent at the government price).
- Removal of restrictive controls on the imports of most items and lowering of the tariff. The import duty on capital goods was further reduced to 35 per cent from 55 per cent, with a special 25 per cent rate on capital goods destined for priority sectors. The import-weighted tariff was to be reduced to 25 per cent in two to three years.[15]
- Abolition of the internal licensing system in all but 18 industries.
- Preparation for sale in principle of up to 49 per cent of the government's share in state enterprises.
- In 1993, the floating of the rupee on trade account in 1993.
- Reduction of the excise duty.
- Reform of the financial sector.
- A substantial reduction in the rate of company taxation in 1994.[16]

The smartest move of the 1991 economic policy was the implementation of globalisation, liberalisation and privatisation. The primary focus of these reforms was to attract Foreign Direct Investment and foreign trade by bringing back the derailed economy on track. Consequently, market economy replaced with a socialistic society which was backed by Congress for a long time being the means to develop India's public sector domestically and insulating global market forces from India. These reforms were initiated in 1991, thus constitute a turning point in the history of the Indian economy.

Obligations of India to Look East

In the early 1990s, the radical change political and economic development, appeared in the relations among countries resulted in the appearance of the globalisation era. Globalisation integrated the economies and societies of the developed and developing countries as well as opened numerous opportunities and challenges. This globalisation of world economies greatly intensified international competition and had, at the same time, given rise to a new wave of regionalism.[17] Thus, Regionalism has proved an effective method to assist economic and commercial objectives. During this process, new organisations were formed to acclimatise with the changing world in an economic and political context. Political commitment, economic complimentary, geographical proximity, infrastructure development and policy coordination are the vital components which are ingredients in the formation of such groups. Therefore, various states of the world combined themselves into regions to take a fresh impetus to a vast collection of cooperative ventures backed by regionalism. In this evolving context, India needs to analyse the international order to adjust its political and economic policies to draw benefit line for itself. There were three vital objectives of India's foreign policy.

- Preserving India's territorial integrity.
- Creating a stable atmosphere of peace for ensuring its geopolitical security.

- Stability in the region and to build a framework for the well-being of the people by encouraging a healthy external economic environment.[18]

India and it's neighbouring countries in the South Asian region have made several efforts for regional cooperation. The South Asian Association for regional cooperation (SAARC) was established on December 8, 1985, to speed up the process of social and economic development among the member states. There have been several endeavours to improve trade in the region through South Asia Preferential Trade Agreement (SAPTA) and Free Trade Agreement (SAFTA) despite such efforts trade within the countries continues to be abysmally low.[19] Till date, Pakistan has not ratified the Free Trade Agreement (FTA). Economic relations and cooperative ties were constrained in SAARC, if not stopped by Pakistan-India conflict. SAPTA and SAFTA negotiations pace were disappointing which forced India to see beyond the line of South Asia regional economic cooperation.

The collapse of the Soviet Union brought severe repercussions for India. India was one of the largest receivers of supplies of arms, petroleum and sometimes economic aid from the former Soviet Union. The Soviet Union had been a reliable partner for India and provided a huge market of Indian consumer goods. The collapse of the Soviet system deprived India not only of a valuable partner, where the Rupee Trade Area accounted for about one-fourth of its exports and always supported India diplomatically through United Nations votes, but also of an important model of centralised planning.[20] One of the major concerns for New Delhi was that it could no longer rely on Soviet diplomatic support at the Security Council of the United Nations. Thus, India was exposed to international pressures to vital interests like disarmament, non-proliferation and the Kashmir issue.[21] India faced a significant loss in strategic, economic and political terms.

The oil economy in Gulf region was temporarily dislocated followed by the crisis in Kuwait brought to India as the significance of diversifying its options of energy supply to reduce dependency on the traditional suppliers in erstwhile Soviet Union and Gulf. Australia, Brunei, Indonesia and Myanmar were the available alternative sources of energy in the Asia-Pacific. Thus, it was natural for Indian decision-makers to look for a new international role and to turn to the most economically dynamic region of the world: Southeast Asia.[22]

India is facing three main issues in the Southeast Asian region. First, stabilising the Northeast, its clandestine flows and develop foreign connections; taking advantage of the proximity of Southeast Asian nations especially Myanmar, to step onto the Asian diplomatic and economic scene; and finally measuring the impact of China's influence on the Myanmar regime and its consequences for the country's interests.[23] China's increasing economic and military influence in Myanmar and its assertive policy in the Asia-Pacific region regenerated India's concern regarding the outcomes of powerful and antecedent China and its bearing on India's security. India requires an overall mechanism which must have a military, economic and diplomatic tool to handle such strategic geopolitical and sensitive issues.

During the cold war years, India's foreign policies were driven by political factors and decided to stay at a distance from the two opposing blocs of ideology by engaging itself in the Non-Alignment Movement (NAM). Economic dimensions of foreign relations were not given much importance to the Ministry of External Affairs.[24] India's central tenet of foreign policy became obsolete by the end of the cold war. India was one of its co-founder influential members; one can assume the position of another leader among developing countries who were enjoying some reputation at the international level in the cold war period. The concept of NAM was undermined by the end of the cold war, US victory and its policies; free-market economic system and political world view raised a new challenge for India. Although military power was still one of the deciding factors in the international equation later on gradually, economic capability started to exert its influence over it which changed the balance of power as it was shifting from military to the economic sphere. Many countries in the developed and developing world were convinced with the shift and implemented the same in their foreign policy by limiting defence orientation to enhance economic orientation. Thus, the

Nehruvian model of foreign policy autonomy vis-a-vis imperialism and capitalism have come under severe strain and there are intense pressures from several influential quarters in India and abroad to link it with the Western economy.[25]

The economy has become a vital factor in international relations with the end of cold war and trends in free-market reforms. The international status of a country depends much on its wealth. Therefore by the end of 1991 Prime Minister, Narasimha Rao issued a note asking foreign office and its diplomatic posts abroad to focus more on the economic aspects of India's external relations.[26] Therefore, India adopted economic diplomacy in its foreign policy.

India's Look (Act) East Policy

There was a strategic shift in India's vision worldly. It was an external economic policy which would place India in a better position in the global economy and this move named India's Look (Act) East Policy which was followed by other Prime Ministers of India and renamed Act East Policy in 2014 by the present Prime Minister Narendra Modi. India explored the opportunity to uplift its relations with the major powers after coming milestones in the international system and post-cold war in the absence of political rival blocs and globalisation. During this time, India initiated its Look (Act) East Policy which was corroborated by economic liberalisation reforms.

Southeast Asian countries appreciated India's efforts towards them. Till the early 1990s due to India's compulsion towards Pakistan and its preoccupations by China. India could not be explored out of the box opportunities. It was in 1990 when India realised the benefit of growth in the market of Southeast Asian nations especially Indonesia, Malaysia and Singapore. India also realised the fact that China has already established itself profoundly in most Southeast Asian countries over the period. Though some analysts pointed out that by launching this policy India was trying to balance China's influence in this region. India had often reiterated that it was not competing with China in any manner.[27] Despite that, the Indian policy makers realised the fact that India had to go beyond the confines of SAARC if it had to reap the benefits out of the economic potential of the South East Asian region and establish itself as a regional power.[28]

India's Look (Act) East Policy, which was initiated in 1991, pronounced a strategic change in India's visual aspect of the world. It was formulated and enacted during the PV Narasimha Rao government and strictly pursued by the consecutive governments of Sri Atal Bihari Vajpayee and Dr Manmohan Singh. It has been realised that Look (Act) East Policy is an attempt to forge closer and deeper economic integration with its eastern Northeast neighbours as a part of the new *realpolitik* in evidence to India's foreign policy, and the engagement with Association of South East Asian Nations (ASEAN) is a part of the recognition on the part of India's elite of the strategic and economic importance of the region to the country's national interests.[29]

It is preferable to recall the critical instances that existed when the Look (Act) East Policy was launched.

- First, the Soviet Union disintegration ended the cold war.
- Second, new relationships emerged with the changing global scenario.
- Third, the US emerged as a sole global superpower.
- Fourth, China appeared important player in East Asia.

At this time the ASEAN countries have dramatically transformed their economies by opening up to each other and came up with the strategy of engaging China by forging increasingly close economic ties with it and encouraging it to become involved in an increasing web of regional institutional linkages.[30] There is no doubt that India and ASEAN tried to engage with each other but could not get through. Meanwhile, India was also facing economic and financial crisis. These aspects mentioned above insisted India to rethink about its economic reforms in 1991. Thus, India launched its reforms process by liberalising, deregulating and restructuring its economy.

On the other side, China's influence over Southeast Asia has become a major concern for India. China has been providing defence support to the Northeastern neighbours of India including the significant nuclear programme assistance to Pakistan. This is a serious destabilising factor for India. A country in control of the Indo-China region would threaten India's security, as many as Southeast Asian states have adjoining borders with India.[31] Consequently, India started its endeavour to improve its linkages with Southeast Asia by reviving long lost connections with ASEAN. The Look (Act) East Policy represents the Indian response to this new and changing strategic milieu in the region as Policy was welcomed because it dovetailed very well with ASEAN's fundamental strategic requirements.[32] It was ASEAN who always desired to engage with India in the region due to Chinese assertive behaviour. However, India was reluctant and avoided ASEAN inception while continued to direct policies which ensured engagement. Thus, when India launched its Look (Act) East Policy the ASEAN appreciated it and responded favourably to the Policy through the decision to accord sectoral dialogue partner status to India in 1992.[33] After India's initiative, ASEAN deserves an applaud for their greater efforts for linking with India in reaching new heights in the relationship which scaled only in a decade. It is particularly note worthy that ASEAN's decision to accord full dialogue partner status to India in 1995 at the ASEAN summit in Thailand was made without India being given any prior indications whatsoever.[34] Thereafter in 1996, India was duly accepted as a full and regular member of ASEAN Regional Forum (ARF).[35]

India has been engaging Myanmar in multifarious activities and with Vietnam, it started exploration work in the South China Sea for oil and gas. China exerts much dominance in Vietnam and Myanmar; it has registered the resistance against India's presence in the region where sovereignty is to be claimed. The dual factors make China issue crucial to India's engagement with those countries, but the mutual needs of economic interest's importance must not be ignored. India requires the assistance of Myanmar in accessing its Northeast portion where links are encouraged by the insecure status of the 23-km corridor, famously called Chicken's Neck. Bangladesh and Myanmar are the way out for India when it has to reach the Northeast region if loses Chicken's Neck.

India's gateway to Southeast Asia is via Myanmar. During President Thein Sein's visit, the feasibility of establishing rail links and speed up progress on two hydroelectric projects would be examined. India's vision is entirely related to that India proceeds with other Northeastern neighbour countries; Bangladesh, Bhutan, Sri Lanka, and Nepal, marking security concerns for each other and maintaining relations in telecommunication, power, and interconnectivity by road, sea, air and railways. India and Myanmar are working actively upon the Moreh-Mae Sot road project to connect Thailand, Myanmar and India, besides fastening up their projects with Southeast Asian region for Ganga-Mekong corridor, it is also known to heighten the industrial activities and connectivity.

Although India does not vocally propagate the China factor beyond a point, Western analysts see India as a remedy to China in the Southeast Asian region.[36] Virtually, China is far ahead of India in all the aspects. On the other hand, India should hold its position in the areas where it has dominance and influence. China-India enmity is more or less on silent mode in Myanmar but vocally active in Vietnam. Chinese media have accused India of "fishing in troubled waters" where China claims complete sovereignty that has been disputed by others.[37] Recently, Global Times realised India's deep political motives in Vietnam while conducting exploration. India wishes to accumulate bargaining bits over issues with China. It averred that Chinese protests were "unlikely to work" on India and recommended that Beijing deploy "non-military forces to disturb their work, and cause dispute or friction to halt the two countries' exploration."[38] India and Vietnam are maritime Northeastern neighbour countries and face similar security issues such as natural disaster, piracy and terrorism though the security and safety of sea lanes of communication have become a vital concern for both countries. India and Vietnam agreed to have regular interactions for strengthening exchanges in these fields. The Indian Prime Minister further stressed that the Look (Act) East Policy is not about economics alone; however, it also encompasses efforts to deepen security ties.[39] The Look (Act) East Policy has been intensified by China's alarming rise for India, East Asia and Southeast Asia. Recently, China has proved to be more obtrusive in the region, especially prompting India to move quicker.

India-ASEAN Engagement

Look (Act) East Policy is the driving force behind India-ASEAN engagement. It has been primarily focused on trade and investments connections. In 2003, India became more comprehensive in extending coverage from East Asia to Australia, ASEAN at its core. During this period, the focus was shifted from trade to broader economic and security cooperation, physical connectivity via rail and road link and political partnership.

Today, India covers a wider area of trade and investments, tourism, transportation and infrastructure, science and technology, health and pharmaceuticals and human resource development. India signed "Long-Term Cooperative Partnership for Peace and Prosperity" with ASEAN, which is the corner-stone of India's Look (Act) East Policy.[40] India chooses to exercise the Comprehensive Economic Cooperation Agreement as a model for Free Trade Agreements (FTAs) because of its comprehensive extent of goods and services trade and investments as well. While discussing FTAs, India has always believed that service trade is as needed as trade in goods. Indian policy makers believe that India's strength covered in its service sector, India-ASEAN trade has been flourishing significantly. India finally signed the ASEAN-India Free Trade Agreement with the ten members of ASEAN in August 2009.[41] India has taken various initiatives to enhance economic cooperation with ASEAN. India signed a 'Trade in Goods' agreement with ASEAN in 2009, which became operational from January 1, 2010. Agreements on Trade in Services and Investment as part of FTA are the central fields. India has also negotiated a Free Trade Agreement (FTA) with the Bay of Bengal Initiative for Multi-Sectoral Technical and Economic Cooperation (BIMSTEC). Trade and investment relations between India and ASEAN are growing firmly, as ASEAN has become a 4th largest trading partner of India. India's trade with ASEAN accounts US$ 81.33 billion, which is approx. 10.6 per cent of India's overall trade.[42] India's export to ASEAN accounts at 11.28 per cent of total exports of India. Investment flows are also substantial both ways, with ASEAN accounting for approximately 18.28 per cent of investment flows into

India since 2000. FDI inflows into India from ASEAN between April 2000 to March 2018 was about US$ 68.91 billion, while FDI outflows from India to ASEAN countries, from April 2007 to March 2015 as per data maintained by DEA, was about US$ 38.672 billion. The ASEAN-India Free Trade Area has been completed with the entering into force of the ASEAN-India Agreements on Trade in Service and Investments on July 1, 2015.

Initially, India was not sure to join ASEAN. ASEAN provided a cold shoulder to India due to the post-cold war dimensions and the Pakistan-China factor, although these factors have not much impact in the present time on India. Political will and vision with implementation make the best use of the opportunity. Present leadership seems to have had a will with other elements which reflect in their efforts to have an FTA with the ASEAN. India has to cope up with the pace of China in the areas of diplomatic skills, military preparedness and economic well being if India wishes to play an influential character in ASEAN. There is a traditional influence of the US and Japan in ASEAN. India is regarded as a potential country. China's high performance and Japan's lacklustre economic performance have created an expectation for India in the region that India needs to play a balancer in the Asian region. US-India engagements would truly complement India's endeavour in the Asia-Pacific for being a role player. The US dominance in this region has been accepted and appreciated by a number of players. Whereas China sought to be revisionist power, India feels the same, but the reality is:

> India is incapable of playing the role of a revisionist power now. It needs to take care of the points as mentioned above to be able to emerge as a meaningful partner of the ASEAN—the most successful regional cooperation arrangement in Asia.[43]

India and ASEAN are focussing on the economics of relationship to accomplish new heights, and India has much scope to gain beyond this area. India shares its maritime boundaries with Thailand and Indonesia whereas land frontier with Myanmar. India-ASEAN are connected in many forms and share common concerns of sea-lane protection, counter-narcotics, counter-terrorism and anti-piracy. In the sea, the primary shared security interest is protecting the Strait of Malacca, which connects the South China Sea to the Indian Ocean and is one of the world's busiest sea routes carrying goods that are vital to the economic viability and energy security of India. ASEAN, acts as insulators in the sea lanes from piracy and crime, is thus a key concern for both sides.[44] India and ASEAN also share concerns regarding terrorism and organised crime, although both sides have intensified their suppression in the past few years. Mumbai attacks in 2008 for India and bombing of JW Marriott in 2009 and Ritz-Carlton Hotels in Jakarta exemplify that terrorism is a great threat not just for a country but humanity. Therefore, there was much scope for India and ASEAN to cooperate in various fields, set up arrangements for sharing technologies and intelligence in 2003 under the Joint Declaration on Cooperation to Combat International Terrorism.

India and ASEAN have a convergence between them on Non-Traditional Security Challenges especially in the field of natural disaster management and climate change. Southeast Asia has a densely populated coastline which is dependent on irrigation, though vulnerable to climate change. As per ADB and World Wide Fund projections, few ASEAN countries are impoverished like Laos and Cambodia, facing predictable risk in energy shortage and dropping crop yields in the coming future, whereas lowland mega cities such as Manila and Jakarta would be intensely fragile to increasing sea level tropical disturbances, heat waves and drought. Meanwhile, monsoon seasons in India are difficult to predict and may appear shorter in duration. Cyclones may get over frequently with great intensity and the yielding crop may drop by 30 per cent by 2050.

Both sides share a mutual commitment to assist each side in disaster relief. An approach for cooperation was demonstrated in 2004 when the Indian Ocean earthquake and tsunami disturbed South and Southeast Asia, the deadliest natural disasters in recorded history. India and ASEAN have facilitated cooperation in the fields of non-traditional security. India-ASEAN have set up a network for climate change and the Green Fund for collaboration in the agriculture sector to secure the food challenges.

BIMSTEC: A Growth-oriented Mechanism

Contemporary BIMSTEC, the brainchild of Thailand, was launched in Bangkok on June 6, 1997, with Bangladesh, India, Sri Lanka, and Thailand Economic Cooperation (BIST-EC) as members. Myanmar was an observer in the inaugural meeting and joined the bloc as a member on December 22, 1997, which led to change in its name to BIMST-EC. Nepal and Bhutan were added in 2003 and were granted full membership. In the first Summit on July 31, 2004, leaders of the group renamed it as BIMSTEC. Its emergence was well-timed as it coincided with the continuing wave of regionalism and regional groupings in Asia since the 1990s, where a concerted effort was on for a harmonious blending among the South and Southeast Asian economies.[45]

The vision of BIMSTEC is to improve connectivity among India, Bangladesh, Myanmar, Thailand and other members through a network of multi-modal transport corridors. These networks would facilitate trade, exchange of energy through oil and gas pipelines, promotion of tourism and the increase of communication links leading to what can be termed as a zone of co-prosperity.[46] BIMSTEC connects the 'Look West' policy of Thailand and Association of Southeast Asian Nations (ASEAN), and 'Look East' policy of India and South Asian Association for Regional Cooperation (SAARC) is thereby linking between the ASEAN and SAARC. BIMSTEC has identified 14 priority areas where a member country takes the lead.[47]

- Trade and Investment
- Technology
- Energy
- Transport and Communication
- Tourism
- Fisheries
- Public Health

- Cultural Cooperation
- Agriculture
- People-to-People Contract
- Environment and Disaster Management
- Climate Change
- Poverty Alleviation
- Counter-Terrorism and Transnational Crimes.

India is the leading country for transport and communication, tourism, environment and disaster management and counter-terrorism and transnational crime. On the other hand, Myanmar is the lead country for energy and agriculture cooperation.

Therefore, BIMSTEC has the potential to increase the trade among member countries by taking advantage of their geographical location in the region of the Bay of Bengal and the Eastern coast of the Indian Ocean.[48] BIMSTEC is home to around 1.8 billion people (22 per cent of global people) with a combined GDP of about US$ 2.7 trillion economies.[49] BIMSTEC as a region has grown faster than the world average of 6.5 percent GDP growth in recent years. FDI inflows in the region rose from 5 per cent in 1995 to 20 per cent in 2011, and it had reached 36 per cent in 2015.[50] The region has three essential elements missing—harmonisation of the railway network, all-weather paved roads and a modern port. These require a sound infrastructure and transport base for movement of goods and people in the region. BIMSTEC underlines seamless connectivity in 5 areas:

- Transport Connectivity
- Trade Connectivity
- Investment Connectivity
- Energy Connectivity and
- People-to-People Connectivity

BIMSTEC is an opportunity for the countries to be a part of the powerful region by exploring and utilising areas for regional economic growth, technological cooperation and trade liberalisation. Trade among

BIMSTEC countries shows positive Compound Annual Growth Rate (CAGR), which is 25.16 per cent (during the period 2005-2014); highest CAGR (during the period 2005-2014) in terms of trade was found with Thailand (30.43 per cent), and the least was found with Bhutan (7.7 per cent). While there was a decline in India's exports in the year 2014 (–3 per cent), the exports growth was at 10.37 per cent with the BIMSTEC countries. The share of BIMSTEC countries in India's total trade was 3.89 per cent, whereas in exports the share was 6.74 per cent, and in imports, the share was 1.94 per cent in the year 2014. This shows that there is huge scope in enhancing India's trade with other BIMSTEC countries; India's share of trade with BIMSTEC countries is significantly low as of now.[51]

The most important driving force should be the BIMSTEC Free Trade Area (FTA). While a Framework Agreement has been signed, it is yet to be fully implemented. The agreed conclusions of the BIMST-EC Economic Ministerial Retreat held in Bangkok, Thailand, on August 7, 1998, mentioned that the BIMSTEC should aim and strive to develop into an FTA and focus on the activities that facilitate trade, increase investments and promote technical cooperation among the member countries. It is driven by the need for strengthening economic cooperation in the region to realise the potential of trade and develop completely for the benefit of the member countries and fill that gap in the region.[52]

India hosted the 2nd BIMSTEC Summit in New Delhi, November 2008. The 2nd Summit took place four years after the 1st BIMSTEC Summit which was held in Thailand. The growth of BIMSTEC as a sub-regional group between the two summits can be traced by the statements of the leaders as they expressed satisfaction at the progress that had been made in the negotiations for FTA in trade in goods, thus called for its early conclusion. They also expressed concern at the threat posed by terrorism to the region and appreciated the finalisation of the BIMSTEC Convention on Combating International Terrorism, Transnational Organised Crime and Illicit Drug Trafficking.[53]

The Third BIMSTEC Summit was held in Myanmar, March 2014, where leaders reaffirmed their commitments in accelerating the pace of regional integration and bringing prosperity to the people in their respective nations. India's then Prime Minister Manmohan Singh underscored the relevance of BIMSTEC, stating that "BIMSTEC is a natural grouping of countries. We are bound by geography and linked by history. Our culture, religions and architecture bear eloquent testimony to our ancient bonds."[54] The region faces many common challenges—from natural disasters to terrorism which has to be collectively addressed to make an important contribution to peace, harmony, security and prosperity in Asia and the world.

The Fourth BIMSTEC Summit was held in Nepal, August 2018, the focus was given on regional connectivity, transport and tourism, space technology and coastal shipping. It was concluded with 18 points Kathmandu declaration that includes cooperation in the field of agriculture technology exchange, increases trade and investment, dropping the impact of climate change, easing visa process for member state people to increase tourism and people to people connectivity. In this summit two more priority areas are proposed: Mountain economy and Blue economy along with FTA. Blue Economy Vision 2025, harnessing business potential for India and International Partners is a pioneering effort by FICCI to sensitise India about the growing global and regional emphasis on sustainability of harnessing the ocean resources. The current estimated asset value of US$ 24 trillion and an annual value addition of US$ 2.5 trillion, would continue to offer significant economic benefits both in the traditional areas of fisheries, transport, tourism and hydrocarbons as well as in the new fields of deep-sea mining, renewable energy, ocean biotechnology and many more, only if we integrate sustainable practices with our business models. Sri Lanka, the current chair of the Bay of Bengal Initiative for Multi-Sectoral Technical and Economic Cooperation (BIMSTEC), has proposed to host the fifth summit of the regional grouping in the first half of January 2021, subject to the improved COVID-19 situation.

India's Northeast Vision

The indispensability of Northeast came in the focus of Indian Policy makers mainly with the initiation of the Look (Act) East

Policy. Before that, the region was merely viewed from security point only. Indeed, situated at the tri-junction of South, Southeast and East Asia. Northeast has geographical importance of its own in the shifting regional economic trends. It is in the transit of many of the newly formed sub-regional groupings with a vast amount of untapped potential, but yet to be fully developed. Today realisation has dawned on the foreign policy makers in India that any proper physical connectivity with Southeast Asia, the main decisive factor for the success of Look (Act) East Policy, could be possible only through this region.

In the same vein, North Eastern Region Vision 2020 also emphasises the need for refashioning the development process of Northeast to ensure that the region plays the arrow-head role it must play in the vanguard of the country's Look (Act) East Policy.[55] The implication is clear of the long-term potential and importance of the region, at the same time the continuing negligence and indifference towards the same. The unfortunate part of Northeast in the emerging scenario is that India's economic engagement with Southeast Asia has expanded, but nothing has been seen as an advantage to Northeast. Even in the existing bilateral trade among India and eastern countries the share of Northeast forms only about 1 percent of India's total trade with the latter.

Figure 5.1: India's Total Trade with Eastern Neighbours

(figures in Rs crore)

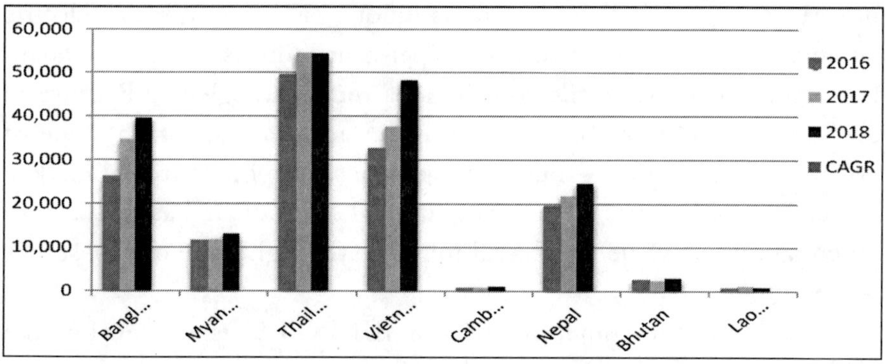

Source: Export-Import Bank of India, Ministry of Commerce

Figure 5.2: India's Total Trade & Share of Northeast

(figures in Rs crore)

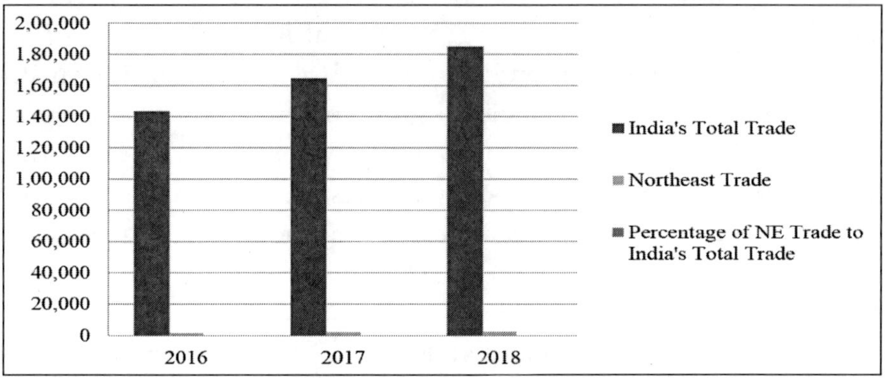

Source: Export-Import Bank of India, Ministry of Commerce

Northeast India, consisting of eight Indian states, is one of the naturally most endowed but highly neglected regions in the country, more to do with the way of governance. It represents 7.9 per cent of the country's geographical area, 3.8 per cent of its total population and 2.7 per cent of GDP, characterised by an extraordinary mixture of ethno-cultural heritage and intertwining realities of ethno-nationalism and sub-regionalism, Northeast is considered to be one of the most complex regions of India with over 200 ethnic groups.[56] Being a latecomer in the national mainstream the questions of transition and alienation always loom large in the mind of its natives—leading to anti-Indian tensions in various stages. Further, despite its unique biodiversity, hydro-electric potential, hydro-carbon reserves (38 per cent), forests wealth, abundant flora and fauna and fertile soil the area remains neglected because of geographical bottlenecks and lack of an adequate and right type of policy implementation—thus limiting its access to international market. Nevertheless, because of its geographical location it has got a high potential market value which will roll once the right type of exposure is made.

India's primary objective within BIMSTEC is to develop the Northeast region by integrating it with existing trade networks while capitalising on future opportunities. BIMSTEC could be a "potential game changer" for the Northeast's overall development. While considering the potential of BIMSTEC to bring trade, transport, tourism and other linkages to the states of the Northeast. "It is in India's interest to make sure that Northeast does not fall behind, that it develops as well in a manner that is commensurate to its potential."[57]

The integration of the Northeast with the fast-developing economies of ASEAN is fundamental to peace, security and development within the region. BIMSTEC has the potential of producing trade worth US$ 43-50 billion under a proposed Free Trade Agreement (FTA) that the grouping is in the process of finalising.[58] An early conclusion of the planned FTA among BIMSTEC member states is of the utmost necessity for the acceleration of trade and investment in the Bay of Bengal region. "We should aim for an early conclusion of the BIMSTEC Free Trade Agreement for trade in goods and extend it to investment and services. Most of us are connected through one or more regional economic arrangements and it should not be difficult for us to conclude one for BIMSTEC."[59]

The Northeast is pivotal to this vision as it shares international borders with five Northeast neighbouring countries and is home to many ethnic groups, languages and dialects. People of some of the bordering states have close familial and community links with those across international borders, especially in Myanmar. Despite its economic focus, BIMSTEC is also aimed at the integration of people of different sociocultural and politico-economic backgrounds throughout the region via greater people-to-people contact among citizens of all member states.

Thus, in the present era of globalisation where distances are decreasing, and boundaries are changing into gateways the potential of Northeast can no longer be sidelined with transnational dimension gradually picking up. In the present context, the Northeast has to explicitly act as India's land bridge to Myanmar and outlet to the rest of Southeast Asia.

BIMSTEC and India Equation

BIMSTEC offers India an opportunity to get its ties with its eastern Northeast neighbours reinforced, much in conformity with the core of

India's Look (Act) East Policy. Describing BIMSTEC importance to India, Prime Minister of India stated, "We consider our participation in BIMSTEC as a key element in our Look (Act) East Policy and long-standing approach of good Northeast neighbourliness towards all our Northeast neighbours—by land and sea. The challenges before us are to transform the richness of our human and natural resources into cooperative regional activities promoting development, enhancing prosperity and the well being of our people, and ensuring our collective security in all its multifarious dimensions."[60] BIMSTEC in order to act as a proper linkage between South and Southeast Asia needs.

Even after many years of developmental strategy required a level of necessary infrastructure growth which is missing in Northeast. In this background balanced and sustainable economic growth under the new market equation becomes difficult. Development of the potentials are always curtailed by various challenges such as ethnic insurgency, inefficient and corrupt governance, the militarisation of the region or a warehousing atmosphere, lack of financial discipline, lack of proper marketing channel and all mode connectivity. Thus, what is hoped is that regional grouping like BIMSTEC will be a means to pull it in the average international economic flow by gradually overcoming the existing development deficit. It is regarded as a growth mechanism for transforming the Northeast by making it a gateway to the East with the right type of linkages. Indeed sub-regional developments link adjacent areas with different factor endowments and different comparative advantages. In this scenario, the Northeast is very much suited for the BIMSTEC initiatives.

The success of BIMSTEC will definitely contribute and complement to the development of India's Look (Act) East Policy in general and Northeast in particular. Indeed, for India, this regional grouping acts as a medium for achieving the three-pronged strategy of its Look (Act) East Policy:

- Closer link with its proximate and immediate Northeast neighbours.
- Economic integration with Southeast Asia.
- Security considerations of Northeast and development of its untapped potential.

Various infrastructural efforts will be enhanced with the participation of the member countries which in turn will also bring out reciprocal benefits. Effective and progressive cooperation is much in demand between BIMSTEC and India's Northeast so that when the Free Trade Agreement materialised Northeast does not lag or it poses a hurdle to the grouping itself.

The Myanmar Factor

India and Myanmar relations are rooted in shared historical, cultural, ethnic and religious ties. In addition to these similarities, both these Asian countries share a long geographical land border and maritime boundary in the Bay of Bengal. One of the most integral parts of India's Look (Act) East Policy is its Myanmar policy with the apparent reality that in the process Northeast comprehensive concerns need to discuss with the nearby regional groups—BIMSTEC being not an exception. India looked upon Myanmar as an indispensable medium for acquiring more economic benefits as well to put India in a strategically more advantageous position through its Northeast. It is Northeast transnational dimension which brought to its fold both problematic as well as prospective facets, especially associated with Myanmar. The proper synergy between India's Northeast and BIMSTEC thus calls for an understanding of these facets and dealing with them thereof.

Myanmar is crucial to India's economic engagement with Southeast Asian countries. The country shares a 1643 km border with the Northeast states of Manipur, Mizoram, Nagaland and Arunachal Pradesh. Under the Indo-Myanmar Trade Agreement of 1994, formal border trade is conducted through the designated custom posts at Moreh in Manipur to Tamu in Myanmar, and Zowakhatar in Mizoram to Rhi in Myanmar.[61] In enhancing sub-regional cooperation, extending current transit and transport connectivity is vital. While several trade routes existed between India and Southeast Asian countries before British colonial intervention, they were disrupted as a result of the narrow business and imperial interests of the British. In the post-Independence period, trade and cultural exchanges have for the most part remained stagnant and the road to connectivity between India and Myanmar is underdeveloped. The planned extension of the Indo-Myanmar Friendship Road will link Mandalay with the Trans-Asian Highway, while states that possess modern medical facilities such as Assam and Manipur are being routed as possible destinations for medical tourists from Myanmar.[62]

Regional Economic Integration

BIMSTEC economic relevance in the region could be further enhanced when India would establish proper cooperation with Myanmar. It becomes imperative in the changing economic architecture of the region. Closing the gap between India and Myanmar in the realm of economic relations could be traced to the signing of an MOU on trade and economic cooperation, particularly in terms of border trade in 1994. Subsequently, the Moreh-Tamu Border Trade was opened in April 1995, followed by steps to materialise the Zowakhatar (Champhai) Border Trade Post in Mizoram State adjoining Rhi in Myanmar, which was inaugurated in January 2004. Besides, in March 2007 India approved the setting up Border Trade Centres (BTC) along the Indo-Myanmar border in the state of Nagaland. In recent trade meetings between the two countries, it was decided that the present border trade at the Tamu-Moreh and Rhi-Zowakhatar border points to be converted into regular trade and to expand the list of items that can be legally traded.[63] Although Moreh-Tamu Border Trade does not form a substantial share of the total trade capacity between India and Myanmar, yet it is considered significant from the angle of India's move toward Southeast Asia through the Northeast.

Diversification and expansion in trade cooperation continue between India and Myanmar. India is the 4th largest trade partner of Myanmar (3rd largest export destination for Myanmar and 7th largest source of imports into Myanmar).[64] India has already given preferential tariff to most of the items imported from Myanmar namely wood products, legumes, gems, etc. It also supported the setting up of various factories and plants. Here, most of India's economic cooperation with BIMSTEC touching Northeast is inclusive of its initiative for promoting vibrant economic partnership with Myanmar. To promote the existing multilateralism presently effort is being extended by India for early materialisation of the BIMSTEC FTA.

Ventures in Infrastructure Sectors

The BIMSTEC Transport Infrastructure and Logistics Study (BTILS) has identified as many as 100 projects that would promote connectivity within the region. These projects are to be funded by the Asian Development Bank.[65] Apart from these, there are Kaladan Multi-Modal Project that would connect India to ASEAN countries and is expected to be completed by the end of 2020, and India-Myanmar-Thailand Trilateral Highway is expected to be also completed by 2020 and the ESCAP dream project of Asian Highway. Infrastructure in the form of transport and communication constitutes one of the priority sectors of BIMSTEC with India as the leading country. Entry of Northeast in the BIMSTEC initiative means opening up through proper infrastructure development with proper coordination with Myanmar. In the first meeting of BIMSTEC Expert Group on Transport and Communication Sector, held in New Delhi in April 2001, the discussion was made on issues concerning transport and cross-border facilitation, multi-modal transport and logistics, infrastructure development, aviation, maritime transport, as well as communication linkages and networking.[66] Consequently, several infrastructure projects between India and Myanmar emerged as an integral part to move above. Changing Northeast from being a mere border point to profitable economic gateways has become an urgent imperative for India for which a proper infrastructural link is much needed with Myanmar.

In road sector, India has extended assistance for road development projects which include upgradation of the Tamu-Kalewa-Kalemyo road (about 160 km); Kaladan Multi-Modal Transit Transport Project which envisages the development of road and inland waterways from Sittwe port in Myanmar to Mizoram. Border Road Organisation has completed the resurfacing and maintenance work of 132 km Tamu-Kyigone-Kalemyo stretch of the road and handed over to Myanmar.

Several BIMSTEC centres are being launched throughout the region, including three in India, to foster greater technical exchanges between member countries. Another significant move in this direction is the initiative for earliest materialisation of the India-Myanmar-Thailand Trilateral Highway linking India's Moreh to Mae Sot of Northern Thailand through Bagan in Myanmar. This is an important BIMSTEC project. The handing over of the Tamu-Keygone-Kalemyo stretch of road built with Indian assistance to Myanmar in October 2009 was another big development. The effort is also on for the development of "Stillwell Road" (the old Burma Road). Further, India and Myanmar are engaged in completing the missing links in the Trans Asian Railways (TAR) in different parts of their countries. Several corridors have been identified to make this project successful and reality, India and Myanmar have completed their most of the projects which will be adjoining the routes in respect to TAR. In this direction, India has already approved the signing and ratification of the Inter-Governmental Agreement on TAR on March 8, 2007. With all these, an Optical Fibre Telecommunication project to run along the Trilateral Highway is coming up under the aegis of BIMSTEC. The viability will improve multi-fold once the India-Myanmar-Thailand Trilateral Highway (part of the AH1) project of ADB connects with the Sittwe deepwater port in Myanmar, and India's plans to extend the railway connectivity to Moreh on the Myanmar border and beyond to the proposed Trans-Asian Railways are executed. Efforts have also been made between India and Myanmar for the early materialisation of other joint infrastructure projects within the framework of the BIMSTEC development programme. Tamanthi Hydro-Electric Power Project in the Chindwin River, once completed could supplement the power needs of the Northeast; and the Dawei Deep-Sea port. According to an official of the External Affairs Ministry of India, the schedule for all these projects is the next 5-10 years so that by the time India-ASEAN and BIMSTEC FTAs are fully operational the infrastructure is in place to sustain the anticipated much higher level of trade and economic interaction.[67] This grouping project in the form of BIMSTEC Transport Infrastructure and Logistics Study (BTILS) undertaken under the Asian Development Bank also proved helpful in this direction by identifying the bottlenecks that need to be overcome. In all these equal share and eager support from the side of Myanmar is vital.

India's Energy Quest

Growing Indian economy needs sustained energy supplies. Its need is estimated to climb up to 400 million standard cubic meters per day by 2025.[68] India's economic diplomacy is charged with due importance to energy security. Myanmar provides the nearest and the most feasible source. India is the sixth largest energy consumer in the world while Myanmar has enough gas to last for another many years at the current rate of extraction. According to figures from the Energy Information Administration of USA, Myanmar has an abundant amount of crude oil reserves approximating to the tune of 150 million barrels, while its natural gas reserves are around 10 to 13 trillion cubic feet. Lobbying for this huge quantity of gas has become an important objective of India's diplomatic equation. Presently, India's public sector undertakings GAIL and ONGC Videsh Ltd and private enterprise Essar are engaged in gas extraction work. An agreement was signed between the two countries on September 23, 2007, in Nay Pyi Taw to this effect.[69] Moreover, in this pursuit for energy security, India's Northeast has an importance of its own because of its geographical importance for any future transportation of oil and gas to India from Myanmar. Further, as Bangladesh is also determined to ensure regional cooperation, the Myanmar-Bangladesh-India gas pipeline can be a reality.

Greater understanding with Myanmar in the area will also help in bringing better economic cohesion within BIMSTEC with energy as the linking basis. Myanmar as a lead country in the energy sector of the grouping and India with its expertise could contribute to the overall objective of BIMSTEC by using the energy demand-supply aspect for regional resource cooperation with related reciprocity.

Tourism Partnership

Tourism is one of the priority sectors of BIMSTEC where India is the leading country; developing tourism forms another area of India-Myanmar cooperation with India emphasising its Northeast. Tourism is one particular sector in which India's Northeast and Myanmar are rich and have an abundance of untapped business potential. The region is an exceptional tourism destination with the exotic flora and fauna, natural scenic beauty, unique performing arts and varied cuisine and handicrafts. The presence of a large number of religious places of different cultures in the region could also help in promoting pilgrim tourism. India is gradually trying to add this dimension to its Look (Act) East Policy. The motive is to rejuvenate the age-old historical and cultural ties between the people of India's Northeast and Southeast Asia through Myanmar for enhancing the avenue for tourism growth. A declaration known as the Kolkata Declaration on Tourism Cooperation was also adopted in February 2005 with Indian initiative. The Proposed Plan of Action includes the suggestion to establish the BIMSTEC Tourism Information Centre in India as well as to explore the possibility of setting up a BIMSTEC Tourism Fund with financial contributions from each member country.[70] A BIMSTEC Tourism Working Group has also been formed to initiate common steps in the issue. Thus, when these features open up with proper linkages and infrastructure, Northeast could become one of the best tourism hubs of the world, which in turn will show the flow of income and investment.

Chinese Presence in the Equation

China is the largest trading partner of Myanmar with a trading volume of US$ 7.42 billion.[71] China commercially persuades three goals in having closer relations with Myanmar namely:

- China's direct entry to the Indian Ocean via Myanmar in order to avoid dependence on the vulnerable Malacca Strait.
- Unlocking its remote Southern province of Yunnan.
- Strengthening its energy security to congregate the booming economy.

China's influence is so strong in the country that the entire Northern and Central Myanmar are gradually being transformed into a Chinese economic zone.[72] Chinese cheap goods enter Northeast India via Myanmar that may undermine national commercial interests of India. The present tendency continues in the region may altogether be transformed into a marketing ground for low-priced Chinese manufactured durable users.

Furthermore, China-Myanmar relations have appeared much prominent when it comes to security and military domain. China has become the largest arms supplier to Myanmar. The engagement of Chinese military since 1989 in upgrading and developing of Myanmar's naval facilities in its islands in the coastal field and the Bay of Bengal is also a sincere concern for India. India senses the need to counter the 'String of Pearl strategy' of China whereby the latter is trying to have affable naval bases all around the coastal areas of India. Besides from a strategic point, India's Northeast is also on the Chinese radar. India needs to explore all these angles. Including security rapport with Myanmar is thus very much realised. Through more engagement, India is trying to bring Myanmar closer to it and at the same time freeing the country from the 'dependency syndrome' it has towards China.[73]

Advantages from BIMSTEC and its members will have less gain for India in general and Northeast in particular unless China's foray is checked through proper synchronisation and understanding with Myanmar. The ever-changing sub-regional geopolitics with China emerged as a firm directive force is a critical, decisive factor compelling India to go for a change in its existing Myanmar policy. The concern for the competitive dynamics with China is always there in the mindset of the foreign policy mandarins in South Block.

As per India's former diplomat Rajiv Sikri, "Should Myanmar get irreversibly locked in China's tight economic and strategic embrace, this would pose serious security dangers to India.... A China sponsored link-up between Myanmar and Bangladesh would bring China right on India's doorstep and complete China's encirclement of India from the East."[74]

In the same wavelength Professor Mohan Mallik, Asia-Pacific Center for Security Studies Hawaii, expressed, "China's forays into Myanmar are a part of a Grand plan, to expand its economic and strategic interest in South and Southeast Asia."[75]

It has an impact on regional security and economic environment. Though Nay Pyi Taw never wants itself to be entirely under the influence of China, yet in the aftermath of '1988 Uprising' China became the main partner of Myanmar, in turn, giving a boost to the former Southward Policy. China is heavily investing in the development of Myanmar's industrial, infrastructure and energy sector. Subsequently, large-scale Chinese aid, capital and types of equipment pouring into that country which India perceives encroachment in its sphere of influence.

Challenges and Opportunities for India

Security challenges whether it is natural or human-made require collective efforts and firmness needs to be overcome. In the security sphere, India steadily set in place sanctioning legal instruments for regional approaches to transnational crime, international terrorism, drug trafficking and mutual legal assistance in criminal matters. Cases of Islamic terrorism, internal insurgency, small arms infiltration and ever-growing Narco-trafficking are the main domains of serious security concern in India's Northeast with Myanmar aspects. In this atmosphere, one could not be optimistic about the benefits of BIMSTEC contributing to the growth of the region. India shares a 1643-km long border with Myanmar which lies entirely in its Northeast inhabited by trans-border tribes and very porous. On the other hand, the whole of the Northeast is linked with the mainland by a very narrow 22-km wide 'Siliguri Corridor'. Ample potential for a much better link is open towards its Eastern side.

Numbers of states of Northeast are grappling with the problem of endemic insurgency which is sustained mostly by the availability of cheap weapons and secure sanctuary from the Myanmar side. It is believed that at present there are still about 30 camps belonging to ULFA, NSCN (K), CNF and UNLF insurgents inside Myanmar, with or without the awareness of the local government, despite Myanmar's repeated assurance that it will not allow them to work inside its territory.[76] In the absence of a proper controlling mechanism, the number of multilateral and bilateral cooperation initiated by India touching this region become less practical. Curbing insurgency, small arms proliferation and Narco-smuggling became an urgent requirement. Collateral damage in the form of mass-scale drug addiction and AIDS/HIV has become an ordinary happening in the region. Overall the security problem of Northeast forms an important aspect which possibly will have a direct impact on any India-BIMSTEC cooperation where again full support from Myanmar is required.

Maritime surveillance was required in the Bay of Bengal as its sea lanes were being used by terrorists to transport arms, ammunition and drugs. A significant step in this direction was the endorsement and signing of a Convention on Cooperation in Combating International Terrorism, Transnational Organized Crime and Illicit Drug Trafficking in the 12th BIMSTEC Ministerial Meeting held in Nay Pyi Taw, December 2009.[77] India raised the issue of insurgents groups operating from Myanmar soil with the Government of Myanmar on the sidelines of the same meet.

Emphasising on BIMSTEC economic cooperation must not underplay the security and politico-strategic dimensions. Security and Political issues still form the basis of economic cooperation among many of the member countries. So, what needs to be taken care of is that bilateral political and security issues are not to be endorsed to disrupt the course of India's Northeast-BIMSTEC initiatives. Since Myanmar is a deciding factor confidence-building measures are needed. Improving relations between India and Myanmar coupled with the BIMSTEC initiative, inclusive of the special consideration for India's Northeast, could be taken as a manifestation of the bridging gap between South Asia's 'Look (Act) East Policy' and Southeast Asia's 'Look West Policy' which may gradually contribute to a Pan Asian Movement. With the right mechanism, the BIMSTEC FTA which is in the anvil could also materialise at the earliest so that liberalisation of trade in goods could be initiated.[78]

In the ever-evolving scenario, the enduring growth factor of India's Northeast is of utmost significance since in the long-run programme towards the same will prove self-enhancing for India in its bilateral as well as multilateral programmes. The new changes in and around the BIMSTEC region must be used for promotion of the development of infrastructure, trade, border trade, proper linkages and tourism which in turn will promote economic activity in Northeast, with lots of positive multiplier effects. For India, development of the Northeast and its integration with broader regional integration processes have developed an imperative and security aspects. However, insurgency, sense of alienation, health hazards, drug trafficking, excessive militarisation, porous border with unscrupulous activities remain issues that create cracks from time to time in all these initiatives. This is heightened when the benefits which should be for the common people is diverted to the existence of a bureaucrat-politician-insurgent nexus. India's Northeast especially needs to be viable from a security angle as this region is to be the focal point for many of the bilateral and multilateral cooperation projects coming up. A right type of synergy in the India-Myanmar relation and adjusting it with BIMSTEC efforts will go a long way in pulling up this region towards sustained economic growth and socio-political stability. This could be supplemented more effectively, by overcoming two lasting deficiencies of the region: the deficit of democracy and development.[79]

Besides, there is the prevailing view among some scholars that all these processes of regionalisation will not bring any proactive change for Northeast. They are dubious of all these moves of India under its Look (Act) East Policy and are considered to be devoid of the ground reality. Instead, they believe that it will ensure more negative multiplier effects in the form of corporatisation and squandering away of local resources, surrendering of the rights, corridor station of the region, benefits of the local people and coercive policies. This may not be the whole picture but at the same time cannot be taken as completely uprooted particularly in the context of the sensitiveness surrounding Northeast.

Thus, for transforming the potentials of Northeast to definite growth by dispelling the apprehensions around it, the need of the hour is to have a long-term policy perspective with certain level of sincerity in governance and vision, support from the masses, emphasising on removing economic bottlenecks, developing infrastructures on one hand and overcoming security challenges on the other. Also, what is needed is proper connectivity between the Northeast and the mainland of India, psychologically and physically. Efforts for proper understanding among all who are part of the development process is must in order to attain the long-period vision of shared growth and prosperity through cooperative action, with due consideration of the ground realities.

Last but not the least, what could be deduced is the fact that despite the problems which need to be tackled with support from Myanmar there are many critical areas in which mutual beneficial arrangements among the stakeholders could be pursued further. The Northeast-BIMSTEC equation within the broader perspective of Look (Act) East Policy with Myanmar playing a critical role which could move towards enhancement of pragmatic and rational policy. The urgent demand lies in finding a mechanism to rough out all the negative cracks. Myanmar is not an all in all factor, yet it still forms one of the most decisive factors when it comes to Northeast, and could be an enterprising potential within BIMSTEC if put in the right track for all-round growth. Transcending nature of BIMSTEC must be used for the promotion of bilateral relations ultimately leading to moderate regional growth and multilateralism. It could change Northeast from being merely a security issue to a more productive and vibrant economic hub. This will be the overall interest of India in the long run and will make its Look (Act) East Policy more meaningful, enabling Northeast to take the arrowhead role while Myanmar provides the required bridge.

Notes

1. Rajiv Sikri (2009), *Challenge and Strategy: Rethinking India's Foreign Policy*, Sage Publication, New Delhi, India, p. 66.
2. Thongkholal Haokip (2015), *India's Look (Act) East Policy and The Northeast,* Sage Publication, New Delhi, p. 34.
3. Imankalyan Lahiri (2011), "Evolution and Rationale of India's Look (Act) East Policy with Special reference to BIMSTEC," *South Asian Survey,* Vol. 2(18), pp. 239-57.
4. Thongkholal Haokip (2015), *India's Look (Act) East Policy and The Northeast*, Sage Publication, New Delhi, p. 42.
5. Hamish Telford (2001), "Counter Insurgency in India: Observations from Punjab and Kashmir," *The Journal of Conflict Studies*, Vol. 21(1). Available at https://journals.

lib.unb.ca/index.php/jcs/ article/view/4293/4888 (Accessed on July 4, 2017).
6. Sreedhar (1994), "Southern Asia Security Situation," *Strategic Analysis*, Vol. 16(11), p. 1436.
7. Matthew J Webb and Albert Wijeweera (2015), *The Political Economy of Conflict in South Asia*, International Political Economy Series, Palgrave Macmillan Publishers, London, p. 102.
8. Thongkholal Haokip (2010), "India's Look (Act) East Policy and Northeast India," Ph.D Thesis, Department of Political Science, North-Eastern Hill University, Shillong, p. 105.
9. Union Budget and Economic Survey (1990-91), Ministry of Finance, Government of India. Available at https://www.indiabudget.gov.in/es1990-91/esmain.htm (Accessed on September 14, 2017).
10. Marcus Manuel (1991), "The Impact of the Gulf Crisis on Developing Countries," *Overseas Development Institute*, Briefing Paper. Available at https://www.odi.org/sites/odi.org.uk/files/ odi-assets/publications-opinion-files/6770.pdf (Accessed on August 10, 2016).
11. Vijay Joshi and I M D Little (1994), "India: Macroeconomics and Political Economy 1964-91," World Bank Report. Available at http://documents.worldbank.org/curated/en/259451468772490617/India-Macroeconomics-and-political-economy-1964-1991 (Accessed on September 12, 2017).
12. Thongkholal Haokip (2015), *India's Look (Act) East Policy and The Northeast*, Sage Publication, New Delhi, p. 59.
13. K S Bajpai (1992), "India in 1991: New Beginning," *Asian Survey*, Vol.32(2), pp. 207-216.
14. Nikita Dutta, "Major Economic Crisis in Indian Economy," Economic Discussion. Available at http://www.economicsdiscussion.net/economic-crisis/major-economic-crisis-in-indian-economy/6483 (Accessed on October 21, 2017).
15. Thongkholal Haokip (2015), *India's Look (Act) East Policy and The Northeast*, Sage Publication, New Delhi, p. 60.
16. Sandy Gordon (1995), *India's Rise to Power in the Twentieth Century and Beyond*, Palgrave Macmillan Publishers, London, p. 38.
17. R Harshe (1999), "South Asian Regional Co-operation: Problems and Prospects," *Economic and Political Weekly*, Vol. 34 (19), pp. 1100-06.
18. Annual Report of 1991-92, MEA Library, Ministry of External Affairs, GOI, p.13. Available at https://mealib.nic.in/?2520?000 (Accessed on September 28, 2017).
19. Nisha Taneja (2004), "Informal Trade in the SAARC Region: Implications for FTAs," *Economic and Political Weekly*, Vol. 39 (51), pp. 5367-72.
20. Christophe Jafferlot (2003), "India's Look (Act) East Policy: An Asianist Strategy in Perspective," *India Review*, Vol. 2 (2), pp. 35-68.
21. I.S. Mezard (2003), "The Look (Act) East Policy: An Economic Perspective," in Frederic Grare and Amitabh Mattoo (ed.), *Beyond the Rhetoric: The Economics of India's Look (Act) East Policy*, Manohar Publishers, New Delhi, p. 98.
22. Frederic Grare (2003), "In search of a Role: Indian and the ASEAN Regional Forum," in Frederic Grare and Amitabh Mattoo (ed.), *Beyond the Rhetoric: The Economics of India's Look (Act) East Policy*, Manohar Publishers, New Delhi, p. 72.
23. Renaud Egreteau (2004), *Wooing the Generals: India's New Burma Policy*, Authors Press, New Delhi, p. 108.

24. P Malik (1997), *The Changing Face of India's Economic Diplomacy: The Role of Ministry of External Affairs*, Foreign Service Institute and Konark Publishers, p. 232.
25. J N Mahanty and J K barla (1992), "India and Gulf Crisis: A response of minority government," *Pacific Affairs*, Vol. 65 (3), pp. 368-84.
26. J N Dixit (1997), *My South Block years: Memoirs of a Foreign Secretary*, UBS Publication, New Delhi, p. 72.
27. Baladas Ghosal (2013), "China's Perception of India's Look (Act) East Policy and Its Implications," *Institute for Defence Studies and Analysis*, Monograph series No. 26, October.
28. C.S. Kuppuswamy (2010), "India's Look (Act) East Policy—A Review," *South Asia Analysis Group*, Paper No: 3662.
29. Thongkholal Haokip (2011), "India's Look (Act) East Policy," *Third Concept—An International Journal of Ideas*, Vol. 25 (291), p. 15.
30. Atish Sinha and Madhup Mahota (2007), *Indian Foreign Policy: Challenges and Opportunities*, Academic Foundation, New Delhi, p. 59.
31. Sajnani M Vashi (2003), "India's Policy Towards Southeast Asia: 1992-2002," Dissertation Deptt. of Political Science, National University of Singapore, p. 128.
32. Mukul G Asher (2007), "India's Rising Role in Asia,"*Research and Information Systems for Developing Countries,* RIS Discussion Paper No. 121.
33. Ranjit Gupta (2007)," India's 'Look East' Policy: Indian Foreign Policy: Challenges and Opportunities," *Foreign Service Institute*, pp. 351-81.
34. Atish Sinha and Madhup Mahota (2007), *Indian Foreign Policy: Challenges and Opportunities*, Academic Foundation, New Delhi, p. 84.
35. Ibid., p. 98.
36. Imankalyan Lahiri (2011), "Evolution and Rationale of India's Look (Act) East Policy with Special reference to BIMSTEC," *South Asian Survey,* Vol. 2(18), pp. 239-57.
37. Jianming Shen, "China's Sovereignty over the South China Sea Island: A Historical Perspective." Available at https://watermark.silverchair.com/1-1-94.pdf?token=AQECAHi208BE49Ooan9kkhW_Ercy7Dm3ZL_9Cf3qfKAc485 (Accessed on June 25, 2018).
38. Global Times (2011), "India-Vietnam Joint work must be halted," October 14. Available at http://www.globaltimes.cn/content/679263.shtml (Accessed on August 14, 2017).
39. Indian PM's statement at the Joint Press conference with the President of Vietnam, October 12, 2011, New Delhi. Available at http://pmindia.nic.in/speech-details.php?nodeid=1068 (Accessed on August 12, 2017).
40. A Sundaram (2013),"Look (Act) East Policy,"International Journal of Advancements in Research and Technology, Vol. 2 (5), p. 169.
41. Parthapritam Pal and Mitali Das Gupta (2009), "The ASEAN-India Free Trade Agreement: An Assessment," *Economic and Political Weekly*, Vol. 44 (38), p. 12.
42. Ibid., p. 14.
43. Chintamani Mahapatra (2007), "India-ASEAN Relations: Catching up with China," Indian News and Feature Alliance, November 22. Available at http://www.infa.in/index.php?option=com_content&task=view&id=493&Itemid=45 (Accessed on August 20, 2017).

44. L Chatterjee (2010), "Security Raised in Malacca Strait after Terror Warning," *Reuters*, 4 March.
45. T Nirmala Devi (2007), *India and Bay of Bengal Community—The BIMSTEC Experiment*, Gyan Publishing House, New Delhi, p. 73.
46. A Report prepared by *Centre for Studies in International Relations and Development & Institute of Foreign Policy, University of Kolkata*, "BIMSTEC-What is Achieved and Where to go?" (2013). Available at http://www.csird.org.in/rep/Final%20 Report%20of%20BIMSTEC.pdf (Accessed on May 12, 2017).
47. Mahfuz Kabir and Ruhul Salim (2010), "Can Gravity Model Explain BIMSTEC Trade?," *Journal of Economic Integration,* Vol. 25(1), p. 146.
48. M Habibur Rehman (2007), *Legal Regime of Marine Environment in the Bay of Bengal*, Atlantic Publishers & Distributors Pvt. Ltd, New Delhi, p. 86.
49. Rahul Mazumdar (2016), "Exports from West Bengal: Potential and Strategy," *Export-Import Bank of India,* Working Paper No. 48. Available at http://www. eximbankindia.in/ sites/default/files/Research%20Brief/WEST%20BENGAL%20 WP.pdf (Accessed on October 5, 2017).
50. MD shafiqur Rehman (2014), "Promoting Transport Connectivity in Southern Asia: A BIMSTEC Perspective," UNESCAP. Available at http://www.unescap.org/ sites/default/files/Rahman-Shafiqur-RPDST CSA-20nov2014.pdf (Accessed on September 28, 2017).
51. Rahul Mazumdar (2016), "Exports from West Bengal: Potential and Strategy," Export-Import Bank of India, Working Paper No. 48. Available at http://www. eximbankindia.in/ sites/default/files/Research%20Brief/WEST%20BENGAL%20 WP.pdf (Accessed on October 5, 2017).
52. Final Draft Framework Agreement on the BIMST-EC Free Trade Area on 15 January, 2004. Available at http://investmentpolicyhub.unctad.org/Download/ TreatyFile/3099 (Accessed on December 8, 2017).
53. Ministry of External Affairs, Government of India, "Joint Press Conference after the Second BIMSTEC Summit," November 13, 2008 Available at http://www.mea.gov.in/SpeechesStatements.htm?dtl/2800/Joint+Press+ Conference+after+the+Second+BIMSTEC+Summit (Accessed on November 19, 2017).
54. Ministry of External Affairs, GOI, Statement by Prime Minister at 3rd BIMSTEC Summit, Nay Pyi Taw, Myanmar, March 4, 2014. Available online at http://www.mea.gov.in/infocusarticle.htm?23028/Statement+by+Prime+Minister +at+3rd+BIMSTEC+Summit+Nay+Pyi+Taw+Myanmar (Accessed on March 13, 2018).
55. Aparna Sharma (2015), "BIMSTEC and BCIM Initiatives and their Importance for India," *CUTS Centre for International Trade, Economics and Environment,* Discussion Pape. Available online at http://www.cuts-citee.org/pdf/BIMSTEC_and_BCIM_ Initiatives_and_their_Importance_for_India.pdf (Accessed on May 23, 2018).
56. Thongkholal Haokip (2015), *India's Look (Act) East Policy and The Northeast*, Sage Publication, India, p. 121.
57. C Raja Mohan, "From Looking East to Acting East," Ministry of External Affairs, Government of India, January 29, 2015. Available online at http://www.mea.gov. in/in-focus-article.htm?24714/From+Looking+East+to+Acting+East (Accessed on March 22, 2018).

58. Baladas Ghoshal (2013), "China's Perception of India's Look (Act) East Policy and Its Implication," *IDSA* Monograph Series, No. 26 Available at http://www.idsa.in/system/files/monograph26.pdf (Accessed on May 1, 2017).
59. Statement by Indian Prime Minister Manmohan Singh, India at 3rd BIMSTEC Summit, Nay Pyi Taw, Myanmar, 04 March, 2014. Available at https://drive.google.com/file/d/ 0Bw5iVdDDVNCROFU3ekVGMWlrdWM/view (Accessed on March 11, 2018).
60. Ibid.
61. V.S. Shisadri (2014), "Transforming Connectivity Corridors between India-Myanmar into Development Corridors," *Research and Information System for Developing Countries Publication,* p. 77.
62. Heinrich Boll Stiftung, Institute of Social Science and Burma Centre Delhi Conference Report on India-Myanmar Relations- Looking from Borders, 28-29 September, 2015 Available at https://in.boell.org/sites/default/files/india-myanmar_relations_looking_from_the_border.pdf (Accessed on March 24, 2018).
63. The 3rd International Conference on ASEAN Connectivity: Current Issues and Future Prospects towards ASEAN Community, November 2014 Available at http://copag.msu.ac.th/ conference/files/Proceedings.pdf (Accessed on May 14, 2018).
64. Embassy of India, Yangoon, Myanmar, "Bilateral and Economic Relations." Available at http://www.indiaembassyyangon.net/index.php?option=com_content&view=article&id=60&Itemid=189&lang=en (Accessed on June 12, 2018).
65. Moe Thuzar, Rahul Mishra, Francis Hutchinson, Tin Maung Maung Than, and Termsak Chalermpalanupap, "Connecting South and Southeast Asia: Implementation Challenges and Coordination Arrangements," *Asian Development Bank Institute*, Working Paper 501, September 2014. Available at http://www.adb.org/sites/default/files/publication/156356/adbi-wp501.pdf (Accessed on March 15, 2018).
66. M Rahmatullah (2007), "BIMSTEC-Japan Cooperation in Transport: Bangladesh Perspective," *Centre for Studies in International Relations and Development*, Discussion Paper 31. Available at http://www.bntt.org/Discussion/DP31.pdf (Accessed on March 17, 2018).
67. Rajiv Sikri (2005), "India's Relations with Its Eastern Northeast neighbours" MEA at the Bangladesh Enterprise Institute, Dhaka. Available at http://mea.gov.in/Speeches-Statements.htm?dtl/2518/Indias+Relations+with+its+Eastern+Northeastneighbours+Address+by+Shri+Rajiv+Sikri+Secretary+Ministry+of+External+Affairs+at+the+Bangladesh+Enterprise+Institute+Dhaka (Accessed on June 19, 2017).
68. P Garg (2012), "Energy Scenario and Vision 2020 in India," *Journal of Sustainable Energy and Environment.* Available at http://www.jseejournal.com/JSEE%202012/PDF%20file%20JSEE%203(1)%202012/7.Energy%20scenarios%20pp.%207-17.pdf (Accessed on April 18, 2018).
69. Avtar Singh Bhasin (2013), "India's Foreign Relations-2013 Documents," XPD Division, MEA, Geetika Publishers, New Delhi, p. 189.
70. Department of South Asian, Middle East and African Affairs, Ministry of Foreign Affairs, Kingdom of Thailand, BIMSTEC Agreement detail, December 2013. Available at http://sameaf.mfa.go.th/en/ organization/detail.php?ID=4493 (Accessed on April 15, 2018).

71. Betina Dimaranan and Will Martinr (2017), "China, India and the future of the world economy: Fierce Competition or Shared Growth?," *The World Bank Development Research Group,* Policy Research Working Paper 4304. Available at http://siteresources.worldbank.org/INTDEBTDEPT/Resources/468980-1206974166266/4833916-1206974192224/PRWP4304.pdf (Accessed on April 25, 2018).
72. T Nirmala Devi (2007), *India and Bay of Bengal Community: The BIMSTEC Experiment*, Gyan Publishing House, New Delhi, p. 108.
73. Christopher Roberts (2011), *ASEAN's Myanmar Crisis: Challenges to the Pursuit of a Security Community*, KW Publishers, New Delhi, p. 132.
74. Rajiv Sikri (2009), *Challenge and Strategy: Rethinking India's Foreign Policy*, Sage Publication, New Delhi, p. 66.
75. Mohan Mallik (2000), "Burma's Role in Regional Security," in Morten B. Pedersen, Emily Rudland and R.J. May (eds.), *Burma Myanmar Strong regime Weak State?*, Crawford House Publishing, Adelaide, Australia, p. 88.
76. India-Myanmar Relations, *FPRC Journal,* 2013. Available at http://burmanationalnews.org/burma/images/Documents/fprcjourindmyanrel20133.pdf (Accessed on April 21, 2018).
77. Vijay Sakhuja and Gurpreet S Khurana (2015), *Maritime Perspective 2014*, National Maritime Foundation Publication, p. 89.
78. Vijay Sakhuja and Jane Chan (2016), *China's Maritime Silk Road and Asia*, Vij Books Publication, New Delhi, p. 75.
79. Rajiv Bhatia (2016), *India-Myanmar Relations: Changing Contours*, Routledge Publication, New York, p. 152.

6
Conclusion and the Way Forward

The relationship between India and Myanmar has emerged as a topic of immense interest among academia and policy makers. To understand this reason is not difficult; Myanmar's political transition and its opening-up have resulted in creating a new platform for powerful states to grow their dominance and presence to influence the critical geo-strategic nations in Southeast Asia. When global collaboration and geopolitical competition are increasing in sub-regions such as the Bay of Bengal, the South China Sea, and the Mekong River Basin, India's interests eastward, China's emplacement southwards, the US encountering strategies, Japan's revived interests in the region vis-à-vis increasing Myanmar's geo-strategic significance—occurring in the Indo-Pacific region. The interests of these major powers overlap and come across in and around this region. The significance of India-Myanmar relationship is increasing day by day in these changing dynamics.

India and Myanmar bilateral relations are aspired by national interests, geo-strategic importance and national security aspects. Both countries have shared religious, ethnic, cultural and historical bonds. The collective connections and exchanges through ideas, religious, trade and cultural have provided the foundation of a bridging relationship. India's relations with Myanmar are directed by its Look (Act) East Policy which has served an essential instrument in foreign policy. Myanmar is India's eastern immediate neighbour who shares a long land border of 1,643 km with Northeastern region of India and a maritime border of 1,930 km in the Bay of Bengal and the Andaman Sea.

Myanmar is going through a political and fundamental change with an apparent desire to change its foreign policy which may open up new avenues for itself and India to pursue their national interests. Myanmar is a potential neighbour to become a suitable transit road for growing trade between India and Southeast Asia. India is focusing on Myanmar prominently to place it in the Look (Act) East Policy framework. Prime Minister Narendra Modi, clearly stated that Myanmar holds a critical position in collaboration with Asian nations under the initiative for ASEAN integration and India's Look (Act) East Policy. Besides, Myanmar also has a significant role in the BIMSTEC and is a crucial member of the Mekong Ganga Cooperation initiatives. Myanmar's strategic location provides an opportunity to be the land bridge for India to connect mainland Southeast Asia. This would strengthen the economic growth of Northeast India which remained at the back foot regarding investments and industrial growth due to small-scale connectivity. It is also usually accepted that the poor state of socio-economic development in the Northeast region is the primary root cause of insurgency, which led to a feeling of alienation among the people who armed themselves and chose insurgency.

Geographic location and abundance of natural resources make Myanmar a crucial nation, especially for China and India. China is engaged in spreading its presence in Myanmar, as China has become the largest trading partner and investor in Myanmar. China has invested in billions of dollars in Myanmar in the infrastructure sector as per its needs. Myanmar is a strategically significant nation for China with due regard to its string of pearls policy and One Belt One Road Initiative. China initiated projects making ports in Myanmar to make a strategic axis to enjoy the dominance in the Indian Ocean Region. China's increasing influence in Myanmar may have an adverse effect on India's economic and strategic concerns which led India to launch Look (Act) East Policy in the 1990s. China has always been observing Myanmar through its strategic angle, while India's previous policies mainly focused on human rights and pro-democracy which made India-Myanmar relations stalemate.

Although soft power is one of the edged weapons in India's arsenal. India being a democratic society having Asian culture and tradition, has prominent relevance to endeavours of Myanmar for making and developing a progressive, egalitarian and prosperous society. India should allow full leverage to a long-term mutual relationship with Myanmar. The essential component for India is to make an extraordinary bridge of opportunity, enabling long-term stable relations with Myanmar safeguarding its national interests and flourishing it which ultimately would safeguard India's national interests.

A fundamental convergence is in place between India's recognition of Myanmar's geo-strategic position and Myanmar's quest for an independent and influential nation along with balancing its relationship with neighbours and other powerful states. Therefore, a whole set of factors that push the two countries towards a stable and cooperative relationship will remain potent and unchanged, despite political changes that may occur in Myanmar in the future. Both nations' government are obliged to respect the realities and step towards building a strong foundation which has been laid in past decades, especially since 2011. From the above perspective, the major prospects of the relationship can be concluded in the following areas of cooperation.

Politico-strategic Implications

India is in a potential position to develop close politico-strategic relations with Myanmar. As for Myanmar, maintaining friendly relations with neighbour countries is essential for its independence and active foreign policy. Myanmar is geographically located between two Asian powers, India and China. As India is increasing its power in the region, strong and cordial relations with India is crucial for Myanmar's long term geopolitical reality and national interests of its security concerns. India and China have their legitimate interests to craft close relations with Myanmar. Similarly, Myanmar would not choose between India and China, even having friendly relations with both. The geographical locations of India and Myanmar have facilitated collaboration in multilateral cooperation at the sub-regional level being both members of ASEAN, BCIM, BIMSTEC and MGC. The Northeast part of India is an essential factor in extending linkages with the Southeast Asian countries via Myanmar. However, the lack of connectivity is an essential bottleneck in this regard. A range of measures could be considered as relevant here to deal with such situations.

India and Myanmar should establish 'Strategic Partnership'. Scope and contours of the strategic partnership should be aligned through annual high-level summits. These summits would give a boost to the relationship, provide the platform to align views and stands on bilateral, regional and international issues.

India needs to recreate its impression as a reluctant power before Myanmar and consider taking bold steps to enhance security and defence cooperation, especially with regard to maritime security.

India should maintain close cooperation with the Tatmadaw and help it to remain an appropriate apolitical role in a democracy. This coordination and synergy is also required of the Indian diplomats, political experts, military brass, strategic experts and intelligence officials, so that a harmonious approach can be crafted and executed in this realm.

Recent democratic initiatives to provide capacity-building and training assistance to the Myanmar parliament should be enlarged and sustained.

India can assist in sharing cooperation in the field of elections. Both countries should cooperate in the field of press and digital accessibility.

India has vast experience in handling the centre-state relationships. Hence, India can provide in-depth dialogue and much practical cooperation among stakeholders and expertise to Myanmar.

Political fluctuations and armed group threats are the issues which prohibit investments and also decreased the cross-border infrastructure development feasibility. There should be some measures installed to continue the investments mechanism across the border.

India should continue to assist Myanmar in its interests in ASEAN, particularly the Initiatives for ASEAN Integration, that aimed to bridge the gap between old and new memberships.

There is a substantial gap between the theory of India's Look (Act) East Policy and its practice. This must be addressed to improve its implementation and execution.

Both countries need to work out on practical and tangible ways of increasing their multi-dimensional cooperation in regional and sub-regional organisations such as BIMSTEC, BCIM and MGC.

Economic Cooperation

Economic cooperation covers a vast area, including bilateral trade, border trade, investments, technical cooperation and other many joint ventures. There is a need to assess the current situation concerning economic cooperation. India's economic engagement with Myanmar has been less than satisfactory. As per World Bank reports for 2017, India is the fourth largest trading partner of Myanmar. However, a closer view of the figures reveals the absence of diversity in Myanmar's international trade and also India's weak trade-links with Myanmar. Whereas, China, Thailand, Japan and Singapore account for 38.89 per cent, 19.44 per cent and 6.51 per cent of Myanmar's international trade, respectively. This implies that China and Thailand account for nearly 60 per cent of Myanmar's total international trade. On the other hand, India's trade with Myanmar is a mere 5.10 per cent of the latter's overall trade. The trade between India and Myanmar is way below its potential. Despite geographic contiguity, India's border trade with Myanmar is insufficiently developed and imbalanced. India and Myanmar signed a border trade agreement in 1994, which mandates that the trade between the two would take place through Land Custom Posts in Moreh (India)-Tamu (Myanmar) and Zowkhathar (India)-Rhi (Myanmar). Currently, these two border points are functional, which also need an upgrade with regard to security needs, banking and warehouses. However, the security situation in the porous border region, informal taxes by insurgent groups and the absence of road-rail links tend to hinder greater potential trade between the two countries. In addition to the above situations, the following measures are suggested to enhance more economic cooperation in terms of trade.

India-Myanmar trade is conducted through the Singapore dollar which cost higher for providing its services. RBI must take measures to avoid Singapore route while trading with Myanmar which would be beneficial for both the countries.

Myanmar has an abundance of natural resources, but it is not an industrially developed country. Therefore, India can help in setting up industries such as hotel and tourism industry, forestry and agro-tech based industries, oil and gas explorations, Information Technology and setting up refineries.

India-Myanmar must initiate for Free Trade Agreement to permit the flow of goods and services in both markets. India needs to expand trade by adding more items to the list of products limited up to 22 with forestry and agriculture-based products. India must initiate efforts to establish SEZ between two nations to counter China's SEZ in Kyauk Phyu.

The border town on both sides should be upgraded as per trade demands and projects planning, especially to cater trade with fewer duties on goods for cross-border exchanges.

Border towns of Myanmar are more established and in a robust position to have formal tax less trade. Both countries should have an arrangement of multilateral investment guarantee and protection.

India-Myanmar must open third and fourth proposed border trade point at Nampong in Arunachal Pradesh and Pangsu in Myanmar and Avakhung in Phek, Nagaland and Somra in Myanmar.

In 1994, both nations got a boost in their relationship when a trade agreement was signed. Both countries need to take some measures to legalise informal border trade and should create regulations and institutions for it, including currency-related issues.

The private sector of Myanmar has less capability regarding competing with international business standards which further disturb the investor's intentions. The public and private sectors in Myanmar are not well coordinated. India should provide its assistance and close cooperation in it.

India should provide services in establishing e-governance institutions in Myanmar to facilitate the taxation mechanism, central banking training and other government services. India can assist in establishing a local Export-Import bank in Myanmar with the help of the EXIM Bank of India.

Science and technology sector of Myanmar is developing rather slowly, and they have shown interest in Indian assistance in nuclear reactors for research and launching small satellites; these are potential fields for BARC and ISRO to have a long-time commercial partnership.

For doing profitable business in Myanmar, India needs to have a strong local voice, having a regular and reliable liaison in government ministries, good rapport with the local traders and agents in the business as countries like Thailand, China, Singapore, Japan and Korea have established themselves in Myanmar.

India should offer its expertise and training programmes to the respective regulatory bodies operating in Myanmar for insurance, power, telecommunications and finance sectors.

India and Myanmar agreed to upgrade the status of border trade to normal trade and to expand the list of tradable items from 22 to 62 since November 2012, but the fresh products in the list have not been updated so far. India should also decrease its tariffs in terms of import duties average which is 10 per cent compared to China (6.6 per cent) and Japan (0 per cent).

The border *haats* are installed to encourage local border trade. First, *haat* has been opened at Pangasu Pass, Arunachal Pradesh. The number of *Haats* should be increased to enhance the capacity of border trade.

Health care is another sector where India can explore and invest by building advanced hospitals, clinics and medical institutions. Pharmaceutical products from India are in demand in Myanmar.

Development Cooperation

Infrastructure development and road-rail connectivity beginning from Northeast India running through Myanmar would serve as India's Gateway to Southeast Asia and beyond. It would also act as a crucial trade route for linking the landlocked region of the Northeast to the ports of Southeast Asia. Endeavours have been made in this direction through the Kaladan Project to enhance connectivity between the two countries, especially with the Northeastern states of India. This is supposed to provide a vital access point for linking not only India's hitherto landlocked northeast but also a viable trade route from the countries of Southeast Asia, such as Singapore, Malaysia and Indonesia. The project envisages linking Kolkata seaport with Sittwe port in Myanmar, further linking Sittwe to Mizoram via river and road transport. The Tri-lateral highway links India, Myanmar and Thailand to improve connectivity, increase trade and develop the region economically. Furthermore, renovation and re-opening of the historic Stilwell Road is also significant as it could make the Northeast region a gateway for India's trade along the corridor through Myanmar, running into Kunming in China. These projects are supposed to improve the connectivity between India and Myanmar and beyond, which will lead to the development of trade in the region. It will also improve the situation in Northeast India and the western side of Myanmar. There are some relevant measures suggested below.

India's Northeast region and western flank of Myanmar must be adequately connected especially at border points.

There is an urgent need to execute all developmental projects that are in the pipeline, which require efficient coordination, synchronisation and must be accomplished in a time-bound manner.

Both nations must absorb inclusive engagements to have the faith and self-confidence in their minority sections which would ultimately facilitate them efficaciously, and the execution of cooperation-based projects could be possible which will eventually benefit not only two countries but the whole Southeast Asia and South Asia region.

India should take a close introspection into its ongoing projects as these projects are the foundation of development, trade and commerce in the region. Therefore, if India wants to connect to the Southeast Asian nations, there is a dire need that all the projects must be accomplished in a timely manner.

India should focus on all modes of connectivity, especially road connectivity which would boost trade, commerce and tourism between both countries.

India and Myanmar should develop more systematised air connectivity by increasing the frequency of flights, reasonable airfares and more airlines.

India-Myanmar should have adequate connectivity through ports which would undoubtedly reduce the cost of transportation in trade.

Defence and Security Cooperation

Given the geo-strategic factors as well as defence inter-linkage between India's Northeast region and Myanmar's north-western region, it is natural that defence cooperation should be an essential component of bilateral relations. This has witnessed significant strengthening through a series of regular visits at a high level, provisions of professional and technical training facilities, naval ships visit, the supply of equipment and above all a continuing dialogue on professional matters and strategic issues. Some measures are suggested to enhance defence cooperation between India and Myanmar.

India and Myanmar border region has been the theatre of harmful activities. Operations against the Indian government by Indian Insurgent Groups by using north-western Myanmar as a base or shelter can be countered only by mutual intelligence exchange and security cooperation mechanism.

Indian states, especially Mizoram, Manipur and Nagaland face insurgency problem across the border whereas Myanmar is facing a similar problem from the Khaplang group, KIA and PLA. Both armies had launched a coordinated operation against these groups such operations need to continue to maintain tranquillity in the region.

Ethnic armed groups of India and Myanmar should be involved in ceasefire agreements by respective governments. A system or programme must be organised by the governments to pacify the sentiments of an armed group and bring them for table talks.

India has been offered access to the Coco Island for availing surveillance facility by Myanmar. India should avail this offer by showing their defence power to the small nation so that India can build its market in the region. It is significant for India and Myanmar because both are looking forward to having a sea route trade circuit between Sittwe and Kolkata.

India must explore the opportunities in the maritime domain while developing a capacity building to scrutinise non-traditional security threats and Bay of Bengal challenges.

India should utilise Myanmar's political transformation by establishing a strategic partnership with Myanmar and other ASEAN countries, especially in the Indian Ocean Region to counter Chinese presence.

India should build a rapport with Myanmar Tatmadaw for selling military hardware to tackle its internal security situations.

India's national interests allow it to secure the eastern side of the Indian Ocean from conflicts or any rivalry, especially growing Chinese presence in the Bay of Bengal. Therefore, Myanmar is one of the most significant countries from ASEAN, who holds a strategically crucial location between China and India to maintain the balance of power equilibrium.

India-Myanmar's porous border invite the narcotic trade—Myanmar being a Golden Triangle state, wherein drugs are smuggled to different states of India. India-Myanmar should have agreements to curb this menace.

Insurgents are using the porous border between India and Myanmar for their operations and hideouts. Both countries must take strict actions for securing the borders, like install digital borders between them. This is to curb drug peddlers also, who use this as an other criminal activities take place.

Both countries should conduct regular military exchanges, expand coordination in counter-terrorism and counter-insurgency and security forces vigil in criminal activities especially insurgents and traffickers. India can assist Myanmar in developing and establishing Myanmar's defence production infrastructure.

China Factor

Strategic and development considerations drive China's long-term vision of its relationship with Myanmar. Myanmar's critical geographic location serves as a connecting bridge between China and the Indian Ocean which further allows China to have an approach in this region. Myanmar is believed to be the solution to the Malacca problem of China. China's energy resources needs are mainly met through the Strait of Malacca in the Indian Ocean. China has become one of the major supplier and investor in Myanmar from the last two decades. Under the One Belt One Road Initiative China is constructing ports and other facilities in Pakistan, Myanmar, Maldives and Sri Lanka to provide a platform for China to secure its shipment interests in the region. Some measures are suggested to counter China's presence in Myanmar and the region.

The proximity in the political and diplomatic domain is the foundation of any relationship. India must increase its interaction to gain more and more benefits.

China has scored spectacular success in infrastructure in Myanmar. Chinese assistance in building roads, rails, bridges, dams and ports and their efficiency and commitments towards the projects strengthen their relations with Myanmar. While most Indian projects are under construction and every time completion date is being extended. India needs to complete its projects timely to get better connectivity with more trade.

India needs to improve its itemised list of trade as its imports are dominated by forest and agriculture-based products which account for around 90 per cent of trade with Myanmar.

China's initiative of one belt one road is meant to revive ancient trade routes inland and sea route, India needs to engage countries in the Indo-Pacific region especially the US in balancing China in the region. India's Project Mausam is under dockyard but still should come up with web connectivity.

India is a party to many regional and sub-regional organisations; BCIM, MGC and BIMSTEC which provide India with a potential platform to become an economic power by initiating and exercising on these corridors and networks in the region. They should not remain an accord on paper only; there must be a substantial contribution to the development and the global market.

China is the largest trading partner of Myanmar, whether it is import or export. China has designed its trade structure in a way where there is no trade deficit which China has to face. Approximately 71 Chinese projects are being executed in Myanmar. While other foreign companies including India encountered difficulties in doing business and finding suitable local partners, India needs to understand and create tie-ups at a domestic level so Indian companies can start more and more ventures.

The defence and strategic cooperation between China and Myanmar are due to the rising influence of China in Myanmar. Defence cooperation is the area where ties have a scope for India as Myanmar's large military needs arms and equipment, training, exposure to concepts of modern warfare and counter-insurgency.

Myanmar is aware of China's advantage which it took during sanctions. Myanmar is interested in having relations with other Asian countries and India can be that option against China.

Energy Cooperation

The productive potential of hydrocarbons in the general area of Northeast, western Myanmar and the offshore waters was recognised. However, the involvement of Indian companies in Oil and Gas exploration in Myanmar is only a decade and a half old. Indian public sector companies, ONGC and GAIL, secured their stakes in offshore projects. It is notable that except A 1 and A 3 blocks, other blocks were also offered to India, however, India could not avail the opportunity. Further, Indian authorities came up with the transport of natural gas between India and Myanmar via Bangladesh. However, the proposal did not register success due to the lack of cooperation by Bangladesh. Ultimately, China grabbed the project. Therefore, energy cooperation between India and Myanmar in this context was not as successful as compared to China's success in this field. Though, recent bids have registered the remarkable presence of India in Myanmar. Further, some measures are suggested to heighten energy ties between both countries.

Ministry of Energy, Myanmar, offers onshore and offshore blocks for oil and gas exploration. During the Military Regime in Myanmar, it was a little challenging to get profitable blocks to Indian companies. After the democratic government came into power, it has been changed. Now Indian companies are winning energy projects in the reform era. India should pro-actively get involve in energy-oriented projects to develop stronger ties with Myanmar.

India should utilise its big refineries with the collaboration of Myanmar for refining crude and exporting refined products to Myanmar. India's Paradip, the eastern coast, could also be used in the collaboration.

Myanmar supposedly has the world's 10th largest natural gas reserves accounts nearly 90 trillion cubic feet. Energy demand in India has risen, to meet its requirements, India needs to establish energy-driven long term policies with Myanmar.

India can lead Myanmar in multi-utilisation of renewable energy resources. India can work with Myanmar on the demonstration and training programmes in biomass gasifies and wind energy.

Myanmar is currently facing limited production and refinery capacity issues, apparently not in a position to meet the rising demand for energy. India should establish Liquefied Natural Gas pipelines under its hydrocarbon vision 2030 by resolving concerns with Bangladesh and Myanmar to have a win-win situation.

People-to-people Contacts

Besides the government-to-government and business-to-business facets, there is the third pillar of bilateral relations which needs to be strengthened appreciably. The two governments, as well as a few interested companies and other institutions, may join hand to provide substantial funding for establishing the foundation for people-to-people connections. The following measures may be taken into consideration to increase people-to-people interaction.

Both countries consulates and embassies must develop and implement a set of programmes for strengthening people-to-people contacts.

India should promote Buddhist pilgrimages in India to connect Buddhist people of India and Myanmar along with promoting its tourism for the Northeast which can be considered a tourism hub around the world.

There must be direct connectivity (by air, road and rail) to historical and tourist places between India and Myanmar. There should be proper recreational places for tourists on both sides to promote tourism.

India should promote educational linkages with Myanmar by designing various student exchange programmes in skill development courses and job oriented programmes. India should offer scholarships to meritorious students in the course of medical, management and engineering institutions.

India should utilise the media and social media network platforms to enhance their relationship to another level by organising programmes, releasing statements and conducting studies in the Burmese language.

Indian IT companies and Myanmar IIT can go ahead with commercial spillovers of benefit being set up by both government support. It would cater to people and open many employment avenues. India can also be beneficial to Myanmar in providing vocational education for better startups and its businesses.

Indian think tanks, civil society institutions and trade outfits should be encouraged to engage counterpart groups from Myanmar and develop close collaboration to reap more benefits comparatively as Myanmar has opened its all doors for the world.

From the Diaspora angle, India's interests have risen with the emergence of corporate involvements. Indian Diaspora has a good percentage so they must involve local traders and address their interests in strengthening its position in Myanmar.

These measures and recommendations would enhance the deep relationship between both countries. Given the slow political transition in Myanmar, it offers immense opportunity for India to re-engage and re-design its approach towards Myanmar for strategic and economic advantages in the region. However, it is not free from complexities. The path ahead is full of challenges as three critical gaps are identified that need to be bridged through immediate intervention. These are: security and stability at the borders, connectivity of India's Northeast with the mainland and with the western region of Myanmar and expansion of bilateral trade. These endeavours would undoubtedly go a long way in strengthening the partnership and boosting ties between the two countries. It has become necessary for India to carefully deal with the encircling security threats and draw a balance in its engagement with China both at the western and the eastern flanks. Therefore, India needs to engage positively with Myanmar by strengthening the economic and strategic ties between each other.

Selected Bibliography

Official Records/Documents-Government of India/Myanmar

Lok Sabha/ Rajya Sabha Debates

Directorate of Investment and Company Administration, Myanmar

Ministry of Corporate Affairs

Ministry of Defence

Ministry of Development of North Eastern Region

Ministry of External Affairs

Ministry of Foreign Affairs, Myanmar

Ministry of Home Affairs

Ministry of Shipping

Books

Bajpayee, U.S. (1986), *India and its Neighbourhood*, Lancer International, New Delhi.

Behuria, Ashok K., and Dahia, Rumel (2012), *India's Neighbourhood Challenges in the Next two Decades*, Pentagon Press, New Delhi.

Bhatia, Rajiv, Sakhuja, Vijay and Ranjan, Vikas (2014), *Change in Myanmar*, Shipra Publication, New Delhi.

Bhatia, Rajiv and Mishra, Rahul (2015), *BCIM-Economic Corridor: The Road Ahead*, Pentagon Press, New Delhi.

Bhatia, Rajiv (2016), *India-Myanmar Relations: Changing Contours*, Routledge Publication, New York.

Bhattacharya, Rakhee (2015), *Northeastern India and Its Neighbours: Negotiating Security and Development*, Routledge Publication, New Delhi.

Bhattacharya, Swapna (2007), *India-Myanmar Relations (1886-1948)*, K P Bagchi & Co., Kolkata.

Bora, Kumar Padamapani (2014), *North-East India in India-ASEAN Relations*, Discovery Publishing House, New Delhi.

Chandra, Puran (2013), *Burma Past and Present: A Fact Book*, Forward Books, New Delhi.

Chandran, D. Suba, Sinha, Tulsi and Kang, H. Kaur (2011), *An alternative strategy for Southeast Asia: Looking through India's Northeast*, Samskriti Publication, New Delhi.

Chakraborty, Shantanu (2012), *Reappraising India's Look East Policy*, KW Publishers, New Delhi.

Chatterjee, B.R. (1995), *South East Asia in Transition*, Minakshi Publications, New Delhi.

Chopra, V.D. (2006), *India's foreign policy in the 21st Century*, Gian Publishing House, New Delhi.

Christopher, Roberts (2011), *ASEAN's Myanmar Crisis: Challenges to the Pursuit of a Security Community*, KW Publishers, New Delhi.

Das Garudas, Singh N B and Thomas C J (Ed.) (2005), *Indo-Myanmar Border Trade, Status, Problems & Potential*, Akansha Publication, New Delhi.

Das Garudas, and Thomas, C Joshua (2019), *BCIM Economic Cooperation: Interplay of Geo-economics and Geo-politics*, Routledge, New Delhi.

Das Garudas, and Thomas, C Joshua (2016), *Look East to Act East Policy: Implications for India's Northeast*, Routledge, New Delhi.

Das, Gautam (2011), *Securing India's Borders: Challenges and Policy Options*, Pentagon Press, New Delhi.

Das, Sailen D (2015), *Northeast India in India-China Relations*, DVS Publishers, Guwahati.

De, Prabir and Raychaudhary, Ajitava (2017), *Myanmar's Integration with the World: Challenges and Policy options*, Palgrave Macmillan, Singapore.

De, Prabir (2018), *Twenty years of BIMSTEC: Promoting Regional Cooperation and Integration in the Bay of Bengal Region*, KW Publishers, New Delhi.

Devare, Sudhir (2006), *India & Southeast Asia*, Capital Publication, New Delhi.

Devi, T Nirmala (2007), *India and Bay of Bengal Community: The BIMSTEC Experiment*, Gyan Publishing House, New Delhi.

Dixit, J.N. (2001), *Indian Foreign Policy and its Neighbours*, Gian Publishing House, New Delhi.

Dutt, V. P. (1984), *India's Foreign Policy,* Vikas Publishing House, New Delhi.

Feigenblatt, Von Otte F (2012), *The Association of Southeast Asian Nations (ASEAN)*, New Century Publications, New Delhi.

Felfamkima, VL (2011), *Mizoram Border Trade: Emerging Trend and Future Prospects*, Akansha Publishing House, New Delhi.

Haokip, Thongkholal (2015), *India's Look East Policy and The Northeast*, Sage Publication, New Delhi.

Harvey, G E and Temple, Richard Carnac (2010), *History of Burma: From the Earliest Times to the Beginning of the English Conquest*, Cosmo Publications, New Delhi.

Ibrahim, Azeem (2018), *The Rohingyas: Inside Myanmar's Hidden Genocide*, Speaking Tiger Publishing House, New Delhi.

Jha, Ganganath (1986), *South-East Asia & India: A Political Perspective*, National Book Organisation, New Delhi.

Kabi, K and Pattnaik, S N (2015), *Media, Conflict and Peace in Northeast India*, Vij Books Publication, New Delhi.

Keenan, Paul (2013), *By Force of Arms: Armed Ethnic Groups in Burma*, Vij Books, New Delhi.

Khosla, I. P. (2008), *Spotlight on Neighbours*, Konark Publication, Pvt. Ltd., Delhi.

Kipgen, Nehginpao (2015), *Democracy Movement in Myanmar: Problems and Challenges*, Ruby Press & Co., New Delhi.

Kipgen, Nehginpao (2016), *Myanmar: A Political History*, Oxford University Press, Oxford.

Konar, D N and Chakrabarti, Subhabrata (2008), *Developmental Issues of North East India*, Akansha Publishing House, New Delhi.

Kumar, Sanjay (Ed.) (2011), *India's Internal Security Challenges*, Sunrise Publication, New Delhi.

Kumar, Satish (2012), *India's National Security*, Routledge, New Delhi.

Li, Chenyang, and Wilhelm Hofmeister (2010), *Myanmar: Prospect for Change*, Select Books, Singapore.

Malik, Preet (2016), *My Myanmar Years: India's Relations with the Region*, Sage Publication,

New Delhi.
Marwah, Ved (2011), *India in Turmoil*, Rupa & Co. Publication, New Delhi.
Muni, S D and Das, Suranjan (2009), *India and China: The Next Decade*, Rupa & Co. Publishers, New Delhi.
Muni, S D and Mishra, Rahul (2019), *India's Eastward Engagement: From Antiquity to Act East Policy*, Sage Publication, New Delhi.
Myint-U, Thant (2012), *Where China meets India: Burma and The New Crossroads of Asia*, Faber and Faber Limited Bloomsbury House, London.
Myoe, Maung Aung (2009), *Building the Tatmadaw Myanmar Armed Forces Since 1948*, K.W. Publishers, New Delhi.
Nag, Sajal (2002), *Marginality: Ethnicity, Insurgency & Sub-nationalism in Northeast India*, Manohar Publication, New Delhi.
Nanda, Prakash (2008), *Rediscovering Asia: Evolution of India's Look East Policy*, Lancer Publishers, New Delhi.
Narahari, N. S. (2006), *Security Threats to Northeast India: The Socio Ethnic Tensions*, Manas Publication, New Delhi.
Noorani, A G (2014), *India-China Boundary Problems: 1846-1947 History and Diplomacy*, Oxford University Press, New Delhi.
O'Kane, Michael (2014), *Doing Business in Myanmar*, Andalus Publishing, Chicago.
Pant, Pushpesh (2013), *International Relations in the 21st Century*, McGraw-Hill Education, New Delhi.
Pemberton, R. B. (2000), *The Eastern Frontier of India*, Mittal Publications, New Delhi.
Popham, Peter (2012), *The Life of Aung San Suu Kyi of Burma*, Random House Group, UK.
Rajshekhar (2001), *Myanmar's Nationalist Movement (1906-1948) and India*, South Asian Publishers, New Delhi.
Ram, Amar Nath (2012), *Two Decades of India's Look East Policy: Partnership for Peace, Progress and Prosperity*, Manohar Publishers, New Delhi.
Raghavan, V R (2011), *Internal Conflicts in Myanmar: Transnational Consequences*, Vij Books Publication, New Delhi.
Reddy, K. Raja (2005), *India and ASEAN*, New Century Publications, New Delhi.
Rieffel, Lex (ed.) (2010), *Myanmar: Inside Challenges, Outside Interests*, Brooking Institution Press, Washington D.C.
Sakhuja, Vijay and Chan, Jane (2016), *China's Maritime Silk Road and Asia*, Vij Books Publication, New Delhi.
Sharma, Atul and Choudhary, Saswati (2018), *Main-streaming the Northeast in India's Look and Act East Policy*, Palgrave Macmillan, Singapore.
Sikri, Rajiv (2016), *Challenges and Strategy: Rethinking India's Foreign Policy*, Sage Publication, New Delhi.
Singh, Daljit, and Kesavan, KV (2010), *South and Southeast Asia: Responding to Changing Geo-Political and Security Challenges*, KW Publishers, New Delhi.
Singh, Thingnam Kishan (2009), *Look East Policy and India's Northeast: Polemics and Perspectives*, Concept Publication, New Delhi.
Singh, Tenshubam Hemo (2016), *Terrorism in Indo-Myanmar Region*, Akansha Publishing House, New Delhi.
Steinberg, David I (2013), *Burma/Myanmar: What Everyone Wants to Know*, Oxford University Press, New York.

Taneja, Nisha, Das, D Kusum and Bimal, Samridhi (2019), *Sub-regional cooperation between India, Myanmar and Bangladesh: Trade, Investment and Connectivity*, Academic Foundation, New Delhi.

Tripathi, D P and Deepak, B R (2012), *India-China Relations: Future Perspectives*, Vij Books Publication, New Delhi.

Wagh, Popatrao Laxman (2017), *India-Myanmar Relations*, Atul Prakashan, Kanpur.

Yhome, K (2008), *Myanmar: Can the Generals Resist change*, Rupa & Co. Publication, New Delhi.

Articles

Aditya, Vijay (2018), "India's trade and Maritime Policy in the Indian Ocean Region", *Centre for Public Policy Research*, Vol. 12 (2), pp. 35-52.

Amrita, Jash (2017), "China in India's Look East-Myanmar: Strategic Interests and Security concerns", *International Research Journal of Social Science*, Vol. 36 (6), pp. 54-57.

Baruah, Darshana M (2018), "India's Answer to Belt and Road: A Roadmap for South Asia", *Carnegie India*, Paper 05.

Basit, Saira H (2018), "India-Myanmar Relations and the Management of Transmitted Militant Threats", Journal of Strategic Security, Vol. 11 (2), pp. 73-92.

Bert, Wayne (2004), "Burma, China and the USA", *Pacific Affairs*, Vol. 77 (2).

Chang, Y. S. Joseph (2001), "Sino-ASEAN Relations in the Early Twenty First Century", *Contemporary Southeast Asia*, Vol. 23 (3).

Chaturvedi, Medha (2012), "Myanmar's Ethnic Divide: The Parallel struggle", *IPCS Special Report*, # 131.

Chenyang, Li (2012), "China-Myanmar Comprehensive Strategic Cooperative Partnership: A Regional Threat?", *Current Southeast Asian Affairs*, Vol. 31 (1).

Das, R Upendra (2016), "Enhancing India-Myanmar border trade: Policy and implementation measures", Ministry of Commerce and Industry, India.

Dutta, Rangan (2018), "Northeast and China-Myanmar Economic Corridor", ISPSW strategy series: focus on defence and international security, Issue no. 529.

Egreteau, Renaud (2008), "India's Ambitions in Burma: Frustration than Success?", *Asian Survey*, Vol. 48 (6).

Gottschlich, Pierra (2015), "New developments in India-Myanmar bilateral relations", *Journal of Current Southeast Asian Affairs*, vol. 34 (2), pp. 139-163.

Gottschlich, Pierra (2017), "The India-Myanmar relationship: New directions after a change of Government", *International Quarterly for Asian Studies*, Vol. 48 (3), pp. 171-202.

Holliday, Ian (2005), "Rethinking the United State's Myanmar Policy", *Asian Survey*, Vol. 45 (4).

Holliday, Ian (2009), "Beijing and the Myanmar problem", *The Pacific Review*, Vol. 22 (4).

Hong, Zhao (2006), "India's Changing Relations with ASEAN: From China's Perspective", *East Asian Affairs*, Vol. 20 (2).

Hong, Zhao (2007), "India & China: Rivals or Partners in Southeast Asia", *Contemporary Southeast Asia*, Vol. 29 (1).

Jones, Lee (2014), "The Political Economy of Myanmar's Transition", *Journal of Contemporary Asia*, Vol. 44 (1).

Joshua, H. Ho (2006), "The Security of Sea Lanes in Southeast Asia", *Asian Survey*, Vol. 46 (4).

Kapoor, Rajeev (2018), "China-Myanmar Nexus: India's conundrum", *Centre for Land Warfare Studies*, Issue brief no. 157.

Karim, Mohd. Aminul and Islam, Faria (2018), "BCIM Economic Corridor: Challenges and Prospects", *The Korean Journal of Defence Analysis*, Vol. 30 (2), pp. 283-302.

Kumar, Ashok (2017), "India-Myanmar Relations with reference to BIMSTEC", IOSR Journal of Humanities and Social Science, Vol. 22 (7), pp. 28-36.

Lall, Marie (2006), "Indo-Myanmar Relations in the Era of Pipeline Diplomacy", *Contemporary Southeast Asia*, Vol. 28 (3).

Malik, J. Mohan (1994), "Sino-Indian Rivalry in Myanmar: Implication for Regional Security", *Contemporary Southeast Asia*, Vol. 16 (2).

Padmaja, G (2017), "BIMSTEC: Where India's Neighbourhood first and Act East meet", National Maritime Foundation, 6 October.

Palit, Amitendu, Choudhary, Rahul and Tieri, Silvia (2018), "BIMSTEC: Relevance and Challenges", Institute of South Asian Studies, No. 519.

Ramachandran, Sudha (2018), "China-Myanmar Economic Corridor Ambitions meet hard Reality", *Global Research and Analysis*, Vol. 18 (5).

Routray, B. Prasad (2011), "India-Myanmar Relations: Triumph of Pragmatism", *Jindal Journal of International Affairs*, Vol. 1 (1).

Routray, B. Prasad (2013), "Myanmar's National Reconciliation: An audit of Insurgency and Ceasefires", *IPCS Special Report*, # 138.

Sharma, Aparna & Rathore, Chetnak (2015), "BIMSTEC and BCIM Initiatives and their importance for India", CUTS International, Discussion Paper.

Sharma, Sukanya (2005), "Building roads to Myanmar: A Historical overview", *Economic & Political Weekly*, Vol. 40 (48).

Sikri, Rajiv (2009), "India's Look East Policy", *Asia Pacific Review*, Vol. 16 (1).

Singh, Amit (2013), "Diaspora as a Factor in India-Myanmar Relations", *Maritime Affair: Journal of the National Maritime Foundation of India,* Vol. 9 (2).

Singh, Mohindra Pal (2017), "India-Myanmar relations: Time to Act", *Indian Defence Review,* 6 November.

Steinberg, David I. (2012), "China-Myanmar Relation", *Journal of Current Southeast Asian Affairs*, Vol. 31 (1).

Storey, Ian (2009), "Maritime Security in Southeast Asia: Two cheers for Regional Cooperation", *Southeast Asian Affairs.*

Tandon, Pradeep (2018), "Relations between India, China and the Myanmar", International Journal of Research in Humanities, Arts and Literature, Vol. 6 (9), pp. 389-396.

Taylor, Robert H. (2010), "Myanmar in 2009: On the Cusp of Narmality?", *Southeast Asian Affairs.*

Wagner, Daniel and Cafiero, Giorgio (2014), "Can China and India Co-exist in

Myanmar", *Asia Pacific Bulletin,* no. 250.

Wong, John (1997), "Why has Myanmar not developed like East Asia", *ASEAN Economic Bulletin*, Vol. 13 (3).

Xavier, Constantino (2018), "Bridging the Bay of Bengal towards a stronger BIMSTEC", *Carnegie India,* Paper 08.

Yhome, K (2011), "Myanmar's changing Political Landscape: Key Players and Recent trends", *Strategic Trends*, Vol. 1 (1).

Yhome, K (2015), "From Look East to Act East: What it means for India's Northeast", *Eastern Quarterly*, Vol. 11 (1), pp. 18-29.

Selected Webliography

http://www.asiapacificms.com	:	Asia Pacific Media Services Ltd.
http://burmacentredelhi.org	:	Burma Centre Delhi
http://www.burmalibrary.org	:	Burma Library
http://www.idsa.in	:	Institute of Defence Studies and Analyses
http://www.jstor.org	:	JSTOR Digital Library
http://www.tandfonline.com	:	Taylor and Francis Online
http://www.icwa.in	:	Indian Council of World Affairs
http://www.cenjos.in	:	Centre for Joint Warfare Studies
http://www.ris.org.in	:	Research & Information System for Developing Countries
http://www.myanmarisis.org	:	Myanmar Institute of Strategic and International

Newspapers

Asia Times, Hong Kong
Global New Light of Myanmar, Yangoon
The China Times, Taiwan
The Conversation, Melbourne
The Diplomat, Tokyo
The Economic Times, Mumbai
The Guardian, London
The Hindu, Chennai
The Myanmar Times, Yangoon
Washington Post, Washington

Journals/ Magazines

Economic and Political Weekly, Mumbai
Extraordinary and Plenipotentiary Diplomatist, Noida
Foreign Policy Research Centre, New Delhi
Indian Defence Review, New Delhi
Indian Foreign Affairs Journal, New Delhi
India Quarterly, New Delhi
Institute of Peace and Conflict Studies, New Delhi
South East Asia Politics, Singapore

Strategic Analysis, New Delhi
Strategic Digest, New Delhi
USI Journal, New Delhi
World Affairs, New Delhi